Git Recipes

Włodzimierz Gajda

Git Recipes

ISBN-13 (pbk): 978-1-4302-6103-2

ISBN-13 (electronic): 978-1-4302-6104-9

President and Publisher: Paul Manning
Lead Editor: Michelle Lowman
Technical Reviewer: Patrick McConnell
Editorial Board: Steve Anglin, Mark Beckner, Ewan Buckingham, Gary Cornell, Louise Corrigan, Jonathan Gennick, Jonathan Hassell, Robert Hutchinson, Michelle Lowman, James Markham, Matthew Moodie, Jeff Olson, Jeffrey Pepper, Douglas Pundick, Ben Renow-Clarke, Dominic Shakeshaft, Gwenan Spearing, Matt Wade, Steve Weiss, James T. DeWolf
Coordinating Editor: Christine Ricketts
Copy Editor: Judy Ann Levine
Compositor: SPi Global
Indexer: SPi Global
Artist: SPi Global
Cover Designer: Anna Ishchenko

Distributed to the book trade worldwide by Springer Science+Business Media New York, 233 Spring Street, 6th Floor, New York, NY 10013. Phone 1-800-SPRINGER, fax (201) 348-4505, e-mail orders-ny@springer-sbm.com, or visit www.springeronline.com. Apress Media, LLC is a California LLC and the sole member (owner) is Springer Science + Business Media Finance Inc (SSBM Finance Inc). SSBM Finance Inc is a Delaware corporation.

For information on translations, please e-mail rights@apress.com, or visit www.apress.com.

Apress and friends of ED books may be purchased in bulk for academic, corporate, or promotional use. eBook versions and licenses are also available for most titles. For more information, reference our Special Bulk Sales–eBook Licensing web page at www.apress.com/bulk-sales.

Any source code or other supplementary materials referenced by the author in this text is available to readers at www.apress.com. For detailed information about how to locate your book's source code, go to www.apress.com/source-code/.

For Beata

Contents at a Glance

Contents

About the Author

Włodzimierz Gajda is an experienced trainer and a highly passionate teacher. During the last 20 years, he has conducted numerous courses on very diverse subjects, ranging from programming in C language and TCP/IP networking to building LEGO robots and developing web applications with PHP. He is currently employed at the Institute of Mathematics and Computer Science, The John Paul II Catholic University of Lublin. His preferred leisure activities are trekking in the Tatra Mountains and playing the blues (http://www.youtube.com/user/gajdaw). He lives in Lublin, Poland with his wife and three children.

Włodzimierz provides git training all over the Europe. You can contact him by email: gajdaw@gajdaw.pl.

About the Technical Reviewer

Patrick McConnell has 15 years of experience designing and supporting systems on various Linux and Unix platforms. Having worked in IT within different industries and across several continents, his experience has led him to build, support, and automate the server, monitoring, backup, and storage infrastructure in organizations of all sizes.

Acknowledgments

For me, the whole adventure of writing for Apress started almost exactly one year ago when Michelle Lowman accepted my proposal to write about git. Thus my first and foremost acknowledgments are due to Michelle. I really cannot say how grateful I am.

Next, I would like to express my sincere gratitude to the Git authors and contributors. I want to thank Linus Torvalds, Junio C. Hamano, and the whole community for the enormous effort that resulted in creating such an amazing tool as git. My humble "Thank you" to all of you!

Finally, I want to thank the staff of Apress that I had the pleasure to work with. They just took me by the hand and taught me everything. I'm grateful to:

- Douglas Pundick for his professional assistance and guidance

- Patrick McConnell and Peter Membrey for their comments and suggestions

- Christine Ricketts and Judy Ann Levine for their efforts in improving the quality of the book

Last, let me add two statements that clarifies my intentions. While many people helped me, directly or indirectly, to write this book, I'm the only one to blame for everything. All errors and mistakes are exclusively mine. Also, it wasn't my intention to gain authority by implying any relationship that could possibly connect me with either with the git community, Github, or Bitbucket. I'm an independent git, Github, and Bitbucket user—I do not contribute nor work for any of them.

—Włodzimierz Gajda
Lublin, Poland
November 19, 2013

■ ■ ■

## CHAPTER 1

Getting Started with Git

The manufacturers of computer software are facing difficult challenges caused by quite trivial reasons. A typical application is produced by a team of developers working on hundreds, if not thousands, of files on a short schedule. Each file needs to be available for modification by all of the developers at any moment. The situation is complicated even more when we supplement the scenario with the time line. Every file can be modified by any developer at any chosen moment. The following three simple factors make the management of a source code a nontrivial task:

- The number of files
- The number of developers
- The time line

These problems have been known for many years, and as you might expect, there are various software tools that make group work on text files a lot of easier. These tools are commonly referred to as *version control software* or *revision control software*. And git belongs to this family.

What is git?

Git is a distributed version control system created to support the development of a Linux kernel. It was started in April 2005 by Linus Torvalds and is now maintained by Junio C. Hamano.

The main features that set git apart among other version control systems are:

- Branching
- Data integrity
- Locality
- Distributed system
- Open source
- Last but not least—popularity

The *branching* model is git's most amazing feature. I consider it alone to be a sufficient reason to switch to git. With git, branches can be created almost instantaneously and can be easily merged and shared with other developers. Although there are many sophisticated operations that can be performed on branches, the basic usage is easy and straightforward. This encourages the extensive usage of branches, and I think I am not exaggerating when I say that the git branching model changed the way developers work.

Data integrity means that git tracks all the files and directories of your project in such a way that it is not possible to introduce unnoticed changes. Even if you want to change a single byte you have to create a revision. When you create a revision, there is no way to hide something inside. This is a built-in feature that cannot be turned off. Therefore you can trust git completely: all the changes are introduced as revisions and every revision can be inspected.

Locality increases git's efficiency and allows you to execute many git commands even if the network is down. When you work with git you are not connected to any server. Most commands, such as commit, branch, merge, and rebase are performed locally in a similar way to typical filesystem commads such as mkdir, ls, rm. They don't carry out any data transfer.

Because git is a *distributed* version control system, every repository is fully functional and can serve both as a sender and a receiver. If there is a channel of communication between the computers, their repositories can exchange the contents in both directions. Therefore, you can create more complicated workflows than just the client/server paradigm that are used by centralized revision control systems.

Added to this is the fact that git is an *open-source* project and it is becoming the most *popular* version control system on the world—you'll see that there is good reason to start learning git.

1-1. Installing git on Windows

Problem

You want to install git on Windows.

Solution

Go to http://msysgit.github.io/ and download the most recent installer version of git for Windows. At the time of writing this was version 1.8.3. The installer was named: Git-1.8.3-preview20130601.exe. Run the installer leaving all options set to default values. After this, git is ready to be run on your system.

How It Works

There are two methods for installing git on Windows:

- Use Cygwin package available at http://www.cygwin.com

- Use the standalone installer called msysgit.

In this procedure we use msysgit package.

When you run the msysgit installer downloaded from http://code.google.com/p/msysgit/ you will be asked two questions:

- How to configure the paths?

- How to configure the conversion of end of line character?

The dialog box titled *Adjusting your PATH environment* sets the path environment variable. Msysgit installer contains not only git binaries but also a number of Linux programs such as ssh, curl, ls, mkdir, rm, and find. With default settings the installer copies git and these programs to the following directories:

C:\Program Files (x86)\Git\bin

This folder contains ls, mkdir, ssh, curl, find, etc.

C:\Program Files (x86)\Git\cmd

This folder contains the git binary file and the shell script to run git

The first choice in the dialog box is *Use Git Bash only*. With this setting the path variable is not modified. When you start a Windows command line and type git, the command line will respond with a message that the git command does not exist.

The second choice, *Run Git from the Windows Command Prompt*, adds the C:\Program Files (x86)\Git\cmd folder to your path. Thus, you can use git command in the windows command line. When you type ssh in the windows command line, however, the system will respond with an unknown command message.

The last choice is *Run Git and included Unix tools from the Windows Command Prompt*. This choice adds two folders C:\Program Files (x86)\Git\bin and C:\Program Files (x86)\Git\cmd to your path. Now, you can use all the included tools in the Windows Command line: ssh, git, ls, curl, and so on. But some commands in C:\Program Files (x86)\Git\bin, such as find, overlap with the original commands available in Windows. The original find is not available now in the command line.

When I was writing this book my intention was to present the commands that can work in exactly the same way on all platforms. Thus I decided to use the bash command line. If you work on Windows and want to use bash command line, then you can leave the default first choice *Use Git Bash only*.

The second dialog box, which is titled *Configuring the line ending conversions*, sets the configuration option named core.autocrlf to one of these values: true, input, or false. The meaning of this setting is summarized in Table 1-1.

Table 1-1. *All values of the core.autocrlf option and their influence on the checkout and commit operations*

Value	Checkout	Commit
True	LF => CRLF	CRLF => LF
input	None	CRLF => LF
false	None	None

When you choose the first setting, the value true, git will convert the end-of-line characters in your files during the checkout and commit operations. When you check the files out, git will convert LF to CRLF and when you commit git will convert CRLF to LF.

The second choice, input, turns the conversion of new lines only when you commit. In this case git converts the line endings from CRLF to LF.

The third setting (false) turns all the conversions off.

The conversion of end-of-line characters is explained in greater detail in Recipes 13-2 through 13-6. No matter which is your current choice, you can always change the setting using one of these commands:

```
$ git config --global core.autocrlf true
$ git config --global core.autocrlf input
$ git config --global core.autocrlf false
```

When the installer finishes, run the git bash application available in the Start menu. To verify that the installation was successful, you can run the command:

```
$ git --version
```

It should print the version of git installed on your system.

■ **Hint** If you want to change the current directory to the root directory of drive c use the following command: $ cd /c
This is the equivalent of the command: c:

3

1-2. Installing git on Linux

Problem

You want to install git on Linux.

Solution

Depending on your system run one of the commands:

```
# for Ubuntu
$ sudo apt-get install git

# for Fedora
$ sudo yum install git
```

How It Works

The easiest way to install git on Linux is to use the available packages. If you want to compile and install git using its source follow the procedure described in Recipe 11-3.

To verify that the installation was successful, you can run the command:

```
$ git --version
```

It should print the version of git installed on your system.

1-3. Installing git on OS X

Problem

You want to install git on OS X.

Solution

Visit the http://code.google.com/p/git-osx-installer/ site and download the most recent available version of git. Run the downloaded installer leaving all options set to the default values.

How It Works

The easiest way of installing git on OS X is to use the graphical installer. To verify that the installation was successful, you can run the command:

```
$ git --version
```

It should print the version of git installed on your system.

1-4. Accessing the manual

Problem

You want to access the git manual.

Solution

Run the following commands:

```
$ git help
$ git help -a
$ git help -g

$ git help commit
$ git commit --help

$ git help merge
$ git merge --help
```

How It Works

Git commands are divided into two major groups:

- Porcelain commands
- Plumbing commands

Porcelain commands are high-level commands meant for every day use. This group includes, among the others:

```
$ git add
$ git commit
$ git help
$ git push
```

The other group, called *plumbing*, contains low-level commands. Here are some examples:

```
$ git receive-pack
$ git update-index
$ git upload-pack
```

By default, the command `$ git help` lists only porcelain commands. If you want to the list plumbing commands as well as the porcelain commands, use -a switch `$ git help -a`.

You can access the documentation for a specific git subcommand using the following syntax:

```
$ git help [COMMAND]
$ git [COMMAND] --help
```

Here are the commands to access the documentation of the `$ git commit` command:

```
$ git help commit
$ git commit --help
```

1-5. Configuring git

Problem

You want to configure git to be ready for work.

Solution

Run the following command:

```
$ git config --global user.name
```

It should print the empty results. That is because right after the installation the user name is not configured. Set the user.name configuration option using the following command:

```
$ git config --global user.name "John Doe"
```

Instead of John Doe type your name and surname.
Next, run the command:

```
$ git config --global user.email john.doe@example.net
```

This command will set your email.

How It Works

If you want to create commits within git repository, you have to configure two settings: user.name and user.email. Otherwise, when you run the $ git commit command, git will print the warning. The strings that you use as values for user.name and user.email will be stored within every commit you create.

CHAPTER 2

■ ■ ■

Working with Well-Known Repositories

We will start our tour exploring existing and quite well-known repositories. The main goal of this chapter is to get familiar with repositories—their types and structure. In this chapter, you will learn the following:

- What are the most popular hosting solutions for git repositories?

- How to create a local copy of a repository that is hosted on Github.com or Bitbucket.org?

Once we know how to clone a repository, we can then analyze its structure. Then we will explore the working directory—the git directory and its contents. At that point we will be able to classify a repository as either bare or non-bare.

Next, we will discuss the various commands that print the information about the repository, such as

- The list of revisions

- The list of contributors

- The number of revisions

- The number of contributors

- The disk usage of the git directory and the working directory

To make the chore of typing long git commands easier, I will define their aliases.

■ **Note**   I have tested all the commands presented in this chapter and in the book on two platforms: Linux and Windows. My aim was to provide one set of instructions that will work regardless of your platform. To achieve this goal, file system operations are performed with Linux commands, such as ls and rm. Moreover, the listings start with $ and paths use / as separator—suggesting that they are prepared for Linux. However, do not worry if you are using Windows. Just use the bash command interpreter distributed with git and all the commands will work fine.

If you are using a Unix-like system that is different than Linux, some commands (i.e., du or echo) can use different switches than those that are presented in this book. Therefore, you will need to customize these commands.

2-1. Cloning a repository hosted on Github

Problem

You want to get a local copy of a jQuery repository.

Solution

Start the command line and create the `git-recipes/` and `git-recipes/02-01/` directories:

```
$ cd /some/where/on/your/system
$ mkdir git-recipes
$ cd git-recipes
$ mkdir 02-01
```

Change the current directory to `02-01/`:

```
$ cd 02-01
```

Then execute the command as shown in Listing 2-1.

Listing 2-1. The command to clone jQuery repository

```
$ git clone https://github.com/jquery/jquery.git
```

■ **Caution**   During a clone command, git copies a complete repository from its original location to your local storage system. Depending on your bandwidth and the project size, this operation can take quite some time. But don't worry about it. The cloning is done only once, when you set up your local repository. All subsequent data transfers are very efficient because git transfers only the missing portions of data. The internals of cloning are explained in Chapter 10 (Recipe 10-1).

After you run the command shown in Listing 2-1, your `git-recipes/02-01/` directory will contain files and directories that are shown in Figure 2-1. Notice that jQuery is stored under the subdirectory `jquery/` and not just within `git-recipes/02-01/`.

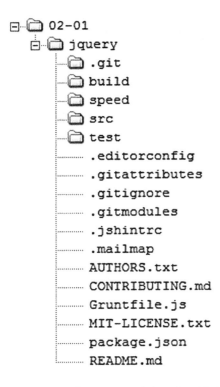

```
⊟ 📁 02-01
   ⊟ 📁 jquery
         📁 .git
         📁 build
         📁 speed
         📁 src
         📁 test
            .editorconfig
            .gitattributes
            .gitignore
            .gitmodules
            .jshintrc
            .mailmap
            AUTHORS.txt
            CONTRIBUTING.md
            Gruntfile.js
            MIT-LICENSE.txt
            package.json
            README.md
```

Figure 2-1. *The contents of git-recipes/02-01/ directory after the git clone command*

■ **Caution** Figure 2-1 was prepared in April 2013. As you can guess, the jQuery project goes forward all the time. Thus the contents of your git-recipes/02-01/ directory may be different.

How It Works

To clone jQuery you have to find the URL that points to its repository. Start your web browser, go to Google.com, and search for "jquery git repository". The results will include:

https://github.com/jquery/jquery

In a similar, way you can find URLs for other popular open source projects. Table 2-1 lists keywords and URLs for three other projects: Linux, git and Mozilla.

Table 2-1. *How to find git repositories for other projects?*

Phrase searched in Google.com	The URL of the repository
linux git repository	https://github.com/torvalds/linux
git git repository	https://github.com/git/git
mozilla git repository	https://github.com/mozilla/mozilla-central

Once you know URL of the jQuery repository, you can start your web browser and visit:

```
https://github.com/jquery/jquery
```

You will see the page presented as shown in Figure 2-2.

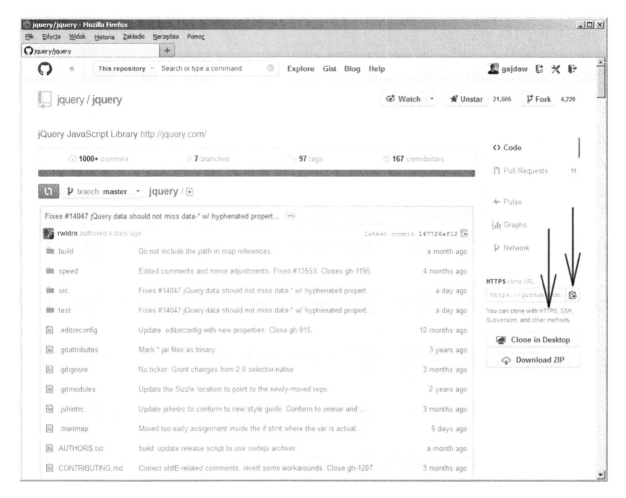

Figure 2-2. *The main page of jQuery repository* `https://github.com/jquery/jquery`

Every repository stored on Github is available under two different URLs: HTTPS and SSH. You can copy them using the buttons pointed to by the arrows in Figure 2-2. The URLs for the jQuery repository are:

HTTPS: `https://github.com/jquery/jquery.git`
SSH: `git@github.com:jquery/jquery.git`

If you don't have a Github account with SSH keys installed you cannot use SSH URL. You have to choose HTTPS URL.

> ■ **Hint** In chapter 13 we will create and configure a Github account. Then you will be able to use SSH URL as well; until then, you must use HTTPS URLs.

In this way you can clone all repositories available on Github.com. Remember this command:

```
$ git clone https://github.com/abc/def.git
```

For it creates the subdirectory def/. And the clone is stored inside it.

However, if you work on Windows and try to clone the Linux source code, for example, you will encounter problems because filename restrictions are different with different systems. We will analyze this in chapter 11.

What will happen if you don't have a Github account with SSH keys configured and use SSH URL? The SSH URL for jQuery is:

```
git@github.com:jquery/jquery.git
```

If you use it for git clone command:

```
$ git clone git@github.com:jquery/jquery.git
```

Then you would get the following error:

```
Permission denied (publickey)
```

2-2. Cloning a repository hosted on Bitbucket

Problem

You want to get a local copy of the Atlassian AUI repository that is stored on Bitbucket.org:

```
https://bitbucket.org/atlassian/aui
```

You want the clone to be saved directly under git-recipes/02-02/, without having an additional aui/ subdirectory.

Solution

Start the command line and create a git-recipes/02-02/ directory:

```
$ cd git-recipes
$ mkdir 02-02
```

Change your current directory to 02-02/:

```
$ cd 02-02
```

Then run the command shown in Listing 2-2. Notice the last parameter—a dot. This dot represents a current directory, thus the clone will be placed directly under git-recipes/02-02/. Without the dot the cloned repository would be stored in a subdirectory git-recipes/02-02/aui/.

Listing 2-2. The command to clone Atlassian AUI repository

```
$ git clone https://bitbucket.org/atlassian/aui.git.
```

■ **Note** The syntax for the git clone command is: `$ git clone URL [directory]`. If used, the optional `[directory]` parameter sets the target directory for the cloned repository.

How It Works

Start your web browser and go to `https://bitbucket.org/atlassian/aui`. The main page of Atlassian AUI repository is shown in Figure 2-3.

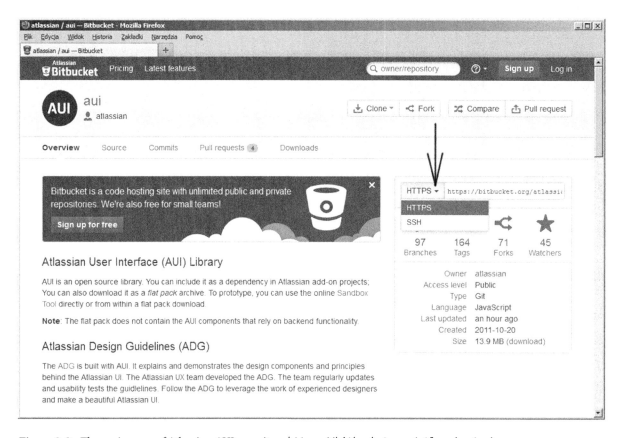

Figure 2-3. *The main page of Atlassian AUI repository* `https://bitbucket.org/atlassian/aui`

Bitbucket offers two URLs for every repository: HTTPS and SSH. Figure 2-3 and the following listing will give you access to both of them:

HTTPS: `https://bitbucket.org/atlassian/aui.git`
SSH: `git@bitbucket.org:atlassian/aui.git`

As with Github, SSH URL can only be used if you have a Bitbucket account with the SSH keys configured.

■ **Hint**   The two most popular hosted solutions for git are `Github.com` and `Bitbucket.org`. Both offer unlimited free accounts for public repositories.

2-3. Cloning a local repository
Problem

You want to clone a repository `git-recipes/02-01/jquery/` that you created in Recipe 2-1, and you prefer to store a new clone directly under `git-recipes/02-03/` without an additional `jquery/` directory.

Solution

Go to your `git-recipes/` directory:

```
$ cd git-recipes
```

Then you need to execute the command shown in Listing 2-3.

Listing 2-3.   The command that clones a local repository

```
$ git clone 02-01/jquery 02-03
```

After the using the command shown in Listing 2-3, the directory `git-recipes/02-03/` will contain the files as shown in Figure 2-4.

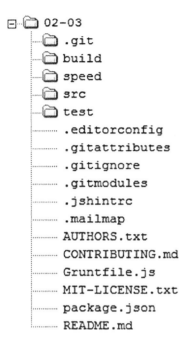

Figure 2-4. *The contents of the git-recipes/02-03/ directory after a succesfull clone*

How It Works

The Git clone command accepts both a URL and a local path that points to the repository. Thus, you can clone a local repository by passing a path instead of a URL to the command.

2-4. Copying a local repository
Problem

You want to clone the repository git-recipes/02-03/ that you created in Recipe 2-3. This time, instead of using a git clone you want to use a standard cp command with a –R flag.

Solution

Enter the directory git-recipes/:

```
$ cd git-recipes
```

Second, you then execute the command:

```
$ cp -R git-recipes/02-03 git-recipes/02-04
```

The command will create the exact copy of files from git-recipes/02-03/. The content of git-recipes/02-04/ is a valid git repository.

How It Works

By using the cp -R command, you can recursively copy a directory. If used on a directory containing a repository it will create a correct repository that is almost identical with a repository created with git clone command. We will explore the difference between repositories created in Recipes 2-3 and 2-4 in Recipe 2-5.

■ **Hint**   Once you know that a repository can be copied with standard filesystem operations such as cp, you can use rsync or scp to achieve the same result. In chapter 11 we will use scp command to start a new project.

2-5. Exploring the contents of a git repository
Problem

What does the directory created by the git clone command contain? To answer this question you will need to explore the contents of git-recipes/02-03/ directory with cd, ls, and cat commands. You also can use your favorite file manager.

Solution

The contents of the git-recipes/02-03/ directory, shown in Figure 2-5, contains jQuery files and directories and a special directory named .git.

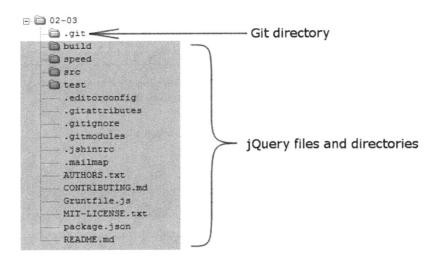

Figure 2-5.   *The repository created in Recipe 2-3*

The directory named .git is called the **git directory**. It contains all the information about the repository. The content of .git directory is shown in Figure 2-6.

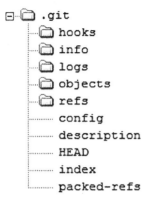

Figure 2-6. *The contents of a .git directory*

How It Works

If you want to display the contents of a .git directory you can use the following commands:

```
$ cd git-recipes/02-03/
$ cd .git
$ ls -l
```

The last command will print the files and directories shown in Figure 2-6. The role of every item is briefly described in Table 2-2. The complete descriptions are included in the recipes dealing with the specific details of git.

Table 2-2. *The contents of a .git directory*

Directory/file	Description
hooks/	Directory contains scripts that can be automatically executed by git when some events occur; for example, before each commit and after each commit.
info/	Directory contains a single file named exclude, which can be used to exclude files from a repository. Unlike the .gitignore file, this file is not shared by others.
logs/	Directory contains logs of local changes made to the repository.
objects/	This is the database that contains all the information about files, directories, revisions, and tags.
refs/	This is where git stores the information about branches and lightweight tags.
config	This is the local configuration file containing the options that will be applied to this repository only.
description	This is the short description of the repository. It is used by the Gitweb CGI application distributed with git.
HEAD	The current branch or revision of the repository
index	The staging area of the repository
packed-refs	The list of references from refs/ in a packed format

Let's now compare the contents of three config files:

```
git-recipes/02-01/jquery/.git/config
git-recipes/02-03/.git/config
git-recipes/02-04/.git/config
```

The first solution, created in Recipe 2-1 is a clone of the original jQuery repository stored on Github. Inside git-recipes/02-01/jquery/.git/config you will find the following lines:

```
[remote "origin"]
    url = https://github.com/jquery/jquery.git
```

The entry [remote "origin"] stores the address passed to the git clone command.

The second solution, git-recipes/02-03/ is a clone of a local directory. The file git-recipes/02-03/.git/config contains:

```
[remote "origin"]
    url = /home/john/git-recipes/02-01/jquery
```

As you can see this time [remote "origin"] points to the local directory.

■ **Hint** I assumed that the full path to your git-recipes/ directory is: /home/john/git-recipes/.

The third solution is an exact copy of git-recipes/02-03/. Thus, the file git-recipes/02-04/.git/config contains:

```
[remote "origin"]
    url = /home/john/git-recipes/02-01/jquery
```

If we had used:

```
$ cd git-recipes
$ git clone 02-03 02-04
```

to create git-recipes/02-04/; the file git-recipes/02-04/.git/config would have instead contained:

```
[remote "origin"]
    url = /home/john/git-recipes/02-03
```

There isn't any difference between git-recipes/02-03/ and git-recipes/02-04/. Later, in chapter 10, we will learn to change [remote "origin"] entries in the config file using the git remote command.

Conclusion

As a conclusion to Recipes 2-4 and 2-5, remember that repositories can be copied and moved to different locations on your drive; just as any other directory. The git directory .git doesn't contain any information that ties the repository to a specific path on your drive.

2-6. Deleting and restoring the contents of the working directory

Problem

You want to verify that git has stored all your files in the database .git/objects. To achieve this you need to delete the contents of the working directory and then restore it from the git database.

Solution

Enter the repository created in Recipe 2-3:

```
$ cd git-recipes/02-03
```

Remove all files and directories, except the .git subdirectory:

```
$ ls -la
$ rm -rf *
$ rm .????*
```

Now, the directory git-recipes/02-03/ contains only one subdirectory .git. You can check it with:

```
$ ls -l
```

Next, execute the command:

```
$ git reset --hard
```

All the files will be restored. The command:

```
$ ls -l
```

now prints the result that is identical with those in Figure 2-4.

How It Works

Usually, the directory containing the git repository consists of two areas. One has already been discussed, the **git directory** named .git. The other is called the **working directory**. They are both shown in Figure 2-7.

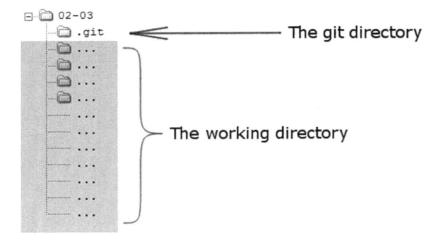

Figure 2-7. *The git directory and the working directory*

The working directory is the temporary storage that contains your work. The git directory, on the other hand, contains the database that stores all snapshots of your project. Recipe 2-6 should convince you that the contents of your working directory can be easily restored from the database.

2-7. Cloning a bare repository

Problem

You want to create a bare clone of a repository from Recipe 2-3.

Solution

Issue the following commands:

```
$ cd git-recipes
$ git clone --bare 02-03 02-06
```

Enter the 02-06/ directory and check its contents:

```
$ cd 02-06
$ ls -la
```

The above command will print the output identical to Figure 2-6.

How It Works

The git clone command takes an optional parameter --bare. You can use the --bare parameter to create a bare repository. A **bare repository** contains only the contents of the git directory. It does not contain the working directory. This type of repository is used for synchronization purposes only. We will use it in chapter 10.

■ **Remember**   The bare repository can be created with the $ `git clone --bare [URL]` command. This type of repository doesn't contain the working directory. Its content is equivalent to the content of a `.git` directory in a non-bare repository.

2-8. Exploring the history with a git log command
Problem

You want to print the following information about a jQuery repository:

- The complete list of the revisions in the repository
- The shortened and simplified list of the latest revisions in the repository
- The list of revisions by John Resig
- The list containing last five revisions in 2012

Solution

Enter the directory `git-recipes/02-01/jquery/`:

```
$ cd git-recipes/02-01/jquery
```

To print the complete list of revisions in the repository execute:

```
$ git log
```

You will see that the output is similar to the one presented in Listing 2-4. This is the complete list of revisions that are accessible from the current revision. You can scroll the output with space and arrow keyboard keys. Press q to quit the git log.

Listing 2-4. The output of git log command

```
commit 18cccd04a6f69018242bce96ef905bc5d3be6ff8
Author: Richard Gibson <richard.gibson@gmail.com>
Date:   Mon Apr 29 13:31:59 2013 -0400

    Fix #13803: domManip remote-script evaluation per 1.9 (AJAX dataType "script")

commit 55e319aa52eb828a3a4c2298aa75b6d15cfa06f8
Author: Corey Frang <gnarf@gnarf.net>
Date:   Wed Apr 24 16:07:15 2013 -0400

    Fixes #13815: Ensure each element has its own private data object - Tests by @rwldrn

commit 3a6194076b8b7ab5a9d9f5e6ec602db2ab427d3e
Author: Oleg <markelog@gmail.com>
Date:   Wed Apr 24 22:15:41 2013 +0400

    Fix #13818: Add wrapMap entry for col element
```

The output shown in Listing 2-4 presents three revisions. The first revision has the name:

```
18cccd04a6f69018242bce96ef905bc5d3be6ff8
```

This revision was created by Richard Gibson on Monday, April 29, 2013. The comment:

```
Fix #13803: domManip remote-script evaluation per 1.9 (AJAX dataType "script")
```

provides the information that the revision contains the fix for issue number 13803.

Shortened and simplified, the list of revisions can be printed with the command shown in Listing 2-5.

Listing 2-5. The command that produces simplified and shortened log information

```
$ git log --abbrev-commit --abbrev=4 --pretty=oneline -10
```

It will print an output similar to:

```
18cc Fix #13803: domManip remote-script...
55e3 Fixes #13815: Ensure each element...
3a619 Fix #13818: Add wrapMap entry for...
78c8 Fix #13819: .parent sort direction...
ad71f Fix #13809: Avoid collisions with...
```

Every line concerns one revision and contains a short abbreviated name SHA-1 and the comment. If possible, the abbreviations are shortened to four characters:

```
18cc
55e3
78c8
```

When necessary, more characters are used:

```
3a619
ad71f
```

Using -10 parameter, the output is restricted to the last 10 revisions only.

The command shown in Listing 2-6 prints the revisions that were authored by John Resig.

Listing 2-6. Revisions authored by John Resig

```
$ git log --author="John Resig"
```

The parameters shown in Listing 2-5 and Listing 2-6 can be used together. The command:

```
$ git log --abbrev-commit --abbrev=4 --pretty=oneline -10 --author="John Resig"
```

prints the last 10 revisions by John Resig in their simplified form.

The command to produce the list of the last five revisions made in 2013 is presented at Listing 2-7.

Listing 2-7. Last five revisions of 2013

```
$ git log --pretty=oneline --since="2012-12-20" --until="2013-01-01" -5
```

How It Works

The history of a git repository consists of a series of revisions. Each revision is a snapshot of the working directory at a particular point in time. The revisions are stored within the .git/objects database.

Every revision is identified by its **name**. Git uses a **SHA-1 algorithm** to generate names. Because the revision's SHA-1 is computed using many different types of data—the author's name, the current timestamp, and the snapshot, among others—we can treat them as unique identifiers. The probability that two different revisions will have the same SHA-1 is so small that it can be disregarded. In fact, SHA-1 uniqness is one of the most basic git assumptions. As you will see in chapter 11. the whole process of synchronization relies on it.

■ **Hint** The user cannot assign a name to the revision. All names are automatically generated by git. Git rules here and you can trust that it will never generate two identical names for different revisions.

SHA-1 names are 20 bytes long, and thus, their hex representation takes 40 characters, for example:

18cccd04a6f69018242bce96ef905bc5d3be6ff8

Later in the book we will need to use the name as a parameter passed to various commands; if that is the case, one will not have to use all 40 characters. Usually, the first seven characters are sufficient. The shortest possible abbreviation of a name has to be four characters long. Remember that abbreviation needs to be unique—if it is not, then you'll have to use more characters.

The list of revisions stored in the repository can be printed with a git log command. Its various options and switches can be used to filter and reformat displayed revisions. The output of a git log command is sorted by the time the revisions were created. The latest revision is displayed at the top of the output.

By default, the git log prints all revisions that are available from your current revision.

The format of the output can be changed with the --pretty parameter. Available values and their meanings are summarized in Table 2-3.

Table 2-3. *The values for --pretty parameter*

Value	Description
oneline	The name and the comment printed in one line.
short	The name, the author, and the comment
medium	Same as short but augmented with the revision's date
full	The name, the author, the committer, and the comment
fuller	The name, the author, the author's date, the committer, the commit's date, and the comment
email	Same as short in email format
raw	Low-level revision's information: the name, the tree, the parent revision's name, the author, and the committer with timestamps
format	User-defined format

The parameters shown in Table 2-3 can be passed to a `git log` command as:

```
$ git log --pretty=oneline
$ git log --pretty=short
$ git log --pretty=raw
```

The value `--pretty=oneline` can be shortened to:

```
$ git log --oneline
```

Additional parameters that influence the format are:

> `--abbrev-commit`—this option turns on abbreviations.

> `--abbrev=n`—this option sets the length of the abbreviated names.

> `--decorate`—this option includes tags and branches for each revision.

The shortest possible abbreviation has to contain four characters. Thus, the minimal value for `--abbrev` is four:

```
$ git log --abbrev-commit --abbrev=4
```

■ **Hint**   The parameter `--oneline` abbreviates SHA-1 to seven characters.

The parameter `--pretty=format` allows you to define the arbitrary output's format. The special string containing placeholders defines the output. The command:

```
$ git log --pretty=format:"%an --- %H"
```

will print the output in this form:

```
Joe Doe --- 123456...
```

The first part of the output (e.g., Joe Doe) is the author's name, while the second part is a full SHA-1 of a revision. This output is produced with two placeholders:

```
%an - author's name
%H - full SHA-1 hash
```

The other useful placeholders include:

```
%h: abbreviated commit hash,
%ae: author email,
%ad: author date,
%cn: committer name,
%ce: committer email,
%cd: committer date,
%e: encoding,
%s: subject,
%n: newline.
```

▦ **Hint**   A full list of placeholders is available in the manual for `git log`. You can access it with the `git help log` command.

Here are some parameters to filter revisions included in the output:

   -n—number of revisions, for example, –7 restricts git log to the last seven revisions

   `--since="yyyy-mm-dd"`—starting date

   `--until="yyyy-mm-dd"`—finishing date

   `--author="John Doe"`—commits by a given author

▦ **Hint**   The dates passed to `--since` and `--until` parameters can be set in `yyyy-mm-dd` format or less formally as `--since="1 week ago"`, `--since="Two months ago"`, `--until="5 days ago"`, `--until="7 hours ago"`, `--until="yesterday"`. To avoid typing quotation marks, you can also use dots for spaces, like in `--since=1.week.ago`, `--since=Two.months.ago`, `--until=5.days.ago`.

2-9. Analyzing a repository with git log and shortlog commands
Problem

You want answers to the following questions for the jQuery project:

- How many revisions does the repository contain?
- How many developers contributed to the project?
- How many days did they work on the project?
- How much space is used by the working directory?
- How much space is used by the git directory?
- How many files are in the working directory?

Solution

Enter the directory `git-recipes/02-01/jquery/`:

```
$ cd git-recipes/02-01/jquery
```

To answer the questions execute the commands shown in Listings 2-8 to 2-13.

Listing 2-8. The command that prints the number of commits in the repository

```
$ git log --pretty=oneline | wc -l
```

Listing 2-9. The command that prints the number of contributors

```
$ git shortlog -s | wc -l
```

Listing 2-10. The command that produces the number of days during which contributions were made

```
$ git log --pretty=format:%cd --date=short | uniq | wc -l
```

Listing 2-11. The command that returns the amount of space used by the git directory

```
$ du -h -s .git
```

Listing 2-12. The command that returns the amount of space used by the working directory

```
$ du -h -s --exclude=.git
```

Listing 2-13. The command that produces the number of files in the working directory

```
$ git ls-files | wc -l
```

▪ **Hint**   Linux and Windows version of du both support --exclude parameter. But some other systems, such as BSD, use other options. In BSD, exclusions are set with -I option (I stands for Ignore).

How It Works

The answers to the above questions can be found using the following commands:

```
git log
git shortlog
git ls-files
du
wc
uniq
grep
```

As we already know, the command:

```
$ git log --pretty=oneline
```

prints the list of all revisions in a simplified form, where every revision occupies one line. Piping the list to wc -l:

```
$ git log --pretty=oneline | wc -l
```

we get the number of revisions.

The git shortlog command presents the information about commits grouped by authors. Without any parameters, its output has the form:

```
Adam Coulombe (1):
      Fix #13150, ...

Adam J. Sontag (7):
      .closest() should
      Add a comment expl
```

```
        Add a comment to e
        Add link to chrome
        shorten the SHA
        Fix tabs vs spaces
        Revert grunt, grun
...
```

The above list contains all the developers and their revisions. The parameter -s prints only the number of revisions and developer's name:

```
1   Adam Coulombe
7   Adam J. Sontag
...
```

Parameter -n prints the results sorted in numeric order by the number of revisions.

To print the number of contributors we pipe the result of git shortlog -s to wc -l:

```
$ git shortlog -s | wc -l
```

The next question is a little more difficult to answer. First, we want to print the output of the git log command in a special form. We want every line to contain only a commit's date in the form yyyy-mm-dd. It can be accomplished by:

```
$ git log --pretty=format:%cd --date=short
```

The above command will produce the list of dates:

```
2013-04-22
2013-04-22
2013-04-20
2013-04-20
2013-04-18
...
```

The date of every commit will be present in the output. Let's remove the duplicates. We can do it using the uniq command:

```
$ git log --pretty=format:%cd --date=short | uniq
```

Thus, we will find out the different dates when contributions to the project were made. If we pipe the result to wc -l:

```
$ git log --pretty=format:%cd --date=short | uniq | wc -l
```

We then get the desired number of days.

■ **Hint** This is the approximate measure that I use to declare the number of days I work on a book. When the command $ git log --pretty=format:%cd --date=short | uniq | wc -l returns 95 it means that I worked on a book not more than 95 days.

The next two questions concern the amount of space that the working directory and the git directory contain. The amount of space the git directory contains is returned by the command:

```
$ du -h -s .git
```

The amount of space the working directory contains is printed by the command:

```
$ du -h -s --exclude=.git
```

Here are the results for the jQuery project:

> The working directory: 1.3 MB

> The git directory: 16 MB

As you can see the git directory uses much more space than the working directory. This is not surprising: the database stored in `.git/objects` contains 5,192 revisions. Every revision can be thought of as a snapshot of a complete working directory.

The last question can be answered with the git ls-files command:

```
$ git ls-files | wc -l
```

The git ls-files command prints the names of all the files in the working directory. We use `wc -l` to count them.

2-10. Defining aliases for the commands discussed in Recipes 2-8 and 2-9

Problem

The commands shown in Listings 2-5 and 2-8 through 2-13 are quite long to type. You would like to define aliases that would be easier to type while returning the same output.

Solution

Open the command line and go to your home directory. Using Linux, Mac, or a bash command line on Windows it can be done with:

```
$ cd ~
```

If you use a standard Windows' command line, then try:

```
$ cd %userprofile%
```

Start the editor of the text files and open the file `.gitconfig`. If you use `vi`, you can do it with:

```
$ vi .gitconfig
```

At the bottom of the file append the contents of Listing 2-14. Save the file and exit the editor.

Listing 2-14. The aliases for the commands shown in Listings 2-5 and 2-8 through 2-13

```
[alias]
    l    = log --oneline --abbrev-commit --abbrev=4 -25

    days = "!days() {
        git log --pretty=format:%cd --date=short | uniq;
    }; days"

    stat = "!stat() {
        echo -n Number of revisions:;
        git log --oneline | wc -l;
        echo -n Number of developers:;
        git shortlog -s | wc -l;
        echo -n Number of days:;
        git days | wc -l;
        echo -n The working directory:;
        du -h -s --exclude=.git;
        echo -n The git directory:;
        du -h -s .git;
        echo -n Number of files in the working dir:;
        git ls-files | wc -l;
    }; stat"
```

■ **Hint**   You don't have to type the aliases presented in Listing 2-14. They are all available in the
`https://github.com/gajdaw-git-recipes/aliases` repository.

■ **Note**   The Listing 2-14 should be typed without newline characters within stat and days aliases. The file should
look like:

```
days = "!days() { ... }; days"
stat = "!stat() { ... }; stat"
```

The newline characters were used only for readability purposes.

When you finish entering the contents of Listing 2-14 at the bottom of your `.gitconfig` file, go to the directory
`git-recipes/02-01/jquery/`:

```
$ cd git-recipes/02-01/jquery
```

and execute the first of the aliases:

```
$ git l
```

You should see an output similar to:

```
18cc Fix #13803: domManip remote-script ...
55e3 Fixes #13815: Ensure each element ...
3a619 Fix #13818: Add wrapMap entry for ...
...
```

Next try the second alias:

```
$ git stat
```

It will produce similar results:

```
Number of revisions:     5192
Number of developers:    190
Number of days: 1246
The working directory:   1.3M    .
The git directory:       16M    .git
Number of files in the working dir:     149
```

■ **Caution**   The alias git stat uses echo with –n parameter to suppress the output of newline characters. If your system doesn't support echo –n, the formatting of the above results will be different.

How It Works

Git allows you to define aliases for arbitrary commands. The aliases should be stored in the user's configuration file. The file should be named .gitconfig and stored in your home directory. If you have already executed any commands to configure git with --global option, for example, git config --global user.name, then the .gitconfig file already exists in your home directory. Otherwise, you will have to create it.

The first of the aliases shown in Listing 2-14 can be created with:

```
$ git config --global alias.l "log --oneline --abbrev-commit --abbrev=4 -25"
```

The command git config –global alias.abc "def" just creates an entry abc = def in the [alias] section of your personal .gitconfing file.

If you want to find the location of your home directory type:

```
$ cd ~
$ pwd
```

The above commands will work well on Linux, Mac, or the bash command line on Windows. If you use a standard Windows' command line use:

```
$ cd %userprofile%
$ cd
```

If you work with vi you can open your git configuration file with:

```
# Linux
$ vi ~/.gitconfig

# Windows
$ vi %userprofile%\.gitconfig
```

The syntax of .gitconfig file

We will start the explanation of aliases with the syntax of a .gitconfig file. The interesting characters are: hash marks, semicolons, quotes, and backslashes.

Inside a .gitconfig file you can use hash marks and semicolons to denote comments that span to the end of the line. Thus the definition:

```
word = lorem ; ipsum
```

sets the property named word with the value lorem. The second word ipsum is skipped because a semicolon starts the comment. Similar rules apply to hash marks. The definition:

```
word2 = dolor # sit
```

sets the property word2 with value dolor.

If you want to define the value containing semicolons or hash marks, you have to use quotes:

```
sentence = "Lorem ; ipsum"
```

The above defines a property named sentence with value:

```
Lorem ; ipsum
```

It is not surprising that quotation marks should be escaped. The line:

```
person = "John \"Moo\" Cowboy"
```

defines the property person with the value:

```
John "Moo" Cowboy
```

The same escaping procedure applies to backslashes. The definition:

```
str = "a\\b"
```

sets the value of the str property to:

```
a\b
```

The above description clarifies the following notation:

```
something = "x ; \"y\" ; \\ ; z"
```

Surrounding quotes are necessary because we use semicolons. The quotes inside are escaped. Double backslash is an escaped backslash, hence the property something has the value:

```
x ; "y" ; \ ; z
```

Remember, that these rules apply to everything you store in your `.gitconfig` file.

Hint   The syntax of `.gitconfig` file is described in the manual in the section on Syntax: $ git help config

---

The alias syntax

The syntax to define a git alias in a `.gitconfig` file is either:

```
alias = command
```

or

```
alias = !command
```

The first version—the one without exclamation mark—applies to git subcommands. Alias:

```
abc = def
```

defines the command that can be named as:

```
$ git abc
```

When executed, `git abc` will produce the same effect as:

```
$ git def
```

Thus we can define alias:

```
l = log --pretty=oneline
```

that when called:

```
$ git l
```

will be expanded to:

```
$ git log --pretty=oneline
```

The second syntax for aliases—the one with exclamation mark—applies to arbitrary shell commands. The alias:

```
list-files = !ls
```

31

can be called:

```
$ git list-files
```

This call will result in the following command:

```
$ ls
```

I use aliases prefixed with exclamation mark together with shell functions. The alias:

```
foo = "!bar(){ }; bar"
```

can be called:

```
$ git foo
```

The exclamation mark tells git that this alias should be passed to shell. The next part:

```
bar(){};bar
```

consists of a function definition:

```
bar(){};
```

and a function call:

```
bar
```

Inside the braces you can place an arbitrary number of complete shell calls, separated with semicolons, for example:

```
foo = "!bar(){ echo abc; ls; }; bar"
```

This alias can be called:

```
$ git foo
```

It will result in two commands:

```
$ echo abc
$ ls
```

In a similar way, the alias:

```
info = "!funInfo(){ git --version; git log --pretty=oneline -3; }; funInfo"
```

can be called:

```
$ git info
```

It will produce the same output as two commands:

```
$ git --version
$ git log --pretty=oneline -3
```

Because of the semicolons, the alias using the shell function needs to be enclosed in quotes.

The aliases from Listing 2-14

The first alias presented at Listing 2-14 is:

```
l = log --oneline --abbrev-commit --abbrev=4 -25
```

It doesn't use the exclamation mark; therefore, it refers to a git subcommand. When called:

```
$ git l
```

it will be expanded to:

```
$ git log --pretty=oneline --abbrev-commit --abbrev=4 -25
```

Git allows you to pass additional parameters to aliases. Therefore, if you want to produce a simplified list of revisions by John Doe, call the alias with the --author parameter:

```
$ git l --author="John Doe"
```

You can pass any other parameters in the same manner.
The next alias is:

```
days = "!days() {
    git log --pretty=format:%cd --date=short | uniq;
}; days"
```

Because of the exclamation mark it is expanded to a shell command. The command defines and calls the function named days(). When you type:

```
$ git days
```

it will eventually execute:

```
$ git log --pretty=format:%cd --date=short | uniq
```

The last alias is a shell function that calls a number of other commands.

```
stat = "!stat() {
    echo -n Number of revisions:;
    git log --oneline | wc -l;
    echo -n Number of developers:;
    git shortlog -s | wc -l;
    echo -n Number of days:;
    git days | wc -l;
```

```
    echo -n The working directory:;
    du -h -s --exclude=.git;
    echo -n The git directory:;
    du -h -s .git;
    echo -n Number of files in the working dir:;
    git ls-files | wc -l;
}; stat"
```

Notice, that we produce the number of days with the subalias:

```
$ git days | wc -l
```

▪ Hint There are two methods for creating aliases in git. The first method is discussed in Recipe 2-10 and the second in Recipe 5-3. I prefer to define aliases inside .gitconfig files, as shown in Recipe 2-10. This method doesn't depend on user platform or permisions making it is easier to adopt during classes and training.

2-11. Analyzing one of the popular repositories
Problem

One of the most popular Github repositories is twitter/bootstrap, available at:

```
https://github.com/twitter/bootstrap.git
```

You want to analyze it using the aliases from Recipe 2-10.

Solution

Open command line and clone twitter/bootstrap:

```
$ git clone https://github.com/twitter/bootstrap.git 02-11
```

The command:

```
$ git stat
```

will print:

```
Number of revisions:    3569
Number of developers:    259
Number of days:          505
The working directory:  4.9M    .
The git directory:       28M   .git
Number of files in the working dir: 254
```

How It Works

Using the $ git clone command you can clone any public repository available on Github or Bitbucket. The alias created in Recipe 2-10 will help you to get some basic information about the project.

2-12. Visualizing the history of a repository
Problem

You want to display the history of the HTML 5 Boilerplate repository in a graphical form using a gitk application.

Solution

Clone the HTML 5 Boilerplate repository:

```
$ cd git-recipes
$ git clone https://github.com/h5bp/html5-boilerplate.git 02-12
```

Enter the 02-12/ directory:

```
$ cd 02-12
```

and run the gitk command:

```
$ gitk
```

■ **Note**   If you append the ampersand $ gitk &, the gitk application will run in the background, and you can use command line to execute other commands.

How It Works

The command $ gitk will display the window shown in Figure 2-8. It contains five panels:

1. The revisions
2. The authors
3. The dates
4. The list of modifications
5. The list of modified files

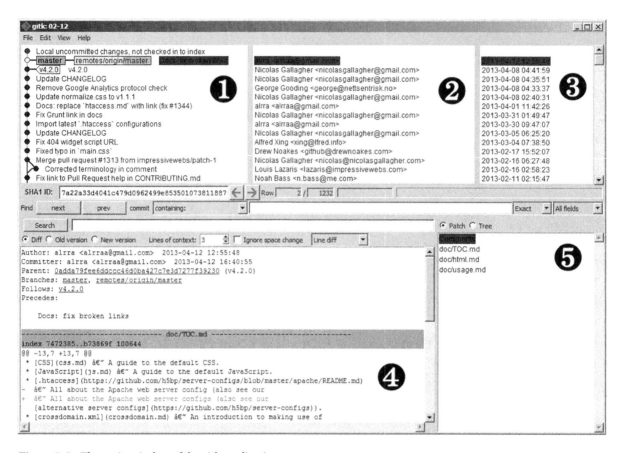

Figure 2-8. *The main window of the gitk application*

Using `gitk` you can easily check not only the list of revisions but also the modifications introduced in every revision.

Try scrolling down the revisions. You will see that the revisions do not necessarily form a linear history. The nonlinear history is shown in Figure 2-9. We will deal with nonlinear histories in chapters 5, 6, and 7.

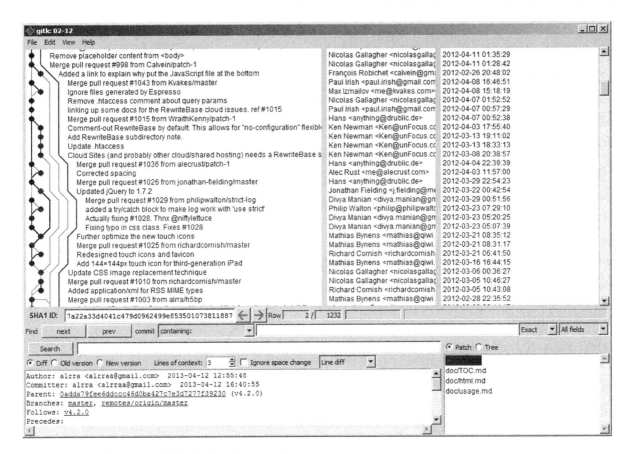

Figure 2-9. *The history of HTML 5 Boilerplate repository*

■ **Note** The $ gitk command accepts all the filters we discussed in Recipe 2-8. You can for example use gitk to display only the commits by a given author: $ gitk --author=john.

2-13. Removing a .git directory
Problem

You wish to discover how removing a .git directory will affect a repository.

Solution

Clone the FontAwesome repository:

```
$ cd git-recipes
$ git clone https://github.com/FortAwesome/Font-Awesome.git 02-13
```

Enter the directory:

```
$ cd 02-13
```

Right now, the directory 02-13/ contains a git repository. Thus, you can list the log entries:

```
$ git log
```

or the project's contributors:

```
$ git shortlog -n -s
```

If you remove .git directory with:

```
$ rm -rf .git
```

you will be left with the contents of the working directory. Git commands do not work anymore. If you issue:

```
$ git log
```

you will get the error:

```
fatal: Not a git repository (or any of the parent directories): .git
```

How It Works

The git directory can be removed with the simple command:

```
$ rm -rf .git
```

After this command you will lose the entire history of your project. The project's directory will contain only the latest version of the files stored in the working directory.

Summary

In this chapter, we've discussed the basic abilities to work with git repositories. You now know how to:

- Clone a repository (both: remote and local).
- Enter the repository and issue various git commands.
- Print the list or revisions stored in the repository.
- Analyze the history with git log and gitk.
- Discover the list and the number of revisions, contributors, and files stored in the repository.
- Define aliases for the most frequently used commands.

You also have learned the role of

- The git directory
- The git database
- The working directory

All of which will be needed to understand the later chapters.

The **git directory** is a special directory named `.git`, which usually is stored inside your project's directory. It contains all the history of your project and various configuration entries necessary for git to operate. Do not modify the contents of the `.git` directory unless you are strictly instructed to do so.

Inside the git directory there is a special subdirectory named `.git/objects`. It is the **git database**, which is also called the **object store**. That is where various git's commands store data. Revisions, different versions of files, directories, their contents, and so forth—they are all stored in this database. From time to time git tries to optimize this database. If you use git improperly, this can cause data loss.

The third area is called the **working directory**. It is the directory of your project excluding the git directory. This is where you work. Once the work is finished you can store the contents of your working directory as the next revision in the database. You will learn how to do this in the next chapter.

Do you remember Recipe 2-6? If not, analyze it once again. This recipe demonstrated a very important aspect of using git. The revisions you stored in the database can be retrieved into the working directory. We used `git reset --hard` to restore deleted files. From now on you should think about the working directory as a temporary storage.

The working directory and the git directory are used to classify every repository as either **non-bare** or **bare**.

A **non-bare repository** contains the working directory and the git directory. The configuration file `.git/config` of a non-bare repository contains the following entry:

```
[core]
    bare = false
```

The **bare repository** consists of the `.git` directory only. Its `.git/config` file contains:

```
[core]
    bare = true
```

As you will see in chapter 10, this type of repository is used for synchronization purposes.

■ ■ ■

## CHAPTER 3

Creating Local Repositories with Linear History

In this chapter you will learn how to create your own repositories, and how to use them in your daily work. This includes

- Initialization of a new repository with `$ git init`

- Storing snapshots as revisions with `$ git add -A` and `$ git commit -m "..."`

- Checking the status of the repository with `$ git status -s -b`

You'll learn how to start a new project from scratch as well as how to import existing files.

Three recipes will focus on restoring the working directory to snapshots stored in revisions. After learning these recipes you should be able to reset the working directory of any repository—such as jQuery—to an arbitrary revision, such as the very first revision in the repository, and then return the working directory to its latest state.

I give special attention to situations that may cause problems. Two recipes describe precisely how and when you can lose uncommitted or committed modifications. This knowledge should build your confidence. If you adhere to some simple rules, you will never lose what you store in your git repository.

In chapter 2, we characterized the repository as either non-bare or bare. This characterization was based on the presence of a working directory. Here we will introduce another classification: **clean** or **dirty**. This classification applies only to non-bare repositories. A repository is **clean** when its working directory contents are identical to the snapshot stored in its latest revision. If, on the other hand, the files in the working directory were modified and not committed, we call that repository **dirty**. To find out whether a repository is clean or dirty, we use the `$ git status` command.

3-1. Creating your first repository
Problem

You want to start a new project that will consist of text files with lists of books written by your favorite writers. Let's assume that you plan to store the works of every writer in a separate file. Once you create a file and type its contents, you should save the file and commit it into the repository. Suppose that you create files with the works of Agatha Christie, John Grisham, and Stephen King. The history of your repository would look similar to Figure 3-1.

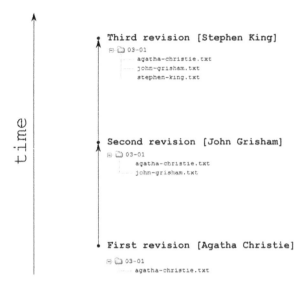

Figure 3-1. *The repository from Recipe 3-1*

Solution

In this recipe you will create your first revisions with the git commit command. Git doesn't allow committing unless you store your identity in a configuration file. If you haven't done it so far, please run the following two commands, replacing John Doe and john.doe@example.net with your personal information:

```
$ git config --global user.name "John Doe"
$ git config --global user.email john.doe@example.net
```

When you are ready to commit, initialize a new repository:

```
$ cd git-recipes
$ git init 03-01
$ cd 03-01
```

Now the directory 03-01 contains the git repository. To verify, run the command:

```
$ ls -la
```

It will print three items:

```
.
..
.git
```

As you will guess, the repository is empty. That means the database contains no revisions. We can verify that with the $ git log and the $ git status commands. First, print the history with:

```
$ git log
```

The answer will be:

```
fatal: bad default revision 'HEAD'
```

Now, check the status with:

```
$ git status
```

The information printed by git status will be:

```
# On branch master
#
# Initial commit
#
nothing to commit (create/copy files and use "git add" to track)
```

The comment # Initial commit means that the repository is ready to store the very first commit. Let's do that. Create the first file:

```
$ vi agatha-christie.txt
```

The file can contain the text shown in Listing 3-1, but that is not crucial.

Listing 3-1. The contents of agatha-christie.txt

```
Novels
    1943 | Five Little Pigs
    1934 | Murder on the Orient Express
```

After the file agatha-christie.txt is saved, check the state of the repository with:

```
$ git status -s
```

You will see the following output:

```
?? agatha-christie.txt
```

The two question marks ?? inform you that the agatha-christie.txt file is not tracked. It is a new file that hasn't been committed. Right now, the repository is dirty.

Create your first revision with the following two commands:

```
$ git add -A
$ git commit -m "First revision [Agatha Christie]"
```

The file is now stored in a new revision. The command:

```
$ git status -s
```

returns the empty output and it means that there are no pending changes in the working directory. In other words the repository is clean. Let's check the log with `$ git log`. The output will be similar to:

```
commit de3680b0a770dd46ede81f46cba0ae32f9e4687c
Author: Włodzimierz Gajda <gajdaw@gajdaw.pl>
Date:   Thu May 2 12:50:19 2013 +0200

    First commit [Agatha Christie]
```

The current state of the repository is shown in Figure 3-2.

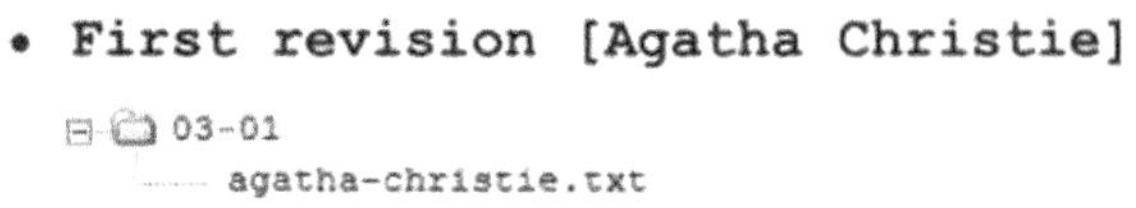

- **First revision [Agatha Christie]**

  ⊟ 🗁 03-01
  ⌐┈ agatha-christie.txt

Figure 3-2. *The repository from Recipe 3-1 after the first revision*

Let's create the second revision. Follow these steps:

1. Create the file john-grisham.txt

    ```
    $ vi john-grisham.txt
    ```

2. Type the contents of the file:

    ```
    Novels
        1989 | A Time to Kill
        1991 | The Firm
        1992 | The Pelican Brief
    ```

3. Save the file and close the editor.

4. Check the status of the repository:

    ```
    $ git status -s
    ```

    The output:

    ```
    ?? john-grisham.txt
    ```

    informs you about one new, untracked file:

    ```
    john-grisham.txt
    ```

5. Save the current state of the working directory as a new revision:

    ```
    $ git add -A
    $ git commit -m "Second revision [John Grisham]"
    ```

6. Check the status of the repository with:

    ```
    $ git status -s
    ```

    The empty output proves that the repository is clean.

7. Check the log of the repository with the alias from Recipe 2-10:

    ```
    $ git l
    ```

The output contains two revisions:

```
0468 Second revision: [John Grisham]
de36 First commit [Agatha Christie]
```

8. The repository should look like Figure 3-3.

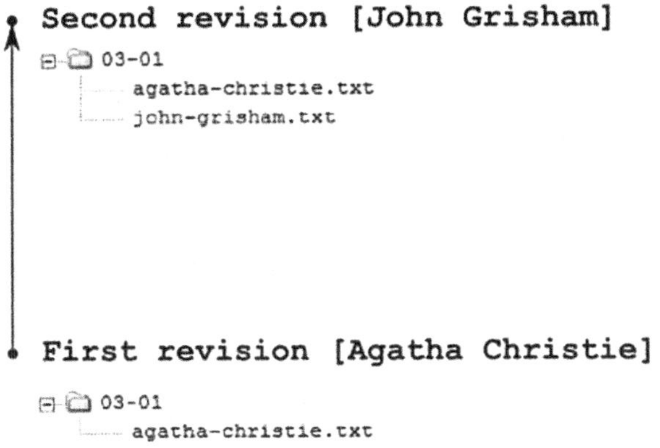

Second revision [John Grisham]

```
⊟ 🗀 03-01
      agatha-christie.txt
      john-grisham.txt
```

First revision [Agatha Christie]

```
⊟ 🗀 03-01
      agatha-christie.txt
```

Figure 3-3. *The repository from Recipe 3-1 after the second revision*

Finish the recipe creating the third file stephen-king.txt and the third revision. Here is the procedure:

1. Create the file stephen-king.txt

   ```
   $ vi stephen-king.txt
   ```

2. Enter the contents:

   ```
   Novels
       1974 | Carrie
       1975 | Salem's Lot
       1977 | The Shining
   ```

3. Save the file and close the editor.

4. Check the status of the repository:

   ```
   $ git status -s
   ```

The repository is dirty:

```
?? stephen-king.txt
```

5. Create the revision for the current state of the working directory:

   ```
   $ git add -A
   $ git commit -m "Third revision [Stephen King]"
   ```

6. Check the status of the repository:

   ```
   $ git status -s
   ```

Now, the output is empty; therefore, we know that the repository is clean.

7. Check the log with:

```
$ git l
```

The output will contain three revisions:

```
ffa6 Third revision [Stephen King]
0468 Second revision: [John Grisham]
de36 First commit [Agatha Christie]
```

8. The repository is shown in Figure 3-1.

Note   The two commands introduced in Recipe 3-1: $ git add -A and $ git commit -m "..." save the current state of your working directory as a new revision. We used them to store one new file in every revision, but that is not necessary. You can create, delete, move, and copy any arbitrary number of files. These two commands store the working directory, no matter how many files were modified or which type of tools were used.

How It Works

The new repositories are initialized with the command:

```
$ git init
```

You can pass a path to tell git where you want your project to be stored. The command:

```
$ git init 03-01
```

creates a new empty directory 03-01 and initializes an empty repository inside. Without any parameters the $ git init command will initialize a new repository in the current directory.

When the repository is initialized, you can work on your project: you can create files and type into their contents. Git is very smart in tracking changes you make in the working directory. It knows all about the modifications you make. If you doubt this, try using this command:

```
$ git status
```

It returns the exact information about the changes that were introduced in the working directory. The shortened form of this command is also very useful. It is shown in Listing 3-2.

Listing 3-2. The command to answer the question: Is the repository dirty or clean?

```
$ git status -s
```

Hint   The repository can be characterized as either clean or dirty. When we say that the **repository is clean**; it means that all the files in the working directory are stored in the latest revision. In this state the command: $ git status -s returns an empty result. The **repository is dirty** means when the working directory contains modifications that are not committed. The command: $ git status -s returns the list of pending changes.

The command from Listing 3-2 prints the list of modifications in a very compact form. You can treat it as a quick answer to the question: is the repository clean? If the output is empty then the repository is clean. Otherwise the repository is dirty and the output lists the modifications.

At some point you will need to make a decision that the current state of the working directory should be saved as a new revision. To achieve this use the two commands shown in Listing 3-3.

Listing 3-3. Two commands that save the current state of working directory as a new revision

```
$ git add -A
$ git commit -m "Comment..."
```

For now, treat them both as one atomic operation. We will discuss their exact role in chapter 4. Right now it is enough to know that when executed, they will create a new revision and leave the repository in the clean state.

If you are new git user, I suggest that at this early stage of learning you should check the status and log of the repository after every revision. As you already know, it can be done with:

```
$ git status -s
$ git log
```

You also can use the $ git l alias defined in Recipe 2-10.

3-2. Creating the git snapshot alias
Problem

As you already know, the snapshot of your working directory can be saved with two commands shown in Listing 3-3. Because we treat it as a single operation, you want to define the alias snapshot that will execute these two commands. Your alias, when executed as:

```
$ git snapshot
```

should store the current state of the working directory as a new revision.

Solution

Open the command line, go to your home directory, and edit your `.gitconfig` file. Follow the procedure given at the beginning of Recipe 2-10.

Type the contents of Listing 3-4 at the end of the [alias] section in your `.gitconfig` file, save the file, and close the editor.

Listing 3-4. Alias git snapshot

```
[alias]
    snapshot = "!snapshot() {
        COMMENT=wip;
        if [ \"$*\" ]; then
            COMMENT=\"$*\";
        fi;
        git add -A;
        git commit -m \"$COMMENT\";
    }; snapshot"
```

How It Works

Similar to Recipe 2-10, the alias was split with newlines. Remember that newlines are here only to make the alias easier to read—you must type the alias as one long line in your .gitconfig file.

The alias uses the shell function snapshot that after parsing of .gitconfig becomes:

```
snapshot() {
    COMMENT=wip;
    if [ "$*" ]; then
        COMMENT="$*";
    fi;
    git add -A;
    git commit -m "$COMMENT";
}
```

The instruction:

```
COMMENT=wip;
```

defines a variable named COMMENT with the value wip. Wip is an abbreviation for work in progress. The special variable $* contains all the parameters passed to the script. Consider the command:

```
$ some-script a b c
```

This call sends to the script some-script three parameters: a, b, and c. You can access all three parameters as one using the quoted $* variable "$*".

The conditional statement if-then-fi:

```
if [ "$*" ]; then
    COMMENT="$*";
fi;
```

checks the parameters passed to the script. If the script was called with parameters they will be assigned to COMMENT variable. Otherwise the COMMENT variable will stay unchanged—it stores the default value wip.

Now you know everything that will enable you to understand how the snapshot alias works. When we run the command:

```
$ git snapshot
```

it creates a revision with comment wip.

If we pass any parameters:

```
$ git snapshot Lorem ipsum dolor
```

then the alias will create the revision with comment "Lorem ipsum dolor".

3-3. Using the git snapshot alias in your daily work

Problem

You want to start a new project that will consist of text files storing songs for children. Similar to Recipe 3-1 you plan to save every new file in a new commit. To avoid typing both $ git add and $ git commit commands, you prefer to use the $ git snapshot alias, defined in Recipe 3-2.

Solution

Initialize a new repository:

```
$ cd git-recipes
$ mkdir 03-03
$ cd 03-03
$ git init
```

Create the first revision containing the lyrics of "Sing a song of sixpence" song.

1. Create the file sing-a-song-of-sixpence.txt

   ```
   $ vi sing-a-song-of-sixpence.txt
   ```

2. Type the contents of the file:

   ```
   Sing a song of sixpence,
   A pocket full of rye.
   Four and twenty blackbirds,
   Baked in a pie.
   ...
   ```

3. Save the file and close the editor.

4. Check the status of the repository with $ git status -s

The repository is dirty.

5. Save the current state of the working directory as a new revision:

   ```
   $ git snapshot Sing a song of sixpence
   ```

6. Check the status of the repository with $ git status -s

The repository is clean.

7. Check the log of the repository with $ git l

The output will contain one revision:

```
7cfb Sing a song of sixpence
```

The repository now looks like Figure 3-4.

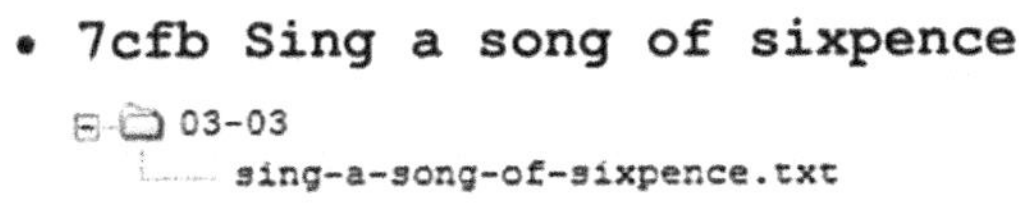

- **7cfb Sing a song of sixpence**
  - 🗀 03-03
    - sing-a-song-of-sixpence.txt

Figure 3-4. *The "Songs for children" project with first revision*

Create the second revision containing the lyrics of "Baa, baa, black sheep" song.

1. Create the baa-baa-black-sheep.txt file:

    $ vi baa-baa-black-sheep.txt

2. Type the contents of the file:

    Baa, baa, black sheep,
    Have you any wool?
    Yes, sir, yes, sir,
    Three bags full;
    ...

3. Save the file and close the editor.

4. Check the status of the repository with $ git status -s

The repository is dirty.

5. Save the current state of the working directory as a new revision:

    $ git snapshot Baa, baa black sheep

6. Check the status of the repository with $ git status -s

The repository is clean.

7. Check the log of the repository with $ git l

The output will contain two revisions:

564f Baa, baa black sheep
7cfb Sing a song of sixpence

The current state of the "Songs for children" project is shown at Figure 3-5.

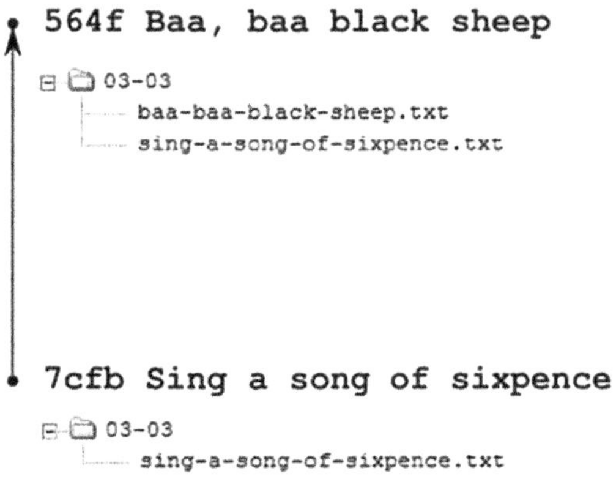

564f Baa, baa black sheep

⊟ 🗀 03-03
    ⊢ baa-baa-black-sheep.txt
    ⊢ sing-a-song-of-sixpence.txt

7cfb Sing a song of sixpence

⊟ 🗀 03-03
    ⊢ sing-a-song-of-sixpence.txt

Figure 3-5. The "Songs for children" project after second revision

Now you decide that this project should store songs in different languages. Create a new directory named EN and move both files into it:

```
$ mkdir EN
$ mv *. txt EN
```

Check the state of the repository:

```
$ git status -s
```

The repository is dirty. Save the current state of working directory as a new revision:

```
$ git snapshot Internationalization: directory EN
```

Now the repository is clean. The command:

```
$ git l
```

returns three revisions:

```
f305 Internationalization: directory EN
564f Baa, baa black sheep
7cfb Sing a song of sixpence
```

The repository we obtained is shown in Figure 3-6.

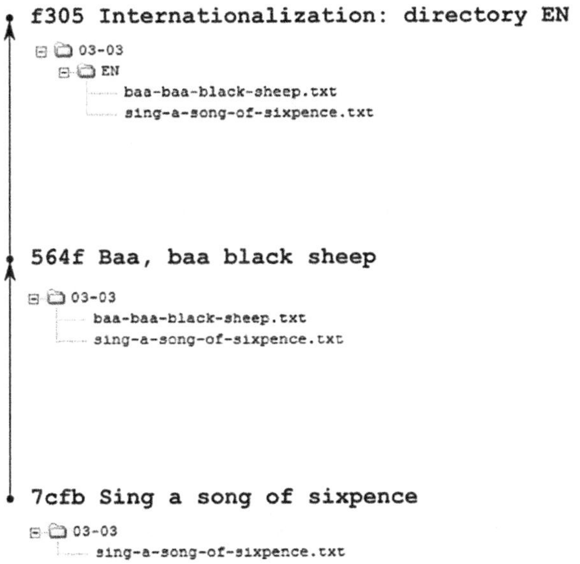

Figure 3-6. *The "Songs for children" project after the third revision*

Create a new folder PL:

```
$ mkdir PL
```

Now, check the status:

```
$ git status -s
```

How strange, the repository is clean! That's because git doesn't track empty directories.

Hint The generally accepted method of circumventing git's restriction forbidding committing empty directories is to create an empty file called .gitkeep.

Now prepare the revision containing a Polish song "Bajka iskierki":

1. Create the bajka-iskierki.txt file:

   ```
   $ vi PL/bajka-iskierki.txt
   ```

2. Type the contents of the file:

   ```
   Na Wojtusia z popielnika
   Iskiereczka mruga....
   ```

3. Save the file and close the editor.

4. Check the status of the repository:

   ```
   $ git status -s
   ```

The repository is dirty.

5. Save the current state of the working directory as a new revision:

   ```
   $ git snapshot [PL] Bajka iskierki
   ```

6. Check the status of the repository with:

   ```
   $ git status -s
   ```

The repository is clean.

7. Check the log of the repository with:

   ```
   $ git l
   ```

The output will contain four revisions:

```
d234 [PL] Bajka iskierki
f305 Internationalization: directory EN
564f Baa, baa black sheep
7cfb Sing a song of sixpence
```

The state of the repository is shown in Figure 3-7.

Figure 3-7. *The "Songs for children" project after the fourth revision*

Now you make the decision that every song should start with a line:

```
TITLE: Abc...
```

Open the EN/sing-a-song-of-sixpence.txt file $ vi EN/sing-a-song-of-sixpence.txt and at the very beginning of the file insert the line:

```
TITLE: Sing a song of sixpence
```

Save the file and close the editor.

In the same manner modify the second file baa-baa-black-sheep.txt. The first line should contain TITLE: Baa, baa, black sheep. Finally modify the third file bajka-iskierki.txt. Enter the text TITLE: Bajka iskierki. Save the file and close the editor.

Right, now all three files are modified. The command $ git status -s prints:

```
M EN/baa-baa-black-sheep.txt
M EN/sing-a-song-of-sixpence.txt
M PL/bajka-iskierki.txt
```

Create the revision that will store the current state of the project:

```
$ git snapshot Titles
```

The history printed by $ git l now prints five revisions:

```
39d6 Titles
d234 [PL] Bajka iskierki
f305 Internationalization: directory EN
564f Baa, baa black sheep
7cfb Sing a song of sixpence
```

As you can see the single revision can store an arbitrary number of modifications. The last revision we created included three modified files. The final repository from Recipe 3-3 is shown at Figure 3-8.

Figure 3-8. *The final repository from Recipe 3-3*

How It Works

You already know how to initialize a new project with $ git init. When executed without parameters the command will create a repository in a current directory.

Once the project is initialized you can proceed with your work using the command:

```
$ git status -s
```

and aliases:

```
$ git snapshot
$ git l
```

Every time you want to save the current state of your working directory as a revision use this command:

```
$ git snapshot
```

If you want to set comments for revisions use the parameters:

```
$ git snapshot A short info explaining the purpose of the revision
```

3-4. Mapping names
Problem

Suppose that during the first contact with git you configure it in such a way, that your name is set to johny:

```
$ git config --global user.name johny
```

You work on your project for some time, and then you decide that you prefer to be identified as John Doe. After another period, during which you commit heavily, you change your mind again. This time you want to be called Paul "Moo" Cowboy. Thus, your revisions are assigned to three different authors: johny, John Doe, and Paul "Moo" Cowboy. You want to reconfigure your repository in such a way that all these names are mapped to your real name. You can achieve this result by preparing a .mailmap file.

Solution

Clone the repository from Recipe 3-3:

```
$ cd git-recipes
$ git clone 03-03 03-04
$ cd 03-04
```

Check the authors of the revisions with:

```
$ git shortlog -s
```

The output will look like:

```
5  Włodzimierz Gajda
```

Of course, my name will be replaced by yours. This output informs you that the person named "Włodzimierz Gajda" authored five revisions.

Open your .gitconfig file and change your name to:

```
[user]
    name = johny
    email = john.doe@example.net
```

Next create the revision as johny. Follow the procedure:

1.   Create the directory FR/ and the file FR/alouette-gentille-alouette.txt:

     ```
     $ mkdir FR
     $ vi FR/alouette-gentille-alouette.txt
     ```

2.   Type the contents of the file:

     ```
     Alouette, gentille alouette,
     Alouette, je te plumerai.
     ...
     ```

3.   Save the file and close the editor.

4.   Create the revision:

     ```
     $ git snapshot [FR] Alouette, gentille alouette
     ```

Right now, the output produced by $ git shortlog -s will include two authors:

```
5  Włodzimierz Gajda
1  johny
```

Follow the same procedure to create a new revision by John Doe:

1.   Change your name in .gitconfig to John Doe:

     ```
     [user]
         name = John Doe
         email = john.doe@example.net
     ```

2.   Create a new file little-skylark.txt:

     ```
     $ vi EN/little-skylark.txt
     ```

3.   Type the contents of the file:

     ```
     Little skylark, lovely little skylark,
     Little lark, I'll pluck your feathers off.
     ...
     ```

4.   Save the file and close the editor.

5.   Save the current state of the working directory as a new revision:

     ```
     $ git snapshot [EN] Little skylark, lovely little skylark
     ```

6.   Check the list of authors with:

     ```
     $ git shortlog -s -n
     ```

Thanks to -n option, the output will be sorted in descending order by the number of revisions:

```
5   Włodzimierz Gajda
1   John Doe
1   johny
```

Next, create the revision under the name of Paul "Moo" Cowboy:

1. Change your name in .gitconfig:

   ```
   [user]
       name = "Paul \"Moo\" Cowboy"
       email = moo@wild-west.example.net
   ```

Notice that you have to escape inside quotes with backslashes.

2. Create a new file frere-jacques.txt:

   ```
   $ vi FR/frere-jacques.txt
   ```

3. Type the contents of the file:

   ```
   Frère Jacques, frère Jacques,
   Dormez-vous? Dormez-vous?
   Sonnez les matines! Sonnez les matines!
   Ding, daing, dong. Ding, daing, dong.
   ```

4. Save the file and close the editor.

5. Save the current state of the working directory as a new revision:

   ```
   $ git snapshot [FR] Frere Jacques
   ```

6. Check the list of authors with:

   ```
   $ git shortlog -s -n
   ```

The output will contain four entries:

```
5   Włodzimierz Gajda
1   John Doe
1   Paul "Moo" Cowboy
1   johny
```

Hint We have four different authors right now, and we will proceed with mail mapping. I encourage you, however, to check the results returned by $ git shortlog -s -n when the repository contains revisions authored by following authors: name = "Paul "Moo" Cowboy", name = Peter ;Moo Cowboy, name = "Peter ;Moo Cowboy", name = "Peter "Moo" Cowboy". These examples are helpful to understand the parsing of .gitconfig file. It is especially helpful to understand the handling of quotes and comments.

To proceed with mapping names and emails, restore your name and email in the .gitconfig file to your original data. I would type:

```
[user]
    name = Włodzimierz Gajda
    email = gajdaw@gajdaw.pl
```

You have to replace the above data with your name and email.

Now, create the file .mailmap:

```
$ vi .mailmap
```

Remember that the .mailmap file has to be stored in the root of the working directory in your current project. Otherwise it will have no effect. Type the following contents (replace my email with your own):

```
My New Extra Name <gajdaw@gajdaw.pl>
```

When you save the .mailmap file the command:

```
$ git shortlog -s -n
```

It will return:

```
5   My New Extra Name
1   John Doe
1   Paul "Moo" Cowboy
1   johny
```

As you can see, my name is mapped from Włodzimierz Gajda to My New Extra Name. Open .mailmap file again and append another line:

```
John Doe <john.doe@example.net>
```

The line:

```
John Doe <john.doe@example.net>
```

changes the name of all the commits by john.doe@example.net to John Doe. The output of:

```
$ git shortlog -sn
```

is now:

```
5   My New Extra Name
2   John Doe
1   Paul "Moo" Cowboy
```

Commits that were previously assigned to johny are now treated as created by John Doe.

How to assign revisions by Paul "Moo" Cowboy to John Doe? You will achieve it with following .mailmap entry:

```
John Doe <john.doe@example.net> <moo@wild-west.example.net>
```

The above entry maps all the revisions by moo@wild-west.example.net to John Doe. Now, the output of $ git shortlog -ns is:

```
5   My New Extra Name
3   John Doe
```

Finish the recipe creating the `.mailmap` entries that will reassign all the revisions to you. Remap your name by adding your second name. The solution to this problem is shown in Listing 3-5.

Listing 3-5. The .mailmap content that reassigns all revisions to me and changes my name by inserting my second name Edmund

```
Włodzimierz Edmund Gajda <gajdaw@gajdaw.pl>
Włodzimierz Edmund Gajda <gajdaw@gajdaw.pl> <john.doe@example.net>
Włodzimierz Edmund Gajda <gajdaw@gajdaw.pl> <moo@wild-west.example.net>
```

Right now the `$ git shortlog -ns` command returns:

```
8   Włodzimierz Edmund Gajda
```

All the revisions are authored by one person—me.
Finish the recipe creating a new revision:

```
$ git snapshot Mapping names with .mailmap
```

Right now the repository contains nine revisions and only one committer. You can verify it with:

```
$ git stat
```

This is the alias we created in Recipe 2-10.
Remember that the `.mailmap` file influences only the `$ git shortlog` command. The command:

```
$ git log
```

will print:

```
commit abda33b8addab96e2016f974765f937f9dac6e3c
Author: Włodzimierz Gajda <gajdaw@gajdaw.pl>
Date:    Thu May 9 10:35:15 2013 +0200

    Mapping names with .mailmap

commit ba805256075eb86cf8a09a1d5c3161dbe6fc63e5
Author: Paul "Moo" Cowboy <moo@wild-west.example.net>
Date:    Thu May 9 10:07:01 2013 +0200

    [FR] Frere Jacques

commit 659ca289a3898eaf210d0c68228a645a74a3dd52
Author: John Doe <john.doe@example.net>
Date:    Thu May 9 10:01:44 2013 +0200

    [EN] Little skylark, lovely little skylark

...
```

Internally all the revisions are denoted with original authors.

How It Works

To change your name you can use the following command:

```
$ git config --global user.name "Your Name"
```

or edit your `.gitconfig` file by hand. The commands:

```
$ git config --global user.name "John Doe"
$ git config --global user.email john.doe@example.net
```

create the following `.gitconfig` entry:

```
[user]
    name = John Doe
    email = john.doe@example.net
```

It doesn't really matter whether you use a `$ git config` command or edit a `.gitconfig` file. The important fact to remember is that name and email entries from `.gitconfig` are used when you create the revision with a `$ git commit` command. Therefore, if you first define your name as:

```
[user]
    name = johny
    email = john.doe@example.net
```

and later decide to change it to:

```
[user]
    name = John Doe
    email = john@doe.example.com
```

then the history of your repository will contain two authors: `johny` and `John Doe`. The command:

```
$ git shortlog -s
```

will return both names because they are treated as different people:

```
13 johny
 8 John Doe
```

This output informs us that johny authored 13 revisions and that John Doe authored eight. You can provide additional information that both names johny and John Doe in fact refer to the same person. This mapping should be stored within the `.mailmap` file in the working directory. Every line of the file defines the mapping of names to names or emails to emails. The line:

```
Proper Name <commit@example.net>
```

defines that commits with author's email set to `commit@example.net` should be labeled with the name `Proper Name`.
The line:

```
<proper@example.net> <commit@example.net>
```

remaps emails. It states that revisions authored by `commit@example.net` should be assigned to the person using the email `proper@example.net`.

The more complicated example:

```
Proper Name <proper@example.net> <commit@example.net>
```

changes both the name and email of the commits with the author's email equal to `commit@example.net` to Proper Name and `proper@example.net`.

The location of the `.mailmap` file can be changed from the root of working directory to an arbitrary location defined by a `mailmap.file` configuration option. Both `.gitconfig` and `.mailmap` files can be utf-8 encoded, thus you can use non-ascii characters, such as ł, ó inside. If you want to analyze the real life `.mailmap` example visit jQuery repository: `https://github.com/jquery/jquery`.

■ **Documentation** The complete specification of the `.mailmap` file is available in the manual of the shortlog command: `$ git shortlog --help`.

Remember that when you define a strange name, such as:

```
Paul "Moo" Cowboy
```

you have to use quotes and backslashes:

```
[user]
    name = "Paul \"Moo\" Cowboy"
    email = john.doe@example.net
```

■ **Hint** The command: `$ git log --pretty=format:"- { name: '%an', email: '%ae' }" | sort | uniq` prints the complete list of all the authors in YAML format. You can use this list to automatically generate your `.mailmap` file for large projects.

3-5. Restoring revisions with git reset
Problem

As you may remember, git is a version control system. That means it stores all versions of the files in your project. You may wonder how can you access versions that were stored some time ago? You want to restore your project to the very first revision, then to a revision that was committed some time ago, and finally to the very last revision.

Solution

Clone the repository from Recipe 3-4:

```
$ cd git-recipes
$ git clone 03-04 03-05
$ cd 03-05
```

and print the history with $ git l. The output will be similar to Listing 3-6. Save the output of $ git l for future reference to use with this recipe. I will refer to Listing 3-6 but because you have different SHA-1 hashes you will need your own copy of the history. Once you learn how to work with reflog, saving will become unnecessary. You will learn how to use reflog in Recipe 3-8.

Listing 3-6. The history of repository used in Recipe 3-5

```
abda Mapping names with .mailmap
ba80 [FR] Frere Jacques
659c [EN] Little skylark, lovely little skylark
348f [FR] Alouette, gentille alouette
39d6 Titles
d234 [PL] Bajka iskierki
f305 Internationalization: directory EN
564f Baa, baa black sheep
7cfb Sing a song of sixpence
```

Now, restore the working directory to the very first revision named 7cfb:

```
$ git reset --hard 7cfb
```

After the successful execution of the above command the working directory contains one file sing-a-song-of-sixpence.txt. You can verify it with the $ ls command. In addition you can check the history with $ git l. The output will contain only one revision:

```
7cfb Sing a song of sixpence
```

That's why I wanted you to copy the output of the $ git l command presented in Listing 3-6. All the revisions are contained in the database, but they are now not included in the history. You can restore them only if you know their SHA-1 names. If you don't know their names you can use reflog—we will learn in Recipe 3-7. The repository now looks like Figure 3-4. There are no revisions other than 7cfb in the history.

I assume that you know the names of revisions printed in Listing 3-6. If not, start the recipe again and this time save the history shown in Listing 3-6.

Now, restore the revision denoted as:

```
f305 Internationalization: directory EN
```

You can do it with following command:

```
$ git reset --hard f305
```

After that command, the working directory contains the following directories and files:

```
.
`-- EN
    |-- baa-baa-black-sheep.txt
    `-- sing-a-song-of-sixpence.txt
```

The repository looks like Figure 3-6. The command $ git l prints three revisions:

```
f305 Internationalization: directory EN
564f Baa, baa black sheep
7cfb Sing a song of sixpence
```

Finally, reset your repository to the latest revision shown in Listing 3-6:

```
$ git reset --hard abda
```

The command $ git l prints the same results as in Listing 3-6. The working directory contains all the files created in Recipes 3-3 and 3-4.

■ **Caution**   Recipe 3-5 clearly shows that the database stored in .git/objects and the history of the repository are not the same thing. After the $ git reset command some revisions are removed from the history but they are still available in the database. The history of the repository is only a subset of all the information available in the database. To obtain something from the database, you need a valid name.

How It Works

The history of the repository can be displayed as a list of revisions. We can use $ git log --pretty=oneline or the alias $ git l. As you already know, every revision is identified by its unique name. To restore the working directory to one of the revisions you can use:

```
$ git reset --hard [REVISION]
```

The command performs the following two operations:

- It resets the state of the working directory to the specified revision, which means that the contents of all the files and directories are restored to exactly the same snapshot as was saved in the revision.
- It removes from the history all the revisions that were created after specified revision.

If you want to restore the original state of the repository, as it was before the $ git reset command, you have to remember the name of the latest revision or alternatively you can use reflog.

3-6. Restoring revisions with git checkout
Problem

The operation of restoring a working directory to a given revision can be performed with a $ git reset or a $ git checkout command. In Recipe 3-5 you restored old snapshots with a $ git reset command. Now, you want to achieve similar results with a $ git checkout command.

Solution

Clone the repository from Recipe 3-4:

```
$ cd git-recipes
$ git clone 03-04 03-06
$ cd 03-06
```

and print the history with $ git l. The output will be identical to Listing 3-6. Save the output of $ git l for future reference.

Now, restore the working directory to the very first revision, named 7cfb:

```
$ git checkout 7cfb
```

This command changes the repository's state into a **detached HEAD**. You can verify this with:

```
$ git status -sb
```

The output should be:

```
## HEAD (no branch)
```

The working directory now contains one file sing-a-song-of-sixpence.txt and the history printed with $ git l consists of one revision only:

```
7cfb Sing a song of sixpence
```

Return it to the normal state with:

```
$ git checkout master
```

Now the history printed with $ git l contains all of the revisions shown in Listing 3-6.
You can use $ git checkout again to switch to some other revision, for example:

```
$ git checkout 564f
```

To return to normal state use:

```
$ git checkout master
```

How It Works

The second method of restoring a previously saved snapshot is to use the following command:

```
$ git checkout [REVISION]
```

This command works differently than $ git reset discussed in Recipe 3-5.
The $ git checkout command performs the three following operations:

- It enters a detached HEAD state.
- It resets the state of the working directory to the specified revision.
- It removes from the history all the revisions that were created after a specified revision.

The detached HEAD is a special state of the repository in which you are not on any branch. We will discuss branches in greater detail in chapter 5, 6, 7, and 10. Right now, to use $ git checkout, you only need to know:

- That the $ git checkout [SHA-1] command enters a detached HEAD state.
- How to check the state of your repository.
- How to return from the detached HEAD to the normal state.

The command:

```
$ git status -b
```

returns the information about the current branch. It outputs:

```
# Not currently on any branch.
```

when you are in a detached HEAD state or:

```
# On branch master
```

when you are in a normal state. You can join two useful switches -s and -b of a $ git status command:

```
$ git status -s -b
```

or even:

```
$ git status -sb
```

When the repository is clean and in a detached HEAD mode this command prints:

```
## HEAD (no branch)
```

While in a normal state the output is:

```
#master
```

If you are in a detached HEAD state you can return to the normal state with:

```
$ git checkout master
```

To summarize, the command:

```
$ git checkout [REVISION]
```

restores the working directory to the specified revision and enters the detached HEAD state.
The command:

```
$ git checkout master
```

returns to the latest revision and restores the normal state.

■ **Hint**   Recipe 3-6 introduces a new characterization of a repository. We can say that a repository is in a **detached HEAD state** or in a **normal state**.

3-7. Creating a git s alias

Problem

How to define an alias that will simplify the execution of a $ git status -sb command?

Solution

Type the contents of Listing 3-7 at the end of the [alias] section in your .gitconfig file.

Listing 3-7. Alias git s

```
[alias]
    s = status -sb
```

You can achieve the same result with the following command:

```
$ git config --global alias.s "status -sb"
```

How It Works

The alias $ git s executes the command:

```
$ git status -sb
```

The output conveys the answers to the following questions:

- Is the repository clean or dirty? In other words, are there any uncommitted changes?
- Is the repository in a detached HEAD state? Or maybe we are on a branch? If so, print the name of the branch.

3-8. Working with reflog

Problem

The procedure of saving the log with SHA-1 names, which was necessary in Recipes 3-5 and 3-6, is very cumbersome. If you know how to use reflog this can be avoided. You will want to create a repository as shown in Figure 3-9. Next, you want to restore the working directory to every commit with the $ git reset --hard [REVISION] command. Instead of copying and pasting SHA-1 names you may prefer to use reflog.

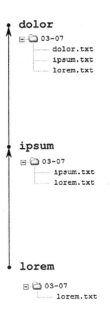

```
dolor
  ⊟ 03-07
        dolor.txt
        ipsum.txt
        lorem.txt




ipsum
  ⊟ 03-07
        ipsum.txt
        lorem.txt




lorem
  ⊟ 03-07
        lorem.txt
```

Figure 3-9. *The repository that is discussed in Recipe 3-8*

■ **Hint** The content of the files shown in Figure 3-9 is not important.

Solution

Initialize a new repository:

```
$ cd git-recipes
$ git init 03-08
$ cd 03-08
```

Create the first file with:

```
$ echo lorem > lorem.txt
```

This command creates a new file named lorem.txt. The file contains a single word lorem. You can verify it with two commands:

```
$ ls
$ cat lorem.txt
```

The first file lists the contents of the current directory (the list will consist of a single file lorem.txt) and the second displays the contents of lorem.txt (it will be lorem, of course).

Now create the first revision with:

```
$ git snapshot lorem
```

Of course, the repository is clean, and the $ `git status -s` returns empty results. Now check the reflog with:

```
$ git reflog
```

The output of this command is shown in Listing 3-8.

Listing 3-8. The output of git reflog after the first commit

```
bb057dd HEAD@{0}: commit (initial): lorem
```

It informs you that the revision with the comment `lorem` can now be referred to as:

```
bb057dd
```

or

```
HEAD@{0 }.
```

Let's create the second revision:

```
$ echo ipsum > ipsum.txt
$ git snapshot ipsum
```

Currently the repository contains two revisions with the comments `lorem` and `ipsum`. The command:

```
$ git reflog
```

now returns the output shown in Listing 3-9.

Listing 3-9. The output of a git reflog after the second commit

```
227c9fb HEAD@{0}: commit: ipsum
bb057dd HEAD@{1}: commit (initial): lorem
```

What happened? We moved from revision `lorem` to revision `ipsum` in the history. The current revision can be addressed as `HEAD@{0}`—right now it is the revision `ipsum`. The previous revision—which is `lorem`—can be referred to as `HEAD@{1}`.

Create the third revision:

```
$ echo dolor > dolor.txt
$ git snapshot dolor
```

and execute:

```
$ git reflog
```

The output is presented in Listing 3-10.

Listing 3-10. The output of git reflog after third revision

```
fe7dbef HEAD@{0}: commit: dolor
227c9fb HEAD@{1}: commit: ipsum
bb057dd HEAD@{2}: commit (initial): lorem
```

The history moved forward. This time HEAD@{0} refers to dolor revision. The previous revision was ipsum, thus it can be referred as HEAD@{1}. The first revision we created—lorem—is now available as HEAD@{2}.

It's time to use reflog names to restore the revisions. First, we want to restore the revision captioned as lorem. You can do it with the following command:

```
$ git reset --hard HEAD@{2}
```

After that, the working directory should contain only one file and the $ git reflog command should return the output shown in Listing 3-11.

Listing 3-11. The output of a git reflog after a git reset --hard HEAD@{2}

```
bb057dd HEAD@{0}: reset: moving to HEAD@{2}
fe7dbef HEAD@{1}: commit: dolor
227c9fb HEAD@{2}: commit: ipsum
bb057dd HEAD@{3}: commit (initial): lorem
```

As you can see in Listing 3-11 all the HEAD@{n} references were updated. Here is what they indicate:

```
HEAD@{0}—points to the revision lorem
HEAD@{1}—points to the revision dolor
HEAD@{2}—points to the revision ipsum
HEAD@{3}—points to the revision lorem
```

Next, reset the repository to the revision captioned as dolor with the following command:

```
$ git reset --hard HEAD@{1}
```

After this, the repository contains three files lorem.txt, ipsum.txt, and dolor.txt; and the $ git reflog command returns the output shown in Listing 3-12.

Listing 3-12. The output of a git reflog after a git reset --hard HEAD@{1}

```
481f34f HEAD@{0}: reset: moving to HEAD@{1}
aae6588 HEAD@{1}: reset: moving to HEAD@{2}
481f34f HEAD@{2}: commit: dolor
84fb524 HEAD@{3}: commit: ipsum
aae6588 HEAD@{4}: commit (initial): lorem
```

How It Works

Git reflog is a special log that stores the information about your movements in the repository. Each time you create a revision, reset the repository, or otherwise change the current revision, the reflog is updated. The name HEAD@{0} always points to the current revision. A previous revision is available as HEAD@{1}. The revision that was current two operations ago is available as HEAD@{2}, and so on. Thus, you can always refer to previous revisions, even if you don't know their names.

3-9. Creating a new repository in an existing project
Problem

You work on a project that already consists of a large number of files and directories. You want to start using git for that project.

Solution

Enter the directory that contains some files you want to track:

```
$ cd my/important/project
```

Initialize a new repository:

```
$ git init
```

And create the revision containing all the files:

```
$ git add -A
$ git commit -m "Initial commit"
```

Of course, you can use the alias:

```
$ git snapshot Initial commit
```

The repository contains a single revision that stores the current state of all the files. Then, you can proceed with your work, storing all modifications with $ `git snapshot` or $ `git add` and $ `git commit` commands.

How It Works

Git's init command can be executed in any directory that doesn't contain a `.git` subdirectory. You can run $ `git init` in a directory that already contains a project consisting of many files and subdirectories. After the repository is initialized, you can import all the files with two commands $ `git add -A` and $ `git commit -m "Initial commit"`. You can use $ `git snapshot Initial commit` as well.

3-10. Losing uncommitted changes
Problem

You want to check what happens to your modifications if you forget to commit changes and reset the working directory.

Solution

Clone the repository from Recipe 3-1:

```
$ cd git-recipes
$ git clone 03-01 03-10
$ cd 03-10
```

Create a new file graham-masterton.txt:

```
$ vi graham-masterton.txt
```

Type its contents:

```
Novels
    1975 | The Manitou
    1977 | The Djinn
    1979 | Revenge of the Manitou
```

Save the file and close the editor.
Then modify the file stephen-king.txt:

```
$ vi stephen-king.txt
```

Append two novels The Stand and The Dead Zone:

```
Novels
    1974 | Carrie
    1975 | Salem's Lot
    1977 | The Shining
    1978 | The Stand
    1979 | The Dead Zone
```

Save the file and close the editor.
Right now, the $ git status command prints:

```
M stephen-king.txt
?? graham-masterton.txt
```

It means that there are two changes in the working directory:

- The file stephen-king.txt was modified.

- The working directory contains one new file graham-masterton.txt.

Print the history with $ git l alias.
The output contains the three revisions we created in Recipe 3-1:

```
ffa6 Third revision [Stephen King]
0468 Second revision: [John Grisham]
de36 First commit [Agatha Christie]
```

Suppose that right now you forget to commit your work. Both files stephen-king.txt and graham-masterton.txt remain uncommitted while you decided to restore your very first revision with:

```
$ git reset --hard de36
```

After that command the working directory contains two files. The command $ ls prints their names:

```
agatha-christie.txt
graham-masterton.txt
```

The file stephen-king.txt has disappeared. You can reset the state of the repository to the revision:

```
ffa6 Third revision [Stephen King]
```

It can be done with the reflog:

```
$ git reset --hard HEAD@{1}
```

The file stephen-king.txt will be restored, but it will now contain only the three books typed during Recipe 3-1. The command:

```
$ cat stephen-king.txt
```

prints:

```
Novels
    1974 | Carrie
    1975 | Salem's Lot
    1977 | The Shining
```

The two new novels you typed during Recipe 3-10:

```
1978 | The Stand
1979 | The Dead Zone
```

were not stored in the database. Do you remember? You forgot to commit the changes. The changes typed in stephen-king.txt are lost and cannot be retrieved.

Display the contents of the new file:

```
$ cat graham-masterton.txt
```

The new file remained unchanged by $ git reset operation.

How It Works

The purpose of this recipe is to warn you that uncommitted changes can be lost. Remember that this command:

```
$ git reset --hard [REVISION]
```

can be safely used only in clean directories. The checkout command:

```
$ git checkout [REVISION]
```

is internally restricted. It can be used only if the operation does not cause data loss. Whenever there is a risk of loosing uncommitted changes you will be warned and the operation will be aborted. This is discussed in detail in Recipes 5-6 and 5-7.

3-11. Creating a git simple-commit alias
Problem

You have noticed that when learning and practicing git, very often you need to create a series of revisions. Very often the content of files is not important and can be neglected. You want to simplify the task of creating this type of commit with the simple-commit alias. When called:

```
$ git simple-commit lorem ipsum dolor
```

the alias should create the three revisions shown in Figure 3-9. Every parameter should be interpreted as a request to create a new revision storing one new file. The call:

```
$ git simple-commit abc
```

should create a revision with the comment abc. The revision should include one new file abc.txt containing the text abc.

Solution

Open your .gitconfig file and at the end of the [alias] section type the aliases shown in Listing 3-13.

Listing 3-13. Aliases: git create-file and git simple-commit

```
[alias]
    create-file = "!createFile() {
        for name in \"$@\"; do
            echo $name>$name.txt;
        done;
    }; createFile"

    simple-commit = "!simpleCommit() {
        for name in \"$@\"; do
            git create-file \"$name\";
            git snapshot $name;
        done;
    }; simpleCommit"
```

How It Works

The first alias creates files. The call:

```
$ git create-file yes no
```

creates two files yes.txt and no.txt. The first file contains text yes and the second contains the text no.
The for loop:

```
for name in \"$@\"; do
    echo $name>$name.txt;
done;
```

processes all the parameters passed to the script. Every parameter is accessible in one pass of the loop as $name variable. Hence the call:

```
$ git create-file yes no
```

is equivalent to:

```
echo yes>yes.txt
echo no>no.txt
```

The second alias contains the identical loop processing all the parameters:

```
for name in \"$@\"; do
    git create-file \"$name\";
    git snapshot $name;
done;
```

With every pass of the loop we call two aliases:

```
$ git create-file $name
$ git snapshot $name
```

The call:

```
$ git simple-commit yes no
```

is equivalent to:

```
$ git create-file yes
$ git snapshot yes

$ git create-file no
$ git snapshot no
```

The call:

```
$ git simple-commit lorem ipsum dolor
```

creates the repository shown in Figure 3-9.

░ **Hint** All the aliases defined in Recipes 2-10, 3-2, and 3-7 are useful in your daily work with git. The aliases defined in Recipe 3-11 are useful only when learning and practicing git.

3-12. Loosing commits

Problem

You want to verify that the revisions not accessible through symbolic references can be lost. You can do it following this procedure:

- Commit the changes.

- Reset the history with $ git reset -hard [REVISION]. Some commits will be no longer returned by $ git log command. They remain unchanged in the database. You can access them using reflog or SHA-1 names.

- Once you clear the reflog, the revisions that are not printed by $ git log become unreachable. It means that they are still in the database but you can access them only if you know their SHA-1 names.

- After the $ git prune command, all ureachable revisions are removed from the database. They are lost. There is no way to get them back.

Solution

Create a new repository:

```
$ cd git-recipes
$ git init 03-12
$ cd 03-12
```

Create three revisions with the comments a, b, c:

```
$ git simple-commit a b c
```

You can achieve the same effect without aliases using the commands show in Listing 3-14.

Listing 3-14. The commands equivalent to git simple-commit a b c

```
$ echo a>a.txt
$ git add -A
$ git commit -m a

$ echo b>b.txt
$ git add -A
$ git commit -m b

$ echo c>c.txt
$ git add -A
$ git commit -m c
```

Print the history with $ git l. The output contains three revisions:

```
5c1e c
4580 b
c4ac a
```

Reset the state of the repository to the first revision:

```
$ git reset --hard c4ac
```

Although the history printed with $ git l now contains only one revision—c4ac a—the other two revisions—5c1ec and 4580b—are still available in the database. You can restore them using their names or reflog. We did this in Recipe 3-8.

Right now the $ git reflog command prints the following output:

```
c4ac743 HEAD@{0}: reset: moving to c4ac
5c1ee9a HEAD@{1}: commit: c
45800dd HEAD@{2}: commit: b
c4ac743 HEAD@{3}: commit (initial): a
```

This means that the revisions 5c1ee9ac and 45800ddb are available under the symbolic names HEAD@{1} and HEAD@{2}. We call this type of revisions *dangling revisions*. Let's clear the reflog with:

```
$ git reflog expire --all --expire=now
```

After this command the reflog becomes empty. The $ git reflog command returns empty results. It means that right now revisions 5c1ee9ac and 45800ddb are available only through their names. There are no symbolic names leading to revisions b and c. If that is the case, git can remove revisions from the database. This type of revisions is called *unreachable revisions*.

Let's check, which objects stored in the .git/objects database are accessible only by SHA-1 names:

```
$ git prune --dry-run
```

The output will contain—among the other things—two revisions:

```
45800ddc19fa325296437fdbd7cc7e5654619597 commit
5c1ee9a3f19f854c783fa87003cb1ecc5508971d commit
```

If you compare the output of $ git l, you will see that the output contains the names of revisions 5c1ec and 4580b. In other words, if you now execute the command $ git prune then the two revisions b and c will be eventually lost. Let's do that. Execute the command:

```
$ git prune
```

If you now try to reset the repository to the revision c using its name:

```
$ git reset --hard 5c1e
```

you will get the error:

```
fatal: ambiguous argument '5c1e': unknown revision or path not in the working tree.
```

The revision is not accessible any more. You have just lost it! Forever!

▦ **Hint**   You can list all inaccessible objects that are stored in a database with $ git fsck --unreachable.

How It Works

Git stores all the revisions in the repository's database `.git/objects`. This database uses SHA-1 hashes to identify revisions, files, and all other entries. It is a content addressable storage, which means that the keys are generated using the contents of stored data. From time to time, the database is cleared and the objects that are not accessible through symbolic references are eventually removed. To get familiar with this process we need to dive deeper into the structure of a repository.

In the previous chapter we divided the git repository into:

- The git directory `.git/`

- The database `.git/objects`

- The working directory

The contents of the database can be further classified into:

- Objects that are available through various symbolic references, such as reflog, branches, and tags are classified as **reachable**.

- Objects that are available only through an SHA-1 name are classified as **unreachable**.

The process of cleaning the database removes all unreachable objects. You can do it by hand using the `$ git prune` or `$ git gc` commands. But even if you don't use those commands, it will be done by git automatically—it's only a matter of time. The exact parameters about how often the repository is cleared can be set in configuration.

When we called:

```
$ git reflog expire --all --expire=now
```

the reflog was cleared. Thus we removed all symbolic references pointing to revisions b and c. This is how revisions b and c became unreachable. Next the call to:

```
$ git prune
```

removed these revisions from the database.

Conclusion

The purpose of Recipe 3-12 was to show you that even committed changes can be removed from the repository. You can avoid this by keeping symbolic references. The easiest solution is to use branches for this purpose. The problem of losing commited changes is discussed in Recipe 5-4 also.

Summary

This chapter is a very important step forward. Now, you can use git for your daily work without any risk of losing data. The simplest workflow with git is to:

1. Modify your files

2. Save the snapshot of the working directory with two commands:

   ```
   $ git add -A
   $ git commit -m "..."
   ```

This operation—as realized by those two commands—is depicted in Figure 3-10.

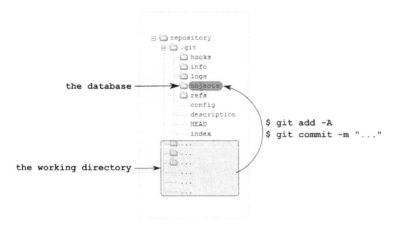

Figure 3-10. *Working with $ git add –A and $ git commit –m commands*

Thanks to:

```
$ git reset --hard [REVISION]
$ git checkout [REVISION]
```

you know how to retrieve one of the previous snapshots. Using $ git checkout or $ git reset you can access every revision stored in your repository. Remember that when using $ git reset the reflog will help you to return to the latest revision.

From now on you should remember two new important ways to characterize a repository. The repository can be:

- Clean or dirty
- In a detached HEAD or in a normal state

Both characteristics are displayed by the $ git status -sb command.

The **repository is clean** when the content of the working directory is identical to the snapshot saved in the current revision.

The **repository is dirty** when the content of the working directory contains uncommitted changes.

The second characterization, normal state and detached HEAD state, is done on the basis of a .git/HEAD file. We will return to this in the chapter about branches. Currently you know how to check states. The **repository is in a detached HEAD state** when the command:

```
$ git status -sb
```

begins with:

```
## HEAD (no branch)
```

Otherwise the **repository is in normal state**.

Another important characterization that appeared in this chapter divided the contents of the database into:

- **Reachable objects**: the objects available through symbolic references
- **Unreachable objects**: the objects available through SHA-1 names only

Remember, that unreachable objects can be removed from the repository during automatic garbage collection process. This is why you cannot work in a detached HEAD state. When you work in a detached HEAD state you create revisions that are unreachable unless you create a symbolic reference (a branch or a tag) manually.

CHAPTER 4

Managing Files

In this chapter we will practice and analyze file system commands used within the working directory. We will create, modify, remove, and rename files, and check how these operations influence the repository.

As you already know, git doesn't automatically register the changes made in the working directory. To create a new revision you have to issue special commands:

```
$ git add -A
$ git commit -m "Some comment..."
```

Up to this point we treated them as one atomic operation that can be described as saving the snapshot of the working directory as a new revision. Now, we will dissect this operation into two separate steps:

```
$ git add -A
```

and

```
$ git commit -m "Some comment..."
```

Git allows you to select which files should go to the next revision—this is the reason why you need two commands to create a revision. The first command selects the files for the next revision. The second command creates the revision using the selected files. The files selected for the next revision are called **staged files**. The list of staged files is stored in the .git/index file called the **staging area** or **index**.

4-1. Staging and committing a new file
Problem

You want to create a new file and commit it into the repository. You also would like to get familiar with the changes performed by every command executed in this recipe. To achieve this you need to analyze the state of the repository with the $ git status and $ git status -s commands.

Solution

Start a new repository with:

```
$ cd git-recipes
$ git init 04-01
$ cd 04-01
```

Then, follow this procedure:

1. Create a new file with $ echo new > new.txt

2. Check the status of the repository. The output of the $ git status will be the following:

    ```
    # On branch master
    #
    # Initial commit
    #
    # Untracked files:
    #   (use "git add <file>..." to include in what will be committed)
    #
    #       new.txt
    nothing added to commit but untracked files present (use "git add" to track)
    ```

    As you can see the new.txt file is listed as **untracked**.

3. Check the shortened output of git status. The command

    ```
    $ git status -s will print:
    ```

    ```
    ?? new.txt
    ```

    Untracked files are denoted with ??.

4. Stage the file using the $ git add new.txt command.

5. Check the status of the repository. The output of $ git status would be:

    ```
    # On branch master
    #
    # Initial commit
    #
    # Changes to be committed:
    #   (use "git rm --cached <file>..." to unstage)
    #
    #       new file:   new.txt
    #
    ```

    This time the file is displayed under the **Changes to be committed** section. This means that the file was staged.

6. Check the status with the $ git status -s command. The command will print:

    ```
    A_ new.txt
    ```

    This new state shown consists of two characters A and space. To make the output more readable, I used an underscore _ instead of a space.

7. Create a new revision with

    ```
    $ git commit -m "Staging and committing a new file"
    ```

8. Check the status with the $ git status -s command. The output is empty, thus the repository is clean.

How It Works

The process of storing a new file in a repository always consists of two steps. There isn't another way to do it. When you create a new file, at first it is **untracked**, which means that git doesn't store the file in the repository and doesn't track the contents of the file. The state of the file returned by $ git status -s command is denoted by two question marks:

```
?? new.txt
```

If you want to store the file in a revision, you first add the file to the staging area. This is done with:

```
$ git add new.txt
```

The **staging area** is a list of modifications that will be included in the very next revision made with the $ git commit command. The staging area is stored in the .git/index file. The files added to the staging area are called **staged files**. After $ git add new.txt the shortened status command $ git status -s prints:

```
A_ new.txt
```

As you can see, new files added to the staging area are denoted by A_.

■ **Hint**   You can use wildcard characters * and ? for a $ git add command.

When the file is in the staging area you can create a new revision with:
$ git commit -m "Some explanation..."
All the changes that were included in the staging area go into the revision. The file is stored in a repository and can be now described as **unmodified**. As you probably noticed the commands:

```
$ git status
$ git status -s
```

did not print any information about unmodified files.
Recipe 4-1 classified files stored in the repository into three groups:

- Untracked

- Staged

- Unmodified

The process of changing the new file from untracked into staged and from staged into unmodified is presented in Figure 4-1.

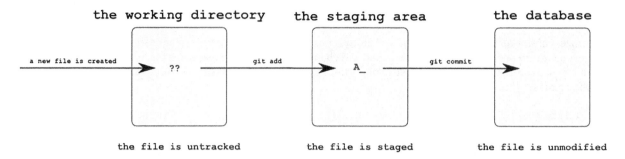

Figure 4-1. *The procedure of committing a new file*

All code returned by the $ git status -s command uses two letters. The first letter describes the staging area and the second letter describes the working directory. When $ git status -s returns ?? you can interpret it as:

- The first ? informs you that the file is unknown in the staging area.

- The second ? informs you that the file is unknown in the working directory.

In a similar fashion, the state denoted by an A_ has the following meaning:

- The first character (A) means that the file was added to the staging area (it was staged and will be stored in a next commit).

- The second character (_) means that the file in the working directory has the same contents as the file stored in the staging area.

Sometimes you may inadvertently stage a new file. How can you reverse staging? In case of a new file it can be done with one of the following commands:

```
$ git rm --cached -- [filename]
$ git reset -- [filename]
```

4-2. Staging and committing a modified file
Problem

You want to modify and commit a file that was already stored in the repository. To become familiar with how this operation is performed you need to use the $ git status and $ git status -s commands before and after every other command.

Solution

Start a new repository with:

```
$ cd git-recipes
$ git init 04-02
$ cd 04-02
$ git simple-commit modified
```

Right now the repository is clean and the working directory contains one file named modified.txt. The file was created and committed by the $ git simple-commit alias defined in Recipe 3-11.

Now, follow the procedure:

1. Modify modified.txt file with $ echo Some other text > modified.txt

2. Check the status of the repository with the $ git status command. The output:

```
# On branch master
# Changes not staged for commit:
#   (use "git add <file>..." to update what will be committed)
#   (use "git checkout -- <file>..." to discard changes in working directory)
#
#       modified:   modified.txt
#
no changes added to commit (use "git add" and/or "git commit -a")
```

   tells you that modified.txt file was modified but was not staged for commit. Notice that as in Recipe 4-1, the file is listed under **changes not staged for commit**.

3. Check the simplified form of status. The output of $ git status -s will be:

```
_M modified.txt
```

   The state is indicated by two characters: a space and the letter M. Again, I used the underscore instead of a space.

4. Add modified.txt to the staging area with $ git add modified.txt

5. Check the status with the $ git status command. The output:

```
# On branch master
# Changes to be committed:
#   (use "git reset HEAD <file>..." to unstage)
#
#       modified:   modified.txt
#
```

   The file is now listed as **Changes to be committed**.

6. Check the simplified form of status with the $ git status -s command. The output will be:

```
M_ modified.txt
```

   The state is denoted by two characters: the letter M and a space.

7. Commit the changes with $ git commit -m "Staging and committing a modified file"

8. Check the status with the $ git status -s command. The output is empty, therefore the repository is clean.

How It Works

Recipe 4-2 starts with a modification of a file that was already stored in revision. We will modify the file with:

```
$ echo Some other text > modified.txt
```

After this operation the file becomes **modified**. To find out what git thinks about the file, we issue the command:

```
$ git status
```

The file is listed under **Changes not staged for commit**. Therefore, we can say that the file is **modified** and **unstaged**. It is also **tracked**. But every unstaged file is tracked and modified. Hence, it is enough to say that the file is **unstaged**. Files that were previously committed after some modifications are labeled as _M by the $ git status -s command.

To add the unstaged file to the staging area we use the $ git add command. After:

```
$ git add modified.txt
```

the file becomes **staged**. Its short label is now M_ (the M letter followed by a space).

Finally, we commit the staged file with:

```
$ git commit -m "Some comment..."
```

And the file is unmodified again.

Recipe 4-2 is depicted in Figure 4-2.

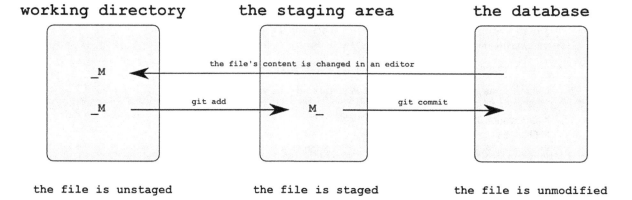

Figure 4-2. The procedure of committing a modified file using the staging area

Two lettered states _M and M_ provide information about the state of the file in the staging area and in the working directory.

The state _M means that:

- The first character (space): the file was not added to the staging area.

- The second character (M): the file was modified in the working directory.

The state M_ can be interpreted as:

- The first character (M): the file was added to the staging area.

- The second character (space): the state of the file in the staging area is identical as the state of the file in the working directory.

If you want to reverse the state M_ again to _M you can use:

```
$ git checkout -- [filename]
```

4-3. Committing a modified file

Problem

You want to modify and commit a file that has already been committed. You want to perform this operation using only the $ git commit command.

Solution

Create a new repository:

```
$ cd git-recipes
$ git init 04-03
$ cd 04-03
$ git simple-commit modified
```

Right now the repository is clean and the working directory contains one file—modified.txt. Now, follow this procedure:

1. Modify the modified.txt file with

   ```
   $ echo Yet another text > modified.txt
   ```

2. Check the status of the repository

   ```
   $ git status
   ```

The output is the same as in Recipe 4-2:

```
# On branch master
# Changes not staged for commit:
#   (use "git add <file>..." to update what will be committed)
#   (use "git checkout -- <file>..." to discard changes in working directory)
#
#       modified:   modified.txt
#
no changes added to commit (use "git add" and/or "git commit -a")
```

3. Check the simplified form of the status. The output of

   ```
   $ git status -s will be:
   ```

   ```
   _M modified.txt
   ```

4. Commit the changes with:

   ```
   $ git commit -a -m "Committing modified file: modified.txt"
   ```

5. Check the status with $ git status -s

The output is empty, thus the repository is clean.

How It Works

We know from Recipe 4-2 that an unmodified file (i.e. a file that was committed and was not modified since then) after the modification becomes unstaged. We can commit all unstaged files with one command:

```
$ git commit -a -m "Some comment..."
```

The flag -a tells git to include in the commit unstaged files. (Do you remember? All unstaged files are tracked!) Notice that using this solution you can not choose which files will go into the commit. The command:

```
$ git commit -a -m "..."
```

will commit all staged and unstaged files. If you want to commit one unstaged file you can pass its name to the $ git commit command as this:

```
$ git commit -m "Some text..." -- [filename]
```

■ **Hint**   The command $ git commit -m "..." creates a new revision containing all the staged files. The unstaged and untracked files are not modified by this command. The command $ git commit -a -m "..." creates a new revision containing all the tracked files (staged and unstaged). The untracked files (i.e., files denoted by ??) are not modified by this command.

The same effect as with the $ git commit -a command can be obtained with two commands:

```
$ git add -u
$ git commit -m "..."
```

The command $ git add -u stages all tracked files.
Remember that you cannot use one command:

```
$ git commit -am "..."
```

to commit new files. New files have to be staged with the $ git add command. There is no other way to commit them.

The procedure described in Recipe 4-3 is presented in Figure 4-3. As you can see the staging area is skipped by both commands.

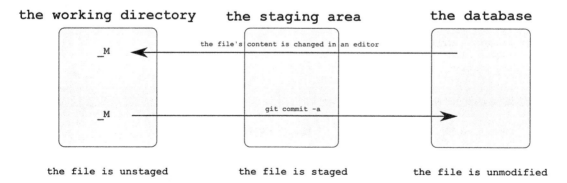

Figure 4-3. *The procedure of committing a modified file (the staging area is skipped)*

> ■ **Caution**   The command $ git commit -a -m "..."can be written as $ git commit -am "...". The order of options is important. You cannot write it as $ git commit -m -a "..."or $ git commit -ma "...".

4-4. Staging and committing a removed file

Problem

Your repository is in a clean state and contains a committed file—deleted.txt. You want to remove the file from the working directory and then commit this operation.

Solution

Start the repository with:

```
$ cd git-recipes
$ git init 04-04
$ cd 04-04
$ git simple-commit deleted
```

Right now the repository is clean and the working directory contains the file deleted.txt.
Follow the procedure:

1. Remove the deleted.txt file with $ git rm deleted.txt

2. Check the contents of the working directory with $ ls. The file deleted.txt was removed.

3. Check the status of the repository with the $ git status command. The output:

    ```
    # On branch master
    # Changes to be committed:
    #   (use "git reset HEAD <file>..." to unstage)
    #
    #       deleted:    deleted.txt
    #
    ```

    lists one file deleted.txt under **Changes to be committed**. This means that the operation of removing the file was **staged**.

4. Check the simplified form of status. The output of $ git status -s will be:

    ```
    D_ deleted.txt
    ```

This time the staged file removal is denoted by two characters: a letter D and a space.

5. Commit the changes with the $ git commit -m "Staging and committing removed file" command.

6. Check the status with the $ git status -s command. The output is empty, therefore the repository is clean. The working directory doesn't contain the deleted.txt file.

How It Works

We start the recipe with a clean repository containing the file deleted.txt. The command $ git rm deleted.txt removes the file from the working directory and stages this operation. Staged and deleted files are denoted by D_ by the $ git status -s command. After another $ git commit command the operation is committed: the snapshot stored in a revision doesn't contain the file deleted.txt.

The flow of Recipe 4-4 is shown in Figure 4-4.

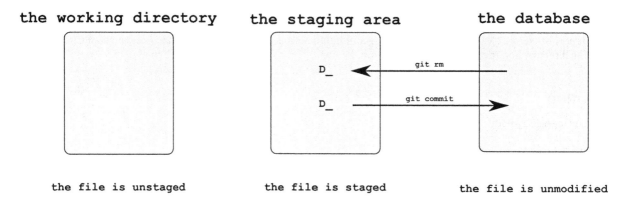

Figure 4-4. *The flow of Recipe 4-4*

The two lettered state D_ means that:

- The first character (D): the file was removed and the operation was staged.

- The second character (space): the state of the file in the working directory is exactly the same as in staging area: the file was removed from the working directory.

How do you reverse the operation performed by the $ git rm [filename] command? The state after $ git rm is indicated by D_. First, we unstage the removal with the following command:

$ git reset -- [filename]

This command converts the state from D_ into _D. In the _D state the file is still missing from the working directory, but the removal is not staged anymore. Thus the file is available in the staging area. To restore the file from the staging area into the working directory execute this command:

$ git checkout -- [filename]

The above command restores the file. We can say that it converts _D state into an unmodified state. The working directory is now clean and the file is restored.

4-5. Committing a file removed with the standard rm command

Problem

Your repository is in a clean state and contains the removed.txt file. The file is committed. You want to remove the file using the standard $ rm command and then commit this modification into the repository.

Solution

Start the repository with:

```
$ cd git-recipes
$ git init 04-05
$ cd 04-05
$ git simple-commit removed
```

The repository is clean and the working directory contains the file removed.txt.
Follow this procedure:

1. Remove removed.txt file with $ rm removed.txt

2. Check the status of the repository. The command:

    ```
    $ git status
    ```

prints:

```
# On branch master
# Changes not staged for commit:
#   (use "git add/rm <file>..." to update what will be committed)
#   (use "git checkout -- <file>..." to discard changes in working directory)
#
#       deleted:    removed.txt
#
no changes added to commit (use "git add" and/or "git commit -a")
```

The file is listed under **Changes not staged for commit**. Therefore, the file is unstaged.

3. Check the simplified form of status. The output of $ git status -s will be:

    ```
     D removed.txt
    ```

The state is denoted by two characters: a space and a letter D.

4. Commit the changes with

    ```
    $ git commit -a -m "Staging and committing removed file"
    ```

5. Check the status with the $ git status -s command. The output is empty, therefore the repository is clean. The working directory doesn't contain the removed.txt file.

How It Works

You can use standard commands such as $ rm to remove files in the working directory. If you want to stage all removed files you can use the -a flag of git commit $ git commit -am "..." or one of the following commands:

```
$ git add -u
$ git add -A
```

You also can stage only selected files removed with the $ rm command; to achieve the use of the $ git rm [filename] command.

To summarize, the following two procedures will have the same effect for filename.txt:

```
# first procedure
$ rm filename.txt
$ git commit -am "..."

# second procedure
$ rm filename.txt
$ git rm filename.txt
$ git commit -m "..."
```

They differ in one aspect: the first procedure will commit all tracked files (staged and unstaged); the second will commit only staged files.

Both procedures are shown in Figure 4-5.

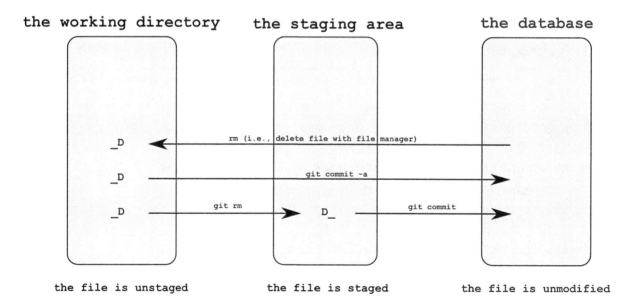

Figure 4-5. *The file removed with standard rm command can be committed with one command—git commit -a—or with two commands—git rm and git commit*

State D_ was thoroughly described in Recipe 4-4. The other state that appears in this recipe, _D, has the following meaning:

- First character (space): the operation was not staged.

- Second character (D): the file was removed from the working directory.

The command $ rm [filename] converts an unmodified file into the _D state. You can reverse this operation with:

```
$ git checkout -- [filename]
```

This command converts a file denoted as _D into an unmodified file. The file will be restored in the working directory.

4-6. Converting an unmodified file into an untracked file
Problem

The repository is in a clean state and the working directory contains one file—untracked.txt. The file is unmodified. You want to convert it into an untracked state.

Solution

Start the repository with:

```
$ cd git-recipes
$ git init 04-06
$ cd 04-06
$ git simple-commit untracked
```

Right now the repository is clean and the working directory contains one file—untracked.txt. Follow this procedure:

1. Remove the untracked.txt file with:

    ```
    $ git rm --cached untracked.txt
    ```

2. Check the contents of the repository with the $ ls command. As you can see the file was not deleted—it still exists in the working directory.

3. Check the status of the repository. The command

    ```
    $ git status prints:
    ```

    ```
    # On branch master
    # Changes to be committed:
    #   (use "git reset HEAD <file>..." to unstage)
    #
    #       deleted:    untracked.txt
    #
    # Untracked files:
    #   (use "git add <file>..." to include in what will be committed)
    #
    #       untracked.txt
    ```

    The file is listed as both **staged** (**Changes to be committed**) and untracked (**Untracked files**).

4. Check the simplified form of the status. The output of

$ git status -s will be:

```
D_ untracked.txt
?? untracked.txt
```

The file is listed twice: as D_ and ??.

5. Commit the changes with $ git commit -m "Committing removed file"

6. Check the status with the $ git status -s command.

The output is: ?? untracked.txt

The file is not tracked anymore and is not included in the latest snapshot.

How It Works

This time the single command:

```
$ git rm --cached [filename]
```

converts one unmodified file into two different states denoted as D_ ??. The first state indicates that the file was staged. To be more accurate, we can say that the file removal operation was staged: the next commit will store the snapshot of the working directory without this file.

The second state, denoted as ??, specifies that the working directory contains a file that is not tracked. This file will not be affected by the next commit operation until the next $ git add command is issued.

Recipe 4-6 is illustrated in Figure 4-6.

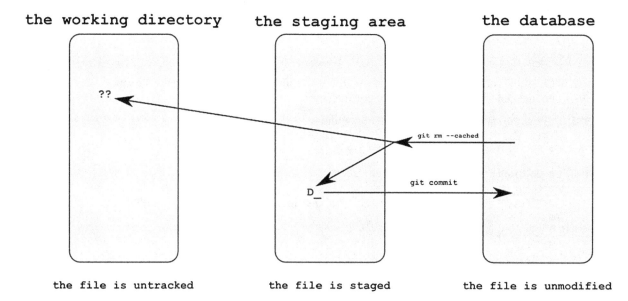

Figure 4-6. The git rm --cached command converts one unmodified file into two states denoted as D_ and ??

4-7. Staging and committing a file renamed with git mv
Problem

Your repository is in a clean state and contains a file named old-name.txt. You want to rename the file old-name.txt to new-name.txt and commit this operation.

Solution

Start the repository with:

```
$ cd git-recipes
$ git init 04-07
$ cd 04-07
$ git simple-commit old-name
```

Right now the repository is clean and the working directory contains one file—old-name.txt. Follow this procedure:

1.   Rename the file with $ git mv old-name.txt new-name.txt

2.   Check the contents of the working directory with the $ ls command. The working directory now contains a file named new-name.txt. The file old-name.txt has disappeared.

3.   Check the status of the repository with the $ git status command. The output:

```
# On branch master
# Changes to be committed:
#   (use "git reset HEAD <file>..." to unstage)
#
#       renamed:    old-name.txt -> new-name.txt
#
```

   explains that the operation of moving a file was staged.

4.   Check the simplified form of status. The output of $ git status -s will be:

```
R_ old-name.txt -> new-name.txt
```

   The state is denoted by two characters: the letter R followed by a space.

5.   Commit the changes with the $ git commit -m "Staging and committing moved file" command.

6.   Check the status with the $ git status -s command. The output is empty, therefore the repository is clean.

How It Works

The syntax of $ git mv is given in the following:

```
$ git mv [old-filename] [new-filename]
$ git mv [filename] [directory]
```

The first command renames a file while the second moves the file to the directory. The files that were renamed or moved with the $ git mv command are denoted by R_.

The operation is depicted in Figure 4-7.

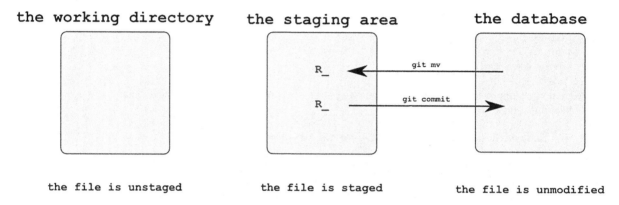

Figure 4-7. *The flow of events in Recipe 4-7*

The two lettered state R_ can be interpreted as:

- The first character (R) indicates the state in the staging area. R means that the file was renamed and the operation was staged.

- The second character concerns the working directory. The space means that the state of the file in the working directory is exactly the same as in the staging area.

How to undo the operation performed by the $ git mv command? The process consists of two steps. First unstage the rename with this command:

```
$ git reset -- [new-filename]
```

This command results in two files:

```
D_ old-file.txt
?? new-file.txt
```

You can restore the old-file.txt with:

```
$ git reset -- [old-filename]
$ git checkout -- [old-filename]
```

The new-file.txt can be removed with:

```
$ rm new-file.txt
```

4-8. Committing a file renamed with the standard mv command

Problem

Your repository is clean and contains one file named old-name.txt. You want to rename and commit the change. You prefer to perform the renaming with the standard $ mv command.

Solution

Start the repository with:

```
$ cd git-recipes
$ git init 04-08
$ cd 04-08
$ git simple-commit old-name
```

The repository is clean and the working directory contains one file—old-name.txt. Follow this procedure:

1. Rename the file with $ mv old-name.txt new-name.txt

2. Check the status of the repository with the $ git status command. The output:

    ```
    # On branch master
    # Changes not staged for commit:
    #   (use "git add/rm <file>..." to update what will be committed)
    #   (use "git checkout -- <file>..." to discard changes in working directory)
    #
    #       deleted:    old-name.txt
    #
    # Untracked files:
    #   (use "git add <file>..." to include in what will be committed)
    #
    #       new-name.txt
    no changes added to commit (use "git add" and/or "git commit -a")
    ```

    informs you about two changes. The first change concerns the file old-name.txt. The file old-name.txt was deleted, but the operation was not staged. In addition your repository now contains a new untracked file named new-name.txt. Thus, when you rename a file, git considers it as two separate operations: a deletion and a creation.

3. Check the simplified form of status. The output of $ git status -s will be:

    ```
     D old-name.txt
    ?? new-name.txt
    ```

    The file old-name.txt was removed; this is denoted as _D. The file new-name.txt is treated by git as a new untracked file. Therefore, it is denoted as ??.

4. Stage a new file with the $ `git add new-name.txt` command. As you remember from Recipe 4-1 there is no other way to stage a new untracked file than to use $ `git add` command. Now the command $ `git status -s` prints:

```
A_ new-name.txt
_D old-name.txt
```

5. Stage the removed file with the $ `git rm old-name.txt` command and check the status with the $ `git status -s` command. The output:

```
R_ old-name.txt -> new-name.txt
```

shows that git is smart enough to guess that the file was moved.

6. Create the revision with $ `git commit -m "Committing a file moved with mv"`.

7. Check the status with the $ `git status -s` command. The output is empty, therefore the repository is clean.

How It Works

The operation $ `mv old-name.txt new-name.txt` results in two changes denoted by:

```
_D old-name.txt
?? new-name.txt
```

The first change can be staged with $ `git rm old-name.txt`
To stage a second change you can use $ `git add new-name.txt`
When both changes are staged, git will guess that there is only one change—the file was renamed:

```
R_ moved.txt -> sudir/moved.txt
```

This proves that in git the way you rename doesn't really matter.

4-9. Staging all files
Problem

The repository is in a clean state and its working directory contains three files: `modified.txt`, `deleted.txt`, `old-name.txt`. You want to:

- Create a new file—`new.txt`.
- Change the contents of `modified.txt`.
- Remove the file—`deleted.txt`.
- Rename the file `old-name.txt` to `new-name.txt`.
- Stage all the changes with a single command—$ `git add -A`.
- Commit the changes with the command—$ `git commit -m "Staging all changes"`.

Solution

Start the repository with:

```
$ cd git-recipes
$ git init 04-09
$ cd 04-09
$ git simple-commit modified deleted old-name
```

The repository is clean and the working directory contains three files: modified.txt, deleted.txt, and old-name.txt. Follow this procedure:

1. Create a new file $ echo new > new.txt

2. Modify the contents of modified.txt file $ echo Some new contents > modified.txt

3. Remove deleted.txt file with $ rm deleted.txt

4. Rename old-name.txt file $ mv old-name.txt new-name.txt

5. Check the status of the repository with the $ git status command. The output:

   ```
   # On branch master
   # Changes not staged for commit:
   #   (use "git add/rm <file>..." to update what will be committed)
   #   (use "git checkout -- <file>..." to discard changes in working directory)
   #
   #       deleted:    deleted.txt
   #       modified:   modified.txt
   #       deleted:    old-name.txt
   #
   # Untracked files:
   #   (use "git add <file>..." to include in what will be committed)
   #
   #       new-name.txt
   #       new.txt
   no changes added to commit (use "git add" and/or "git commit -a")
   ```

   lists all the changes as unstaged. The working directory also contains one untracked file.

6. Check the simplified form of status. The output of $ git status -s will be:

   ```
    _D deleted.txt
    _M modified.txt
    _D old-name.txt
   ?? new-name.txt
   ?? new.txt
   ```

7. Stage all the changes with one command $ git add -A.

8. Check the status with the $ git status command. You will see:

   ```
   # On branch master
   # Changes to be committed:
   #   (use "git reset HEAD <file>..." to unstage)
   #
   ```

```
#        deleted:    deleted.txt
#        modified:   modified.txt
#        renamed:    old-name.txt -> new-name.txt
#        new file:   new.txt
#
```

All the changes were staged.

9. Check the shortened status with the $ git status -s command. You will get:

```
D_  deleted.txt
M_  modified.txt
R_  old-name.txt -> new-name.txt
A_  new.txt
```

10. Commit the changes with the $ git commit -m "Committing all the changes" command.

11. Check the status with the $ git status -s command. The output is empty, therefore the repository is clean.

How It Works

Recipe 4-9 explains the role of the command we already know quite well. It is $ git add -A This command stages all the changes in the working directory. The conversions performed by $ git add -A are summarized in Table 4-1.

Table 4-1. *Conversions performed by git add -A*

The state before $ git add -A	The state after $ git add -A
New unstaged file ??	A_
Modified unstaged file _M	M_
Deleted unstaged file _D	D_
Renamed unstaged file indicated as two changes; one of them is denoted by ??, the other is denoted by _D	R_

4-10. Working with mixed states
Problem

You wish to check what happens when you modify a staged file.

Solution

Start the repository with:

```
$ cd git-recipes
$ git init 04-10
$ cd 04-10
```

The repository is clean and the working directory doesn't contain any files.

Follow this procedure:

1. Create a new file $ echo Some info > file.txt

2. Stage the file with the $ git add file.txt command. Right now the $ git status -s prints:

   ```
   A_ file.txt
   ```

3. Modify the file with $ echo Some other info > file.txt

4. Check the status with the $ git status -s command. The output will be the following code:

   ```
   AM file.txt
   ```

   The code consists of two letters that informs you a file was staged at some point but has been modified since then.

5. Create the revision with the $ git commit -m "First revision" command.
   This command creates a new revision storing the file with the contents Some info.
   The repository remains dirty. The shortened status command prints:

   ```
   _M file.txt
   ```

   The file containing Some other info remains unstaged.

How It Works

Recipe 4-10 underlines a very important aspect of the $ git add command. It stages a file at a given point of time. You can think of $ git add as of special type of $ cp command. Git add command copies the file from the working directory into the staging area. Of course the operation is performed right after you issue the $ git add command. If you modify an already staged file your modifications are not automatically staged. In other words, the version of the file stored in the staging area differs from the version stored in the working directory. The state like this is indicated by two different letters, such as:

```
AM file.txt
```

The first letter, A, specifies that the file was staged. The second letter, M, tells you that the file stored in the working directory was modified. How to return the file to a normal state? If the content that was already staged is important you can follow Recipe 4-10. Otherwise you can redo the $ git add command. The state will become:

```
A_ file.txt
```

In that case, changes that were staged and not committed will be lost.

Usually, I do not use states such as AM during my daily work. The reason is very simple. I do not stage my files and leave them uncommitted. Once the files are staged, I commit. The only example of using an AM state in a real-life scenario is when I restore a deleted file from the repository and then—before commit—modify it. Here is the procedure:

```
$ git simple-commit lorem
$ git rm lorem
$ git checkout HEAD~ -- lorem.txt
$ vi lorem.txt
$ git status -s
```

The command $ git checkout HEAD~ -- lorem.txt restores a deleted file from the next-to-the-last revision. If you edit the file, its state will be indicated by AM.

Summary

This chapter divided all the files stored in the repository into several categories. The division started with the question: whether the file was tracked by git. Every file is either **untracked** or **tracked**. Because git doesn't store any information about untracked files—nothing more can be said about them.

Tracked files can be further categorized as **unmodified** and **modified**.

Unmodified files are files that have already been stored in the repository (i.e., in the database). They have not been modified since then.

Modified files are the files that have been changed after they have been committed. They can be further divided into **staged** and **unstaged** files.

Staged files are files that will go into the next revision, while **unstaged** files will remain unchanged. Unstaged files are not influenced by nor will they influence the next commit command.

Figure 4-8 presents the diagram of the states of files discussed.

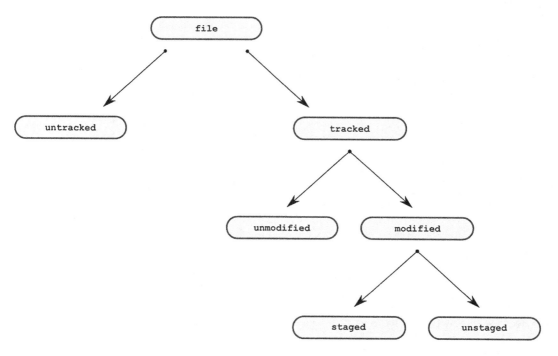

Figure 4-8. *Different states of files*

Notice that:

- Every unmodified file is tracked.

- Every staged and unstaged file is tracked and modified.

Therefore we can unambiguously use these four adjectives to describe files:

- Untracked

- Unmodified

- Staged

- Unstaged

The simplified diagram of states including short codes returned by the `git status -s` command is shown in Figure 4-9.

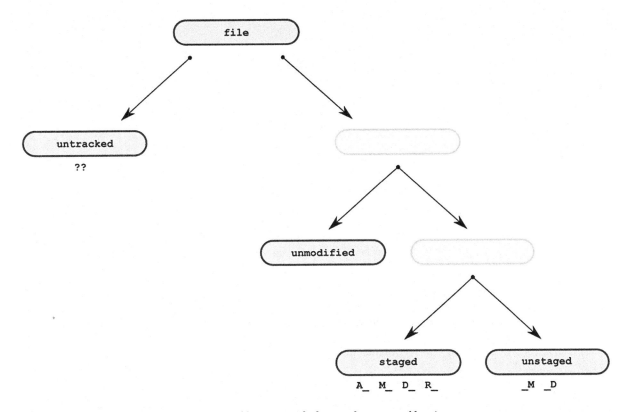

Figure 4-9. *Simplified diagram of different file states with short codes returned by git status –s*

The repository's structure

To introduce the staging area I have extended the structure of a repository. In fact it consists of three different areas, as shown in Figure 4-10:

- The working directory
- The database, which stores objects
- The staging area

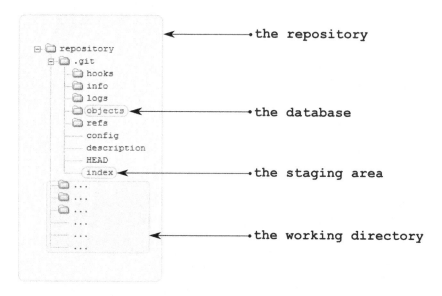

Figure 4-10. *The structure of a repository*

The working directory is the place where you work. As you already know, you can use arbitrary tools and commands to manipulate the files in the working directory.

Once you decide that the current state of the whole working directory or just some files in it should be committed, you stage the files. You do this using $ git add, $ git rm, and $ git mv commands. They all can accept wildcard characters, thus you can write commands such as:

```
$ git add *
$ git rm *.txt
$ git mv .????* tmp/
```

You can avoid using the $ git rm and $ git mv commands because $ git add can stage renames and file removal for you. The $ git add command accepts optional parameters --all or –update, which can be abbreviated as -A and -u, respectively. These parameters influence the default behavior of the $ git add command in a following ways:

- The $ git add * command will stage all new and modified files present in the working directory (deleted files are not staged).

- The git add --update command will stage all modified files (it includes modified and deleted files but excludes new ones).

- The git add --all stages all files (includes new, modified, and deleted files).

Depending on your needs you can stage all files with $ git add –A or tailor revisions as you wish.

Finally you can create the revision using the $ git commit command. If you use the $ git commit command without -a flag only the files manually added to the staging area will be affected. The operations performed by the $ git add, $ git rm, and $ git mv commands are shown in Figure 4-11.

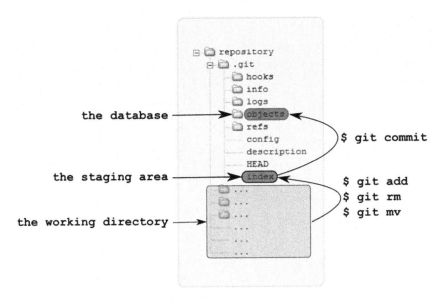

Figure 4-11. *The operation realized by the $ git add, $ git rm, and $ git mv commands*

CHAPTER 5

Branches

Whenever I'm asked about the pros of switching from an older version control systems (VCS), such as CVS or Subversion, to git; I answer with this short statement: git branching model. Once you learn to use it you will ask yourself how on earth did I work without it? Indeed, the way git handles branches sets it high above other (if not all) VCS systems. As a matter of fact, I really believe that this single feature is sufficient reason to switch to git.

What exactly is a branch? *A branch is a line of development.* This is a high-level definition, unconcerned with implementation-specific aspects. Technically speaking, *a branch in git is a pointer to an arbitrary commit in the database.* While it will take some practice to use branches with confidence; you should start right from the first with the most basic feature of branches. They are independent from each other. The way you modify one branch does not influence the other branches. To preserve any point in the project's history it is enough to create a branch. Git will never modify your branch, unless you explicitly ask it to do so.

This chapter will provide you with a strong grasp with most aspects of using branches. We start with creating and switching branches in non-bare repositories. In particular, the discussion includes various aspects of the way git stores branches. This will help you to understand why git branches are so efficient.

Next, we analyze branches in the context of cloning. It will lead us to the following different types of branches:

- Remote branches (i.e. branches in remote repository)
- Local branches (i.e. branches in a repository you are currently working in)
  - Ordinary local branches
  - Local tracking branches
  - Remote tracking branches[1]

All of the branch categories, which may be unclear at the beginning, will become apparent in chapter 10 during the discussion of remote repositories and collaboration. They are introduced here to provide a clear point of view right from the beginning. The subject of cloning with respect to branches will return in the last recipe. There, we consider operating on branches in bare repositories. The recipe will be rarely used, but it further clarifies the process of switching branches in non-bare repositories.

Once again, do not work in a detached HEAD state. This is pointless, especially once you understand branching. Remember, using branches guarantees that your revisions will never be lost.

To get the complete picture of branches I will also show how switching branches—when performed incautiously—can complicate your life. You can recover from these problems using three simple recipes:

- Clear and reset a branch
- Switch a branch avoiding conflicts
- Recover from inadvertent commits

---

[1]Yes, these are local branches, as well. They are local branches that track remote branches.

With these three simple recipes you will be able to take advantage of branching as soon as you finish reading this chapter. These are emergency recipes—you can apply them when you're in trouble.

Once in a while you will face the problem of accessing files from different branches. Two simple commands come to rescue: you can either check out the file from a different branch or display it on standard output. The latter solution used with a stream redirector > allows you to rename a file checked out from a different branch. The recipe presenting these commands underlines the problems you may encounter while working in heterogeneous environments.

The final part of the chapter presents the recipes that explain how to delete and rename branches. This leads us to the very important concepts of merged and not merged branches.

5-1. Creating and switching branches
Problem

You want to create and switch branches in git. To achieve this goal you need to make a repository as shown in Figure 5-1. The figure presents a graph of revisions where every dot stands for a single commit and every rounded rectangle with an arrow represents a branch. You should take good care to create the commits in such a way that commit messages are exactly the same as the label of a corresponding dot. Moreover, every commit should include one new file with the name and contents based on the dot's label. A dot labeled with d2, for example, represents a commit with comment d2. It should include a single file named d2.txt containing the text d2. This method of committing has two important features that will help you practice branching and committing:

- There are no conflicts.

- For every revision you can easily guess the contents of the working directory.

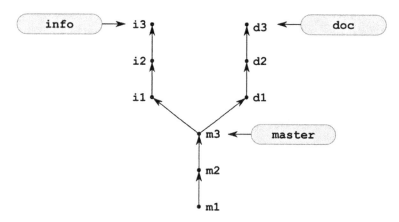

Figure 5-1. *The repository created in Recipe 5-1*

When the repository shown in Figure 5-1 is finished, you want to verify that every branch contains only the files stored in the revision as pointed to by the branch and its ancestors.

Solution

Start the command line and create a new repository:

```
$ cd git-recipes
$ git init 05-01
$ cd 05-01
```

Then create three revisions m1, m2, and m3. You can use the following procedure:

1. Create a new file m1.txt with $ echo m1 > m1.txt

2. Commit the snapshot with $ git snapshot m1

3. Create a new file m2.txt with $ echo m2 > m2.txt

4. Commit the snapshot with $ git snapshot m2

5. Create a new file m3.txt with $ echo m3 > m3.txt

6. Commit the snapshot with $ git snapshot m3

The repository now looks like Figure 5-2.

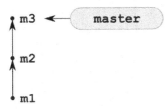

Figure 5-2. *The repository from Recipe 5-1 with the first three revisions created in the master branch*

By default, any newly initialized repository contains a single branch named master. You can verify this with the command:

```
$ git branch
```

This command prints the list of branches. Right now its output will be:

```
* master
```

Let's create a new branch named doc. Here is the command you need:

```
$ git branch doc
```

Now if you list the branches with the $ git branch command, you will notice that the repository contains two branches listed as:

```
  doc
* master
```

The asterisk denotes a current branch. It means that you are still in the master branch. The repository now looks like Figure 5-3.

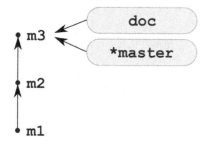

Figure 5-3. *The repository from Recipe 5-1 with the two branches master and doc*

Now you need to create three revisions on the branch named doc. First, you have to switch to this branch with the command:

```
$ git checkout doc
```

Right now the command:

```
$ git branch
```

prints:

```
* doc
  master
```

The above output informs you that you currently are on branch named doc. Your commits will now go to this new branch. You can create three commits d1, d2, and d3 with the following procedure:

1. Create a new file d1.txt with `$ echo d1 > d1.txt`

2. Commit the snapshot with `$ git snapshot d1`

3. Create a new file d2.txt with `$ echo d2 > d2.txt`

4. Commit the snapshot with `$ git snapshot d2`

5. Create a new file d3.txt with `$ echo d3 > d3.txt`

6. Commit the snapshot with the `$ git snapshot d3` command.

The repository now looks like Figure 5-4.

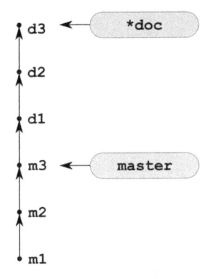

Figure 5-4. *The repository from Recipe 5-1 with revisions d1, d2, and d3*

To create the next branch you can use three commands:

```
# switch to master branch
$ git checkout master

# create a new branch named info
# pointing to the same commit as master branch
$ git branch info

# switch to info branch
$ git checkout info
```

or a single command:

```
$ git checkout -b info master
```

Both solutions will create a new branch named info, which points to the same revision as branch master. The current branch in the repository is now info. You can check it with this command:

```
$ git branch
```

The output of the above command will be the following:

```
  doc
* info
  master
```

The repository now looks like Figure 5-5.

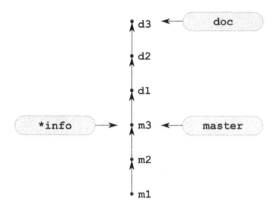

Figure 5-5. *The repository from Recipe 5-1 with a new branch named info*

You can finish the recipe creating three revisions i1, i2, and i3:

1. Create a new file i1.txt with $ echo i1 > i1.txt

2. Commit the snapshot with $ git snapshot i1

3. Create a new file i2.txt with $ echo i2 > i2.txt

4. Commit the snapshot with $ git snapshot i2

5. Create a new file i3.txt with $ echo i3 > i3.txt

6. Commit the snapshot with $ git snapshot i3

The repository is finished. It looks like Figure 5-1. You can verify it with the following command:

```
$ gitk --all &
```

The graph drawn by the gitk application is shown in Figure 5-6. Notice that in this figure the name of the current branch is written in bold font, and the current revision is denoted with a white dot. On your screen the dot will be yellow—that's the convention gitk uses by default.

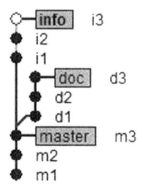

Figure 5-6. *The repository from Recipe 5-1 drawn with the gitk application*

The diagram similar to the one presented in Figure 5-6 can be printed with the $ git log command using additional switches:

```
$ git log --oneline --graph --decorate --all
```

The output of the above command will be similar to:

```
* 0d6501b (info) i3
* ab087d1 i2
* 6f4364e i1
| * 23d9855 (HEAD, doc) d3
| * f7651b8 d2
| * 6042953 d1
|/
* 7c9bc41 (master) m3
* 9cf5f5a m2
* ebf4409 m1
```

The parameter --graph passed to $ git log turns on the visibility of lines connecting commits, --oneline compresses the output to a line pre-commit with SHA-1 shortened to seven characters and --decorate turns on symbolic references such as HEAD, master, doc, and info. The parameter --all for $ git log and $ gitk commands has the same meaning: it causes the revisions stored in all branches available in the repository to be included. By default, only the commits included in the current branch are displayed.

If you now switch to the branch named master with the command:

```
$ git checkout master
```

the working directory will contain only three files m1.txt, m2.txt, and m3.txt. You can verify it with the $ ls command. In a similar fashion, if you switch to the branch doc with $ git checkout doc, then the working directory will contain six files: d1.txt, d2.txt, d3.txt, m1.txt, m2.txt, and m3.txt. And if you switch to the branch info, the working directory will contain the files: i1.txt, i2.txt, i3.txt, m1.txt, m2.txt, and m3.txt. That's why I insist on creating commits such as m1, m2, d1, d2, and so forth. You can easily verify how the commands you issue influence the working directory. A simple $ ls command will show you the complete contents of your working directory—there's no need to inspect the files.

Hint You can list the files stored in the info branch without switching branches with the $ git show info^{tree} command. In a similar way, you can list the files in an arbitrary revision with $ git show SHA-1^{tree}.

When listing branches with $ git branch you can use the additional parameter -v. The command $ git branch -v will print the latest revision in every branch, for example:

```
* doc    23d9855 d3
  info   0d6501b i3
  master 7c9bc41 m3
```

Finish the recipe executing the two commands:

```
$ git checkout master
$ git pack-refs --all
```

The first of them will change the current branch to the master while the second will store the all the references, including all the branches, in a file named .git/packed-refs.

How It Works

Every repository contains the special file .git/HEAD, which points to the current revision. That's how git knows which revision you recently checked out. This is also used as a parent revision during your next commit. The reference stored in .git/HEAD file is written in one of two forms:

- As a symbolic reference to the branch

- As a SHA-1

If you are on a branch then the contents of .git/HEAD is written in symbolic form. When you enter the detached HEAD state the reference is written as SHA-1. Here, we will focus on symbolic references. SHA-1 references will be discussed in Recipe 5-4.

The symbolic form of the reference looks like this:

```
ref: refs/heads/master
```

The above symbolic form of the reference says that your current revision is the one pointed to by the branch named master.

Branches are stored in the .git directory in one of two different formats:

- Loose format

- Packed format

Loose format branches are stored within the .git/refs/heads directory. Every branch is stored in a separate file. In the symbolic reference ref: refs/heads/xyz the part refs/heads/xyz is a path to the file .git/refs/heads/xyz. This file contains the SHA-1 name of the latest revision in branch xyz.

In the packed format many references, such as ref: refs/heads/xyz, ref: refs/heads/foo, and ref: refs/heads/bar, are stored in a single file—.git/packed-refs. In a newly initialized repository the file .git/packed-refs doesn't exist. This means that by default the references are initially stored in a loose format.

When you initialize a new repository it doesn't contain any revisions—its database is empty. The file .git/HEAD contains the entry ref: refs/heads/master and the folder .git/refs/heads is empty—the file refs/heads/master doesn't exist. The new repository contains a single branch named master, which doesn't contain any revisions.

Once you create the first revision with:

```
$ echo m1 > m1.txt
$ git snapshot m1
```

then your repository is not empty any more. The file .git/HEAD does not change—it still contains the same entry pointing to .git/refs/heads/master. But now the directory .git/refs/heads contains a single file named master. This file stores the SHA-1 of the revision labeled m1. You can check it with following two commands:

```
$ git log --pretty=oneline
$ cat .git/refs/heads/master
```

Comparing the output of the above commands you will notice that the SHA-1 stored in .git/refs/heads/master is exactly the same as the one returned by the $ git log command.

Right now the master branch is stored in loose format. The information about its latest revision is saved in a text file .git/refs/heads/master. If you want to convert the format of all the references from loose to packed format you can use the following command:

```
$ git pack-refs --all
```

After the above command, the .git/refs/heads directory becomes empty again; however it doesn't mean that the branch was removed. The repository still contains this branch. You can verify it with the $ git branch command. However, the tip of the master branch is stored in the .git/packed-refs file in packed format.

▪ **Hint** The last commit in a branch is called the tip of the branch. Figure 5-1 presents three branches with following tips: the tip of the branch doc is d3, the tip of the branch master is m3, and the tip of the branch info is i3.

After the next commit created with:

```
$ echo m2 > m2.txt
$ git snapshot m2
```

the file .git/HEAD remains unchanged but the format for storing the master branch is changed from packed to loose again. The file .git/refs/heads/master is recreated and it now contains the SHA-1 of the revision labeled m2. You can check it using the same two commands used previously:

```
$ git log --pretty=oneline
$ cat .git/refs/heads/master
```

You should notice that every revision converts the format of a branch from packed to loose.

The third revision labeled m3 leaves the file .git/HEAD intact while .git/refs/heads/master contains the SHA-1 of the third revision.

What happens when you create a new branch with $ git branch doc? Git creates a new file .git/refs/heads/doc and stores the SHA-1 of your current revision within it. Initially every branch is stored in a loose format.

Think of a branch as a pointer to a single node in a graph of revisions. Because SHA-1 stored in hexadecimal textual format consumes 40 bytes, therefore creating a branch means storing 40 bytes in a text file. This is one of the reasons why branching in git is so efficient. The whole process of branch creation consists of saving a 41-bytes long reference in a local storage system (40 bytes for SHA-1 and a newline character)! Not only isn't there any data transfer, but there isn't any communication. It is instantaneous!

Notice that when you create a new branch with the $ git branch doc command, the file .git/HEAD remains unchanged. This means that git doesn't automatically switch to a new branch. To switch to a new branch you have to issue the $ git checkout doc command. This command changes the contents of .git/HEAD file to:

```
ref: refs/heads/doc
```

As you can see the information about the current branch, the one that is denoted with asterisk in the output of $ git branch command, is stored in .git/HEAD file.

Which internal operations are performed by git when you commit? Git resolves the name of your current branch using the .git/HEAD file. Let's suppose that the file .git/HEAD contains ref: refs/heads/abc. This means that your current branch is named abc. Once the name of the branch is resolved git reads the SHA-1 name of the latest revision stored in the abc branch. If the branch is stored in loose format—the name is read from .git/refs/heads/abc file. Otherwise the branch's name comes from .git/packed-refs. We will denote the SHA-1 of the latest revision in the abc branch as XXXX. The revision XXXX will be used as a parent of a new revision. Next, git creates and stores the new revision YYYY in the database. During the process the name XXXX is used as a parent for the YYYY revision. Finally, the SHA-1 name of a newly created revision, that is YYYY, is stored in the file .git/refs/heads/abc. As you remember, a side effect of every commit is that the current branch is stored in a loose format again.

To summarize, we can say that while you work on branch:

- When you commit the new revision goes to the current branch. The file .git/HEAD doesn't change. The SHA-1 of the newly created revision will be stored in the .git/refs/heads/branch-name file. If the branch was already stored in a packed format, the format is changed to loose.

- When you create a new branch with $ git branch branch-name a new file .git/refs/heads/branch-name is created and it stores the SHA-1 of the revision passed as a parameter to the $ git branch command or the current revision. The file .git/HEAD remains unchanged. The format for a new branch is always loose.

- When you switch branches with the $ git checkout branch-name command, all the files in .git/refs/heads remain unchanged. The symbolic reference to the branch branch-name is stored in .git/HEAD. It has the form ref: refs/heads/branch-name. The command resets the working directory to the state conforming to the latest revision in branch-name branch. The command doesn't change the format for storing a branch tip.

As you have learned in the Solution section of Recipe 5-1, both operations, creating and switching to a new branch, can be achieved with one command:

```
$ git checkout -b new-branch existing-branch
```

This command creates a new branch named new-branch that points to the same revision as an existing branch named existing-branch.

The HEAD plays a very special role in many git commands. Everywhere you need the SHA-1 of the revision that you are currently working on, you can use HEAD instead. Moreover, HEAD is usually a default value used for absent parameters. The commands:

```
$ git reset --hard
$ git reset --hard HEAD
```

are identical. In a similar fashion, you can create a new branch with:

```
$ git branch new-name [REVISION]
```

The [REVISION] parameter defines where a new branch would point to. If you omit this parameter, HEAD will be used. Thus, both commands:

```
$ git branch new-name
$ git branch new-name HEAD
```

are equivalent. The same is true for other commands as well. The following two commands are also equivalent:

```
$ git checkout -b new-branch
$ git checkout -b new-branch HEAD
```

■ **Notice**   The special name HEAD is transformed to a path .git/HEAD. Therefore, if you work on u*ix-like systems you have to type it using capital letters. Readers working on Windows can type HEAD using lower case (i.e., head).

The revisions can be identified in many different ways. You already know that both SHA-1 and abbreviated SHA-1 names can be used. The other ways to reference revisions include branches, reflog entries, ancestor references, n-th parent references, and tags. Here are some more examples how to create branches pointing to particular revisions:

```
$ git branch new-branch info      # existing branch
$ git branch new-branch a1b2c3ef  # abbreviated SHA-1
$ git branch new-branch HEAD@{5}  # reflog entry
$ git branch new-branch doc~5     # ancestor reference
$ git branch new-branch master^2  # n-th parent reference
$ git branch new-branch v1.2.3    # tag
```

Keep in mind, that the above commands do not modify a database stored in .git/objects. They only create a file in .git/refs/heads. This file will contain a SHA-1 of a given revision.

▪ **Hint**   The syntax for the $ git checkout -b command can also be written in a more general form as $ git checkout -b new-branch [REVISION]

When you start working with branches it is worth remembering that the operation of switching branches is stored in a reflog. The commands:

```
$ git checkout doc
$ git checkout master
```

would result in the following output of $ git reflog entries:

```
23d9855 HEAD@{0}: checkout: moving from master to doc
7c9bc41 HEAD@{1}: checkout: moving from info to master
```

The $ git pack-refs --all command packs all the references stored in .git/refs/heads and stores them in the .git/packed-refs file. You can unpack each branch by creating new commits in it.

5-2. Cloning a repository with branches
Problem

You want to create the exact copy of the repository created in Recipe 5-1. You expect the copy to contain all the branches stored in the original repository: master, doc, and info. You also want to create two new branches named foo and bar—they should point to the same revision as master branch.

You will have to deal with difficulties caused by the behavior of the $ git clone command: the cloned repository contains only one local branch named master. During cloning git only creates one local branch for a branch that is stored in .git/HEAD in an original repository.

Solution

Clone the repository created in Recipe 5-1 using the following commands:

```
$ cd git-recipes
$ git clone 05-01 05-02
$ cd 05-02
```

The new repository contains only one branch named master. You can verify it with the $ git branch command. Its tip is stored using loose format in the file .git/refs/heads/master. To create a branch named info that will correspond to the branch with the same name in the cloned repository, execute the following command:

```
$ git checkout info
```

The command will print the message that the branch info is set up to track a remote branch:

```
Branch info set up to track remote branch info from origin.
Switched to a new branch 'info'
```

After the above command the repository will contain two branches: master and info. It can be verified with the $ git branch command.

In the same manner you can create the branch named doc:

```
$ git checkout doc
```

The repository 05-02 now contains three branches master, info, and doc. Finish the recipe creating branches foo and bar:

```
$ git checkout -b foo master
$ git checkout -b bar master
```

The command $ git branch -a -vv outputs the following information:

```
* bar                     7c9bc41 m3
  doc                     23d9855 [origin/doc] d3
  foo                     7c9bc41 m3
  info                    0d6501b [origin/info] i3
  master                  7c9bc41 [origin/master] m3
  remotes/origin/HEAD     -> origin/master
  remotes/origin/doc      23d9855 d3
  remotes/origin/info     0d6501b i3
  remotes/origin/master 7c9bc41 m3
```

The first line:

```
* bar                     7c9bc41 m3
```

informs you that your repository contains an **ordinary local branch** named doc. This is your current branch and it points to the revision identified by 7c9bc41 with comment m3.

The second line:

```
  doc                     23d9855 [origin/doc] d3
```

informs you that your repository contains a **local tracking branch** named doc. The branch that is tracked by this branch is named origin/doc.

The line:

```
  remotes/origin/doc      23d9855 d3
```

informs you that your repository contains a **remote tracking branch** named origin/doc.

Hence, your repository contains three different types of branches:

- Ordinary local branches
- Local tracking branches
- Remote tracking branches

Finish the recipe by deleting the relationship between the new repository and the cloned original. You can do this with:

```
$ git remote rm origin
```

The output of

```
$ git branch -a -vv:
* bar    7c9bc41 m3
  doc    23d9855 d3
  foo    7c9bc41 m3
  info   0d6501b i3
  master 7c9bc41 m3
```

informs you that the repository contains now only ordinary local branches.

How It Works

In this recipe we work using two different repositories. The first repository is named 05-01. This is the original that we cloned. The second repository is named 05-02. It is the copy of the original repository. All the commands in this recipe will be executed in the repository 05-02. The term *local repository* refers to the repository you work in, which is 05-02. The original repository will be referred to as a *remote repository*. You can check this relation using the command $ git remote -v in the 05-02 repository. The output:

```
origin  .../git-recipes/05-01 (fetch)
origin  .../git-recipes/05-01 (push)
```

informs you that the repository you are currently in uses the alias origin that points to the 05-01 repository. Right after the clone operation but before anyone creates new commits their databases stored in .git/objects are identical.

As you remember from Recipe 5-1 the repository 05-01 contains three branches: master, info, and doc. When we work in the 05-02 repository we will call the branches stored in 05-01 repository **remote branches**. You will never interact with them through commit or add commands. Remote branches are unavailable—there is no way to log in and interact with a remote repository from within your current repository. The only method to interact with remote branches is to use push and fetch commands—thorough discussion of these topics is included in chapter 10.

The branches created and stored locally in 05-02 will be called **local branches**. There are three types of local branches:

- **Ordinary local branches**
- **Remote tracking branches**
- **Local tracking branches**

Let me stress this point one more time: **they are all local**. Remote tracking branches, too.

When you issue the commands:

```
$ git checkout -b foo master
$ git checkout -b bar master
```

they create two **ordinary local branches** named foo and bar. To be sure, no one uses the adjective "ordinary." I've just invented it in the "spur of the moment" to make all the types of branches clear to you. They are usually referred to as local branches. But let's stick with this terminology for a while—it will help to avoid confusion.

Remote tracking branches are local copies of remote branches. They preserve the state of remote branches as it was during the initial clone or last fetch operation. The point of creating remote tracking branches is very simple: whenever you want to check the state of remote branch you should consult a remote tracking branch. The remote tracking branches are named remotes/X/Y, where X represents the alias of a remote repository and Y is the name of the remote branch. For a remote branch named lorem stored in the remote repository 05-01 aliased as origin the remote tracking branch would be named remotes/origin/lorem. This name can be simplified to origin/lorem. The remote tracking branches are stored in a packed format; therefore you will not find them in the refs/remotes/origin directory. They are stored in the .git/packed-refs file. You can treat the remote tracking branches as read only—we will not commit in them.

Local tracking branches are used to publish your commits in a remote branch. They are similar to ordinary local branches: you can commit in them. When in loose format they are stored in .git/refs/heads directory, for example. The main difference is that they are connected to remote tracking branches. Every local tracking branch tracks one of the remote tracking branches. Initially, they point to exactly the same revisions as the remote tracking branches. .

Local branches are listed with the $ git branch command. The command prints both local tracking branches and ordinary local branches. To list remote tracking branches use the -r parameter $ git branch -r. You can list all the branches using $ git branch -a command. The additional parameter -v prints the latest revision in every branch. If you want to get the full classification into three groups, ordinary local branches, remote tracking branches, and local tracking branches, use the parameter -vv.

All four types of branches are depicted in Figure 5-7. The properties of the three branches info, origin/info, and foo from the repository 05-02 are summarized in Table 5-1.

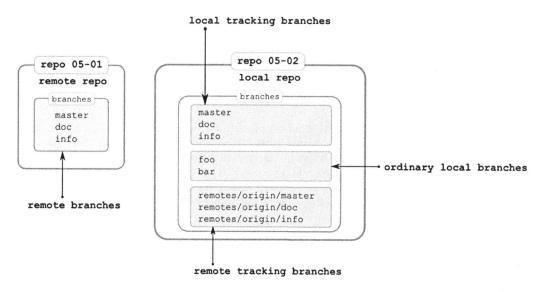

Figure 5-7. *Four types of branches: remote branches, ordinary local branches, local tracking branches, and remote tracking branches*

Table 5-1. *The properties of the three branches info, origin/info, foo from the repository 05-02 shown in Figure 5-7*

name	local/remote	commit	local connection	remote connection	send/receive
info	local	yes	origin/info	—	no
origin/info	local	no	info	info in 05-01	yes
foo	local	yes	—	—	no

■ **Hint**   Remember: remote tracking branches are local branches that act as read-only copies of remote branches.

The columns of Table 5-1 answer the following questions:

- local/remote: is the branch local or remote?
- commit: can I commit in this branch?
- local connection: which local branch is connected with this branch?
- remote connection: which remote branch is connected with this branch?
- send/receive: can I send/receive to/from this branch using a remote branch?

You will notice in Table 5-1 that only remote tracking branches are permitted to interact with remote branches. During cloning git automatically creates:

- One local tracking branch master[2]
- Remote tracking branches for all remote branches

Therefore, right after the $ git clone command the repository 05-02 contains the following branches:

```
* master
  remotes/origin/HEAD -> origin/master
  remotes/origin/doc
  remotes/origin/info
  remotes/origin/master
```

The above is the output of the $ git branch -a command. The line:

```
remotes/origin/HEAD -> origin/master
```

prints the contents of the .git/HEAD file of the remote repository. That's how you would know which branch is considered current by the remote end.

Remember that the new repository created with $ git clone contains the complete database—with all the revisions and other objects. Only the local pointers stored in the .git/refs/heads directory are missing. You have to create them manually. It can be done with the $ git checkout command. As with many other git commands, the $ git checkout command is used to achieve a number of different goals. In this recipe $ git checkout is used to create a new local tracking branch for a remote branch with the same name. Thus the command:

```
$ git checkout info
```

---

[2]The name of the branch can be different—it is the name of the current branch in the remote repository. That's why Recipe 5-1 was finished with $ git checkout master. It guarantees that after cloning, repository 05-02 will contain the master branch.

creates a local tracking branch named info. This branch will be connected with the remote tracking branch remotes/origin/info stored in your local repository. After another command:

```
$ git checkout doc
```

the repository 05-02 contains three local branches master, doc, and info. You can check it using the $ git branch command. These three branches, that is, master, doc, and info, are **local tracking branches**.

■ **Hint** The command $ git branch -a prints local branches, local tracking branches, and remote tracking branches. Although the output clearly shows which ones are the remote tracking branches, the format used for ordinary local branches and local tracking branches is the same. The more precise information is available if you also use -vv option.

You know from the Recipe 2-5 that cloning defines the relationship between a new clone and the repository, which URL you passed to the $ git clone command. The relationship is written in the .git/config file in the form:

```
[remote "origin"]
    url = ...
```

You can also check it with the $ git remote -v command.

We will discuss remotes in greater detail in chapter 10, which deals with remote repositories and synchronization. Right now I only want to delete this relationship otherwise the remote branches from the original repository will blur the output of various commands, in particular $ gitk --all and $ git log --all. To remove the relationship run:

```
$ git remote rm origin
```

This command removes:

- The [remote "origin"] entry from the repository's configuration file
- All remote tracking branches

The command $ git remote -v now returns empty results and the command $ git branch -a prints only five local branches doc, master, info, foo, and bar. Right now, there is no remote repository; therefore all the branches are ordinary local branches.

■ **Hint** Local tracking branches and remote tracking branches exist only in a repository containing at least one remote section in a configuration file. It doesn't make sense to talk about remote tracking branches and local tracking branches in an isolated repository.

5-3. Creating a clone-with-branches alias
Problem

You want to create an alias that will simplify the process of cloning a repository with branches. You want to be able to clone a repository and copy its branches with a single command:

```
$ git clone-with-branches URL directory
```

The first parameter—URL—should point to an existing repository (a URL or a local path). The second parameter—directory—sets the name for the directory you want the clone to be stored in. Here is how we should clone the repository from Recipe 5-1:

```
$ git clone-with-branches 05-01 05-03
```

and jQuery:

```
$ git clone-with-branches git@github.com:jquery/jquery.git jquery-local-clone
```

Solution

Open your .gitconfig file with a text editor and at the end of the [alias] section type the aliases shown in Listing 5-1. Remember that you have to remove all the newline characters. Save the file and close the editor.

Listing 5-1. The aliases to clone a repository with branches

```
list-remote-branches = "!listRemoteBranches() {
    git branch -r | sed \"/->/d; s/  origin\\///g\";
}; listRemoteBranches"

checkout-remote-branches = "!checkoutRemoteBranches() {
    for name in `git list-remote-branches`; do
        git checkout $name;
    done;
}; checkoutRemoteBranches"

clone-with-branches = "!cloneWithBranches() {
    git clone $1 $2;
    cd $2;
    git checkout-remote-branches;
    git remote rm origin
}; cloneWithBranches"
```

You can verify that the alias works as expected by running the following command:

```
$ git clone-with-branches 05-01 05-03
```

How It Works

As you already know, you can list remote tracking branches with the command:

```
$ git branch -r
```

If you clone the repository 05-01 then the above command will print:

```
origin/HEAD -> origin/master
origin/doc
origin/info
origin/master
```

Therefore, we know that the original repository contains three branches named doc, info, and master. The first alias, $ git list-remote-branches, converts the above output in a following way:

- First it removes the item that contains -> characters (this item informs us that in the original repository HEAD contains the symbolic reference to origin/master).

- Then, it deletes the prefixes origin/.

Both operations are performed by the stream editor sed. The following shell command:

```
$ git branch -r | sed "/->/d"
```

removes the line that contains ->. The syntax to filter out some lines with sed is:

```
$ sed "/PATTERN/d"
```

The above command filters out all the lines that contain the PATTERN.
To remove prefix origin/ we use sed's substitution command—its syntax is the following:

```
$ sed "s/PATTERN/REPLACEMENT/"
```

where PATTERN defines the strings that will be replaced, REPLACEMENT is a new string, slashes are used as separators, and s stands for substitute.
The command:

```
$ git branch -r | sed "s/  origin\///g"
```

replaces all occurrences of origin/ with an empty string. Because our PATTERN contains a slash we have to escape it with \.
When we combine both sed commands using a semicolon as a separator into one processing instruction:

```
$ git branch -r | sed "/->/d; s/  origin\///g"
```

the output will contain only branch names:

```
doc
info
master
```

That's how we get the list of names of all remote tracking branches in the cloned repository.
The second alias, $ git checkout-remote-branches, contains a for loop that processes the names returned by the $ git list-remote-branches alias:

```
for name in `git list-remote-branches`; do
    git checkout $name;
done;
```

For every name we execute the checkout command, it creates a local tracking branch. When the loop is finished the newly created clone contains all the branches from the original repository.

The last alias, `$ git clone-with-branches`, performs four operations:

- It clones the original repository: `$ git clone $1 $2`
- It enters the directory with a new clone: `cd $2`
- It creates local branches: `$ git checkout-remote-branches`
- It removes the relationship to the remote repository: `$ git remote rm origin`

Notice, that Recipe 5-3 and Recipe 2-4 both produce similar results. The repositories created with the `$ cp -R` command or the `$ git clone-with-branches` alias contain the same branches as the original repository and no remotes. The main difference between these two procedures is that cloning clears reflog while copying preserves it.

The concept of local tracking branches and remote tracking branches can be unclear if you are new to git. We will discuss both local tracking branches and remote tracking branches in greater detail, emphasizing their role once again in the chapter concerning synchronization. Then, I hope, their purpose will become clearer.

■ **Hint** The alias `$ git clone-with-branches` is useful while learning git. You will probably come to the same conclusion, by the end of this chapter or once we start to practice merging and rebasing.

Creating git subcommands as shell scripts

The aliases you implemented in Recipe 2-10 and Recipe 5-3 were stored in your global `:gitconfig` file. The main drawback of this method is that newlines are prohibited. Every alias, no matter how complicated, has to be stored in a single line of a `.gitconfig` file. This is an internal restriction imposed by `.gitconfig` parsing. You can circumvent this restriction by storing your aliases as separate bash scripts. To prepare the `$ git clone-with-branches` git subcommand using indented syntax, create the file:[3]

```
# on Windows
C:\Program Files (x86)\Git\libexec\git-core\git-clone-with-branches

# on Linux
/usr/lib/git-core/git-clone-with-branches
```

with the contents shown in Listing 5-2. You don't have to remove newline characters while saving Listing 5-2 to a file.

Listing 5-2. Shell script git-core/git-clone-with-branches

```
#!/bin/sh

git clone $1 $2
cd $2
git checkout-remote-branches
git remote rm origin
```

---

[3]The path to the file can be different on your system. On CentOS, for example, it is /usr/libexec/git-core.

5-4. Committing in a detached HEAD state
Problem

You want to commit in a detached HEAD state. You need to clone the repository from Recipe 5-1 and create revisions x1, x2, and x3 shown in Figure 5-8. Notice that the figure doesn't contain any branch pointing to x1, x2, or x3. The revisions that are not accessible through symbolic references (such as branches and tags) are called *dangling revisions*.

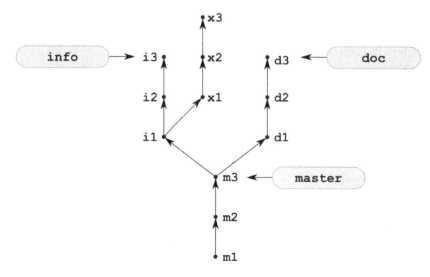

Figure 5-8. *Dangling revisions x1, x2, and x3*

Once you have created these three commits you would like to switch to the master branch and verify that the x1, x2, and x3 revisions are not available. Are they lost? How can you retrieve x1, x2, and x3 back, and how can you ultimately remove them?

Solution

Clone the repository created in Recipe 5-1 with all the branches:

```
$ cd git-recipes
$ git clone-with-branches 05-01 05-04
$ cd 05-04
```

The repository now looks like Figure 5-1. As you can see in Figure 5-8, the parent of revision x1 is i1. As you probably remember from Recipe 3-6 the command $ git checkout [REVISION], when used with SHA-1 name, enters the detached HEAD state and resets the working directory. To use it we need a name for the i1 revision. We could check the name using the following $ git log command:

```
$ git log --oneline --grep=i1 info
```

The first parameter, --oneline, sets the output's format. The second parameter, --grep=i1, acts as a filter. Only the revisions with the comment containing the i1 string are included. The third parameter, info, sets the starting point for the search. Therefore, only the commits available in the branch info will be analyzed. The output of the above command will include only one commit, for example,

```
6f4364e i1
```

There is also a much easier way to refer to i1 than using the abbreviated SHA-1 name. The i1 revision can be addressed as a second parent of the revision pointed to by the info branch. It is formally written as info~2. Thus the command:

```
$ git checkout info~2
```

enters the detached HEAD state and resets the working directory to the commit i1. The command prints clear information about entering the detached HEAD state. Right after the command the .git/HEAD points to i1 commit. This state is depicted in Figure 5-9.

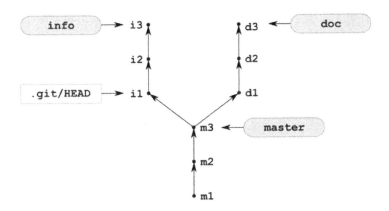

Figure 5-9. *The repository in a detached HEAD state*

Now, create the x1 revision with the alias we created in Recipe 3-11:

```
$ git simple-commit x1
```

The SHA-1 of x1 will be stored in .git/HEAD. The parent of x1 will be i2. This state of the repository is shown in Figure 5-10.

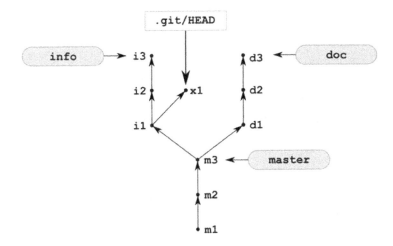

Figure 5-10. *The new commit x1 created in a detached HEAD state*

125

Create two more revisions x2, x3 with:

```
$ git simple-commit x2 x3
```

The repository now looks like Figure 5-11.

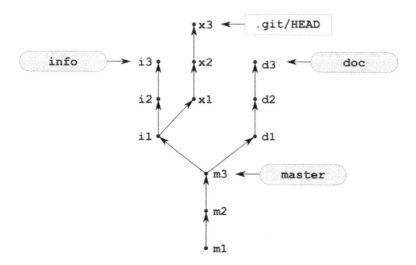

Figure 5-11. *The new commits x1, x2, and x3 created in a detached HEAD state*

In the state shown in Figure 5-11 the .git/HEAD file contains the SHA-1 name of x3 revision. If you now switch to the branch master with the $ git checkout master command then the state of the repository will change as shown in Figure 5-12. This is exactly the state shown in Figure 5-8 with .git/HEAD explicitly shown. The reference to .git/HEAD is usually skipped in the figures because the same information—when necessary—can be presented with an asterisk prepended to the master.

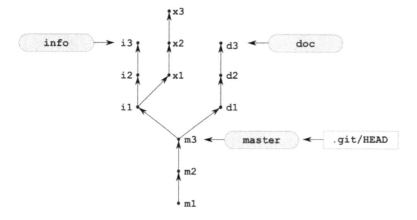

Figure 5-12. *The current branch in the repository can be shown by an asterisk prepended to the master or by including a .git/HEAD reference*

When the repository is in the state shown in Figure 5-12 then the command $ `ls` returns only three files `m1.txt`, `m2.txt`, `m3.txt`—the files `x1.txt`, `x2.txt`, and `x3.txt` are not available.

How to retrieve dangling revisions? First, analyze the output of the $ `git checkout master` command. It contains the detailed information that your three revisions x1, x2, and x3 needs to be retrieved back with the command similar to (surely, your SHA-1 will be different):

```
$ git branch new_branch_name 01f3af0
```

The above command creates a branch named `new_branch_name` that will point to the commit x3 (its SHA-1 name is written as `01f3af0`). If the above information is not available for some reason you can always use the reflog to restore lost commits. Right now you can return to the x3 commit with $ `git checkout HEAD@{1}`.

How can you finally loose dangling revisions? We have already practiced it in Recipe 3-12. If you clear the reflog and prune the database with $ `git prune`, then all dangling revisions will be ultimately lost. Let's do it. Clear the reflog with $ `git reflog expire --all --expire=now`. It can be done with the simple $ `rm .git/logs/*` command. Now, you can check which objects would be lost with either of two commands:

```
$ git prune --dry-run
$ git fsck --unreachable
```

The output should contain three commits (x1, x2, x3), three files[4] (`x1.txt`, `x2.txt`, `x3.txt`) and three trees (one tree for every commit).

▪ **Hint** A tree is a snapshot of given directory. Every commit contains a tree for the main folder of the working directory.

Now, if you run $ `git prune` all dangling revisions will be removed from the database. However, it won't be possible to get them back again.

▪ **Hint** You should treat this recipe as another warning: do not work in a detached HEAD state. You can easily avoid it by using branches.

How It Works

The first problem we have to resolve is how to refer to the revision labeled as i1. Sure, you can find its full or abbreviated name using the $ `git log` or $ `git log --oneline` command. You should be quite familiar with these methods of referring to commits already. In this recipe, however, we used ancestor references—yet another very convenient method to identify revisions.

Every revision except the very first one contains a parent. We can refer to the parent revision using the tilde (~) sign. The notation [REVISION]~ denotes the parent of a given revision. You can use this notation in conjunction with any method to identify a revision. You can write:

```
7c9bc41684455b2b38749ec9cdeed707c07038b2~
7c9b~
master~
info~
HEAD~
```

---

[4]Files are stored in git database as binary large objects (blobs).

The notation:

7c9bc41684455b2b38749ec9cdeed707c07038b2~

refers to the parent revision of the revision pointed to by 7c9bc41684455b2b38749ec9cdeed707c07038b2. The next reference, 7c9b~, points to the same revision using a shortened name. In a similar way:

- master~ refers to the parent of the commit pointed to by master branch

- info~ points to the parent of the commit pointed to by info branch

- HEAD~ refers to the parent of the current revision

- and so forth

Moreover, you can append a number after the tilde—it allows us to point to older ancestors. The reference [REVISION]~n points to the n-th ancestor of [REVISION]. In Figure 5-8, the reference: doc~4 points to the revision labeled as m2, while master~2, info~5, and doc~5 all point to m1. All ancestor references for the branches info, doc, and master are shown in Figure 5-13.

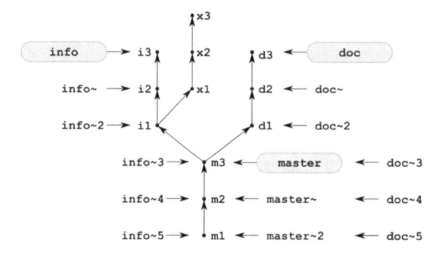

Figure 5-13. *Ancestor references for branches doc, info, and master*

■ **Hint**   References [REVISION]~1 and [REVISION]~ mean exactly the same: the first parent of a given revision.

You learned in Recipe 5-1 that your current revision could always be referenced by symbolic reference HEAD. As you can guess HEAD can be used in conjunction with ancestor references such as HEAD~, HEAD~2, HEAD~3, and so forth. If you switch to the info branch with $ git checkout info, then using HEAD with a tilde would give the results presented in Figure 5-14.

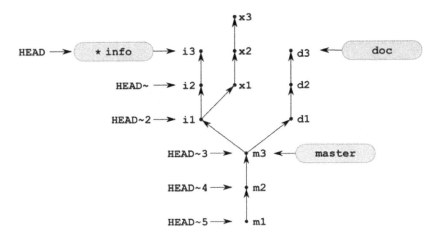

Figure 5-14. *Using HEAD with the ancestor references for the branch named info*

Have you noticed the asterisk in front of *info branch name? As I told you: this is a much easier way to show which branch you are currently on. The asterisk informs you that .git/HEAD now contains the ref: refs/heads/info symbolic reference. This idea is not mine—it is taken from the output of the $ git branch command that would now be:

```
  doc
* info
  master
```

Maybe you noticed that the command $ git checkout [REVISION] works differently depending on its parameter. If the parameter is a SHA-1 name, then the command enters detached HEAD state. If, on the other hand, you pass a branch name, the command will change your current branch. You can force the detached HEAD state with a --detached option, for example $ git checkout --detached master.

The above rules apply even if you pass the SHA-1 of the commit pointed to by a branch. Assuming that $ git log --oneline --decorate prints:

```
7c9bc41 (HEAD, master) m3
```

the command:

```
$ git checkout 7c9bc41
```

enters the detached HEAD state; even though 7c9bc41 points to the master branch.

5-5. Resetting and cleaning a branch
Problem

You are working in a branch—creating, modifying, coping, removing, and renaming files. After making some changes, you realize that all your modifications (they haven't been committed yet) are wrong. You want to reset the state of your branch back to the starting point.

Solution

Clone the repository created in Recipe 5-1 with all the branches:

```
$ cd git-recipes
$ git clone-with-branches 05-01 05-05
$ cd 05-05
```

The repository is now clean and you are in the `master` branch. Modify the working directory using the commands:

```
$ echo foo > bar.txt
$ echo bar > m1.txt
$ cp m1.txt copy.txt
$ rm m2.txt
$ mv m3.txt new-m3.txt
```

The `$ git status -sb` now prints:

```
## master
 M m1.txt
 D m2.txt
 D m3.txt
?? bar.txt
?? copy.txt
?? new-m3.txt
```

You can throw away all these changes with two commands:

```
$ git reset --hard
$ git clean -f
```

Right now the repository is clean, and you can check it with the `$ git status -s` command. All the modifications were lost.

How It Works

You already know the command `$ git reset --hard`. It resets all the tracked files to the state saved in the latest revision. But the `$ git reset` command does not modify untracked files. To remove all untracked files use the `$ git clean -f` command. The parameter `-f` serves as a precaution; without it, the `$ git clean` command only prints a message. It's another level of security that helps to avoid data loss. However, if you want to just list the files that would have been removed without actually deleting them use the `$ git clean -n` command.

5-6. Switching branches in a dirty repository without conflicts
Problem

Suppose that during your work in the repository, you modified some files and want to commit them in a branch that is different from your current branch. You have to switch branches in a dirty repository. Depending on your changes, this operation can be allowed or forbidden by git. In this recipe, we consider the case when switching is allowed.

Solution

Clone the repository created in Recipe 5-1 with all the branches:

```
$ cd git-recipes
$ git clone-with-branches 05-01 05-06
$ cd 05-06
```

The repository is now clean and contains three branches. You currently are on the master branch. Change your current branch to info with:

```
$ git checkout info
```

and then modify the working directory with the following commands:

```
$ echo bar > bar.txt
$ echo foo > m1.txt
$ rm m2.txt
$ mv m3.txt new-m3.txt
```

The file bar.txt was created—it is a new untracked file. The m1.txt file was modified—it now contains foo instead of m1. The next file—i1.txt—was deleted. The last file—m3.txt—was renamed to new-m3.txt. The command $ git status -sb now prints:

```
## info
 M m1.txt
 D m2.txt
 D m3.txt
?? bar.txt
?? new-m3.txt
```

The above changes are not staged, of course. The repository is dirty, and you are in the info branch.

Suppose that you forgot about your changes and for some reason want to checkout the doc branch. The command:

```
$ git checkout doc
```

succeeds. All the changes are preserved, and you are now in the doc branch. The output of $ git status -sb is now almost the same—only the branch name is changed to doc:

```
## doc
 M m1.txt
 D m2.txt
 D m3.txt
?? bar.txt
?? new-m3.txt
```

You still haven't remembered about your changes or about your current branch and you inadvertently stage all the changes with $ git add -A.

Finally, you realize that your changes are still not committed. Moreover, you would like them to go to the master branch. To commit your modifications into the master branch you have to switch the branch and create the revision:

```
$ git checkout master
$ git snapshot Recipe 5-5 Switching branches in dirty repository without conflicts
```

Your repository is clean and all the modifications are stored in the master branch.

How It Works

In all the recipes up to Recipe 5-5 we switched branches when a repository was clean. But git allows switching branches even if repository is dirty. By default, all changes are preserved even if they were staged or not. If git cannot preserve your changes then it will refuse to switch branches. In other words, *switching branches in a dirty repository is permitted if and only if the changes that are not committed do not collide with the contents of the branch you are switching to*. Remember a simple rule of thumb: if the branch was switched, it means that your dirty modifications didn't cause any collisions. However, there is one slight exception: the only situation when you can loose uncommitted changes without any warning during branch switching is when you remove a file that was not present in the branch you are switching to.

You can verify it with the following commands:

```
$ git checkout info
$ rm i1.txt    # removed file i1.txt is not present in doc branch
$ git status -sb
```

The output would contain the information about one deleted file i1.txt. If you switch to the doc branch (this branch doesn't contain the i1.txt file) with:

```
$ git checkout doc
```

Then, git will not warn you about conflicts. The repository becomes clean and the information about the deleted file i1.txt is lost. If you switch to the info branch again the file will be resurrected. In the case of the m2.txt file removed in the recipe with the $ rm m2.txt command, the information that the file was deleted was preserved when we switched to the doc branch. That's because the file m2.txt exists in every branch.

■ **Question**   Can you imagine an alias that restrict switching branches only to clean state?

5-7. Switching branches in a dirty repository with conflicts
Problem

You just modified the working directory and you want to commit changes in a different branch. You have to switch to another branch and then create a new revision. In this recipe we consider the case of when your changes collide with the branch you want to switch to. If that is the case, git doesn't allow you to checkout another branch.

Solution

Clone the repository created in Recipe 5-1:

```
$ cd git-recipes
$ git clone-with-branches 05-01 05-07
$ cd 05-07
```

Switch to the info branch and modify the working directory with the following commands:

```
$ git checkout info
$ echo foo > i1.txt
```

The i1.txt file was modified and it is listed as:

```
_M i1.txt
```

by $ git status -sb. This file is not present in the master branch. If you now execute the command $ git checkout master, you will see the warning:

```
error:
    Your local changes to the following files
    would be overwritten by checkout:
        i1.txt
```

Thus, git refuses to the switch to the current branch to the master because you would lose your changes to the i1.txt file.

Assume that your modifications are important—you want to preserve and commit them in master branch. There are three different approaches you may take:

- You can stash your changes for a while, change a branch, and then retrieve the changes. This is what we will do in this recipe.

- You can merge your changes with a branch you switched to during checkout. This solution is similar to stashing.

- Finally, you can commit in the current (wrong) branch and then move your revision to appropriate branch. This procedure will be discussed in Recipe 5-8.

Stashing uncommitted changes

The command $ git checkout master produces the warning:

```
error:
    Your local changes to the following files
    would be overwritten by checkout:
        i1.txt
```

The settings are as follows: you are in info branch, the file i1.txt is modified, and you want it to be committed in the master branch.

First, save the current state of the working directory with:

```
$ git stash
```

The repository becomes clean, the working directory reflects the latest revision in the info branch, and your modifications to i1.txt file were stored in a temporary area called stash. Because the repository is clean you can safely checkout of the master branch:

```
$ git checkout master
```

The above command doesn't affect in any way your stashed work.
To retrieve your stashed modifications execute the following command:

```
$ git stash pop
```

The state of the working directory will be adjusted to reflect the changes stored with stash command. The above command will produce a warning about conflicting changes:

```
CONFLICT (modify/delete):
    i1.txt deleted in Updated upstream and modified in Stashed changes.
    Version Stashed changes of i1.txt left in tree.
```

General methods to deal with conflicts are presented in chapter 9. The command $ git status -sb prints:

```
## master
DU i1.txt
```

The conflicted file is denoted as DU. To keep i1.txt file in the master branch, you need to stage a file:

```
$ git add i1.txt
```

and then create a new revision:

```
$ git commit -m "i1.txt file..."
```

Merging changes during checkout

To merge your modifications during checkout use the -m parameter:

```
$ git checkout -m master
```

The above command would produce exactly the same result as these three commands:

```
$ git stash
$ git checkout master
$ git stash pop
```

However, by using the $ git stash command you postpone the moment you wish to merge your stashed files.

How It Works

The $ git stash command used in the solution saves the current state of the staging area and the working directory and resets the working directory. The new untracked files are not affected by this command. Therefore, if you want to save all of the files (including untracked files) use the following two commands:

```
$ git add -A
$ git stash
```

The first command adds all modifications to the staging area. When run together, the commands guarantee that all your modifications are stashed.

After saving your changes, the stash command resets the working directory. The repository becomes clean and its working directory reflects the snapshot of the latest revision in your current branch.

To restore the stashed state, you should use the $ git stash pop command. You can execute this command in every branch. Popped stashed changes are merged with your current branch.

Git allows stashing uncommitted changes to be performed an arbitrary number of times—they are stored on stack. Stashed states can be listed with the $ git stash list command. It produces an output similar to the one below:

```
stash@{0}: WIP on info: 0d6501b i3
stash@{1}: WIP on doc: 23d9855 d3
stash@{2}: WIP on master: ae34fcd m4
```

You also can change the default message WIP on XXX to something more meaningful such as:

```
$ git stash save A very descriptive information
```

The command $ git stash is equivalent to $ git stash save WIP on [branch-name]. You have already learned the meaning of WIP in Recipe 3-2. It stands for work in progress.

Although $ git stash is a very convenient tool to use for switching branches in dirty repo, you also can use a forced checkout. There are two switches of the $ git checkout command that will help you: -m or -f. The first one merges your changes with the branch you switch to; the second throws your modifications away.

■ **Hint**   Stashing can be applied if there are no conflicts, of course. Therefore, in Recipe 5-6 you also can use stashing to save and restore your uncommitted changes.

5-8. Committing in a wrong branch
Problem

You have just created a new revision only to find out that it should go to a different branch. If your modifications do not collide while switching branches you can easily forget to check out the appropriate branch before you commit. After creating the revision in the wrong branch you want to move it to its correct destination.

Solution

Clone the repository created in Recipe 5-1:

```
$ cd git-recipes
$ git clone-with-branches 05-01 05-08
$ cd 05-08
```

and modify the m1.txt file

```
$ echo A new text > m1.txt
```

Let's suppose you intended this change to be committed in the master branch. The modification doesn't collide with the doc branch. You can checkout the doc branch without any problems using: $ git checkout doc. The checkout command outputs a line that give you information about the changes:

```
M       m1.txt
```

But it can be easily overlooked.

After some time, you are completely unaware that the current branch is not the master. You create the wrong revision with:

```
$ git snapshot Recipe 5-8: a revision in a wrong branch
```

Now that you realized your failure, you want to move the revision to the master branch.
You can do it in two separate steps:

- Copy the revision from wrong branch to correct one.

- Remove the revision from wrong branch.

Before you proceed with the procedures given below verify that the new revision is present in doc branch and absent from master branch. Here are the commands you need:

```
$ git log --oneline doc
$ git log --oneline master
```

Here is the procedure you need to copy the latest revision from the doc branch to the master branch:

1. Change the current branch to master with the $ git checkout master command.

2. Copy the tip revision from the doc branch to your current branch (which is the master) with the $ git cherry-pick doc command.

As of now, the new revision is present in both branches. The commands $ git log --oneline -1 master and $ git log --oneline -1 doc print the output shown in Listing 5-3. Although your actual hashes will be different, you should notice that the two SHA-1 names of your commits are different.

Listing 5-3. The output of $ git log --oneline -1 for the two branches

```
# the output of $ git log --oneline -1 master
43336a3 Recipe 5-8: a revision in a wrong branch

# the output of $ git log --oneline -1 doc
7ad4187 Recipe 5-8: a revision in a wrong branch
```

Finish the recipe removing the erroneous revision from the doc branch:

1. Change the current branch to doc with the `$ git checkout doc` command.

2. Remove the revision with the `$ git reset --hard HEAD~` command.

The output of `$ git l master` and `$ git l doc` proves that the new revision is included only in the master branch. You also can verify it with one command to display all branches: `$ git log --oneline --graph --decorate --all`.

How It Works

The recipe uses two important commands:

```
$ git cherry-pick doc
$ git reset --hard HEAD~
```

The first command—cherry-pick—makes a copy of a given revision in a current branch. It needs a single parameter that points to the revision to be copied. If you pass a name of the branch to this command, it will copy the revision pointed to by the branch; that is, the tip of the branch. You can use other means to identify a revision, as well, for example:

```
$ git cherry-pick 7c9bc41    # shortened SHA-1 name
$ git cherry-pick info~      # last but one commit in info branch
$ git cherry-pick info~3     # branch name and ancestor reference
```

The term *to copy a revision* can be a little misleading here. Every revision you create has a unique name. There are no exemptions from this rule. You can only:

- Add new revisions to the git's database

- Remove existing revisions from the git's database

Git doesn't implement modification of objects stored in a database. The name of the commit is a SHA-1 hash, which was produced using your name, current timestamp, the snapshot of your files, and the name of the parent revision. When we copy a revision from one place in the history to another we change at least one of these parameters: the name of the parent revision. As a result there is no way to preserve the old SHA-1 for a copied revision. Thus the operation realized by cherry-pick command can be better described as applying the changes introduced by a given revision on top of your current branch. The command creates a completely new revision that reproduces the changes stored in a revision passed as a parameter. The new revision is always created at the top of your current branch—it becomes the latest revision in the branch.

You are already familiar with the second command. We used it in Recipe 3-5. This time we use an ancestor reference HEAD~. The reference points to the last but one revision in a current branch.

5-9. Deleting local branches

Problem

Suppose you have realized that your repository contains stale branches that you will never need again. You decide to delete them.

Solution

Clone the repository created in Recipe 5-1 and switch to the doc branch:

```
$ cd git-recipes
$ git clone-with-branches 05-01 05-09
```

```
$ cd 05-09
$ git checkout doc
```

Let's suppose you decided that master and info branches are not important anymore. To delete the master branch execute:

```
$ git branch -d master
```

Next try to delete the info branch with the same command:

```
$ git branch -d info
```

The above command fails to remove the info branch because it contains some revisions that could be lost. To force the removal use the command:

```
$ git branch -D info
```

How It Works

Every two branches in a repository can be characterized as either *merged* or *not merged*. We say that branch a *is merged* into branch b if all the revisions included in a are also included in b. Figure 5-15 presents two branches a and b. Branch a is merged in branch b. Branch a contains two revisions a1 and a2—both of them can be found starting from the revision pointed to by b and following parent revisions.

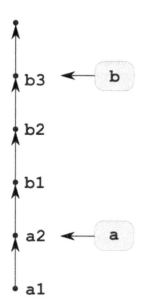

Figure 5-15. *Branch a is merged into branch b; branch b is not merged into branch a*

This relation usually is not reflective. In the repository in Figure 5-15 branch b *is not merged* in the master. As you can see, the revisions b1, b2, and b3 are included in branch b, but not in branch a. The only case when this relation is reflective is when both branches point to the exactly the same revision, as in Figure 5-16.

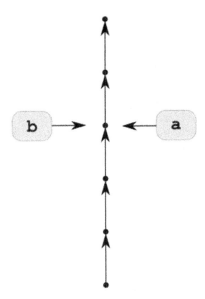

Figure 5-16. *Branch a is merged into branch b and branch b is merged into branch a*

The third case is when neither branch a is merged into branch b nor when branch b is merged into branch a. We say then that branches a and b *have diverged*. This case is shown in Figure 5-17.

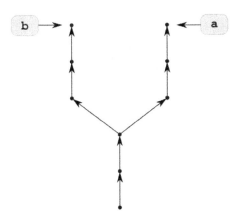

Figure 5-17. *Diverged branches a and b*

The information containing which branches are merged and which are not merged in the current branch can be obtained with the --merged and --no-merged options passed to the $ git branch command:

```
# print the names of branches merged in current branch
$ git branch --merged

# print the names of branches not merged in current branch
$ git branch --no-merged
```

Now that you know about merged and not merged branches you can easily guess that the command:

```
$ git branch -d [branch-name]
```

deletes a given branch only if it is merged in a current branch. If the branch you want to delete is not merged the command prints a warning:

```
error: The branch 'branch-name' is not fully merged.
```

and then exits. The command with the -D option:

```
$ git branch -D [branch-name]
```

removes a branch even if it is not merged.

Let me remind you that a branch is a simple pointer—just a SHA-1 stored in either a loose or packed format. If you create a branch, git stores a new pointer inside the .git directory. When a branch is deleted the pointer is removed. The commands $ git branch -d and $ git branch -D do not modify the database. All the revisions are left intact. Therefore, even if you delete a branch you can retrieve it using reflog.

■ **Note** This recipe describes the way to delete local branches. You can use it to delete ordinary local branches and local tracking branches. All remote tracking branches can be deleted with the $ git remote rm command, as we did in Recipe 5-2. To delete only one remote tracking branch origin/doc you can use $ git branch -d -r origin/doc command. But remote tracking branches deleted with $ git branch -d -r will be recreated after next the fetch command. The commands to delete remote branches will be discussed in chapter 10 concerning synchronization of repositories.

5-10. Using a branch as a backup
Problem

Your repository is in clean state. You start to work on a new feature in your current branch. After some revisions you realize the new idea is not working and want to discard it. You want to cancel the new feature and return your repository to the state just before the feature was started. The best solution to this problem is to use branches.

Solution

Clone the repository created in Recipe 5-1 with all the branches:

```
$ cd git-recipes
$ git clone-with-branches 05-01 05-10
$ cd 05-10
```

The repository is now clean and you are in master branch. This is the starting point. You create a new branch named feature that will be identical as the current master branch:

```
$ git checkout -b feature
```

Now, you are in `feature` branch and create some commits:

```
$ git simple-commit one two three
```

All your modifications are committed, the repository is clean.

Now you decide that the whole concept implemented in the `feature` branch is not working. And you want to get rid of it. You can achieve this with two commands:

```
$ git checkout master
$ git branch -D feature
```

How It Works

You don't need new commands for this recipe. This recipe only underlines the usefulness of branches in a specific scenario. Without risk, git allows you to test new concepts that would otherwise destroy or complicate your work. Every branch is independent of other branches. The modifications you commit in the `feature` branch do not affect the `master` branch or, in fact, any other branch. If some specific state of your repository is important to you, and you want to be absolutely sure that whatever you do, you can always get it back, just create a branch. It's as simple as that. Once you grasp this idea, you will wonder, how on earth you managed to work without it.

Remember that if you are not sure about an idea, you don't have to delete the branch. Superfluous branches don't influence your work in any way. You can leave them alone. A branch written in loose format only consumes 41 bytes, so it does not consume a lot of space.

Finally, if you delete the branch the revisions you created are not removed from a database, even if you prune it. The reason is simple: reflog contains entries that forbid pruning these objects. To completely remove the branch and its revisions you have to delete a branch, clear the reflog, and prune the database.

5-11. Renaming branches
Problem

You work in a repository shown in Figure 5-1, and you want to rename branches:

- `info` to `information`
- `master` to `doc`

Solution

Clone the repository created in Recipe 5-1:

```
$ cd git-recipes
$ git clone-with-branches 05-01 05-11
$ cd 05-11
```

You are in the `master` branch. Change the name of the `info` branch to `information` with:

```
$ git branch -m info information
```

Finally, change the name of the `master` branch to `doc` with:

```
$ git branch -M master doc
```

How It Works

The command `$ git branch -m [old-name] [new-name]` renames the branch named old-name to new-name. If the branch with a new name already exists, then you can overwrite it using `$ git branch -M [old-name] [new-name]`. In this case the existing new-name branch will be lost.

By the way, did you notice? The master branch can be renamed and removed—just as any other branch.

5-12. Checking out a file from a different branch
Problem

While working on a project with many branches, you have just realized that while on one branch you need some files from another branch. You want to checkout files from a branch that is not your current branch.

Solution

Clone the repository created in Recipe 5-1 with:

```
$ cd git-recipes
$ cp -R 05-01 05-12
$ cd 05-12
```

If you prefer, you can create local clones with the `$ cp` command. The clone created with `$ cp` will be slightly different: its reflog is not empty and it doesn't contain a remote. However these differences do not count in this recipe, therefore, you can practice cloning with the `$ cp` command.

I presume you are currently on the master branch. Change the contents of the m1.txt file and commit the change:

```
$ git checkout master
$ echo The new content from Recipe 5-12 > m1.txt
$ git snapshot The new content from Recipe 5-12
```

The only files available in the master branch are m1.txt, m2.txt, and m3.txt. You want a copy of the i1.txt file, which is stored in the info branch. You can achieve this with:

```
$ git checkout info -- i1.txt
```

It may happen that you will need to rename the file during checkout. That's exactly why we modified the m1.txt file in the master branch. Right now, the version of the m1.txt file in the master branch is different than the version in other branches. How to get the m1.txt file from the doc branch without losing the version that is stored in the working directory? You can display the m1.txt file stored in doc branch on stdout by using:

```
$ git show doc:m1.txt
```

To save it with a different name, send the output to a file using stream redirection:

```
$ git show doc:m1.txt > m1-from-doc-branch.txt
```

Finish the recipe by creating another revision with the `$ git snapshot Files from other branches` command.

How It Works

The command $ `git checkout` can be used to checkout just a single file without switching branches. The syntax is following:

```
$ git checkout [REVISION] -- [filename]
```

You can pass an arbitrary revision identifier to it, of course. You can use HEAD, ancestor references, stash references, remote tracking branches, and reflog, to name a few:

```
$ git checkout HEAD~ -- file.txt
$ git checkout stash@{3} -- file.txt
$ git checkout remotes/origin/master -- file.txt
$ git checkout HEAD@{yesterday} -- file.txt
```

The command allows you to use glob wildcards as well:

```
$ git checkout doc -- d*.txt
```

Two dashes separate a filename from commands options. Very often the dashes are not crucial, as in $ `git checkout doc d1.txt`. They are necessary to disambiguate the options from paths. Here the `-f` acts as an option:

```
$ git checkout doc -f
```

And in the example below, the `-f` is interpreted as a path:

```
$ git checkout doc -- -f
```

Arbitrary versions of files stored in a database can also be displayed on your screen without the need to check them out. This can be done with the $ `git show` command. You have to identify the revision and the file. This is done with the two parameters separated by a colon:

```
$ git show [REVISION]:[FILENAME]
```

Using this command you can check out a file and then save it under different name:

```
$ git show [REVISION]:[FILENAME] > [new-filename]
```

This is the way to check out the files with names that are not allowed in your system, for example. If you create a file named `some*strange*name.txt` in Linux, then it won't be able to check out the file in Windows. Working on Windows, you can still checkout this file using a new name for it:

```
$ git show HEAD:some*strange*name.txt > some-strange-name.txt
```

The most astonishing example of problems with filenames I encountered was when I was training someone who was working on Linux and who used filenames with trailing dots, as in:

```
$ echo lorem > lorem.
```

The environment was heterogeneous—trainees were using Windows and Linux. The trainees using Windows couldn't get a clean checkout of the repository anymore. Right after the clone command the repository was dirty. If the revisions such as this are already public, the remedy is to check out the files and change their names. Thanks to $ `git show [REVISION]:[FILENAME] > [new-filename]`, this can be done on any platform.

5-13. Switching branches in a bare repository

Problem

You have cloned a bare repository and its current branch is master. You want to switch to a different branch.

Solution

Clone the repository created in Recipe 05-01 using the following commands:

```
$ cd git-recipes
$ git clone --bare 05-01 05-13
$ cd 05-13
```

The newly created clone will be a bare one. List all the branches with the $ git branch -a command. You will get the output:

```
  doc
  info
* master
```

As you can see, in a bare repository local branches are created for all remote branches. You don't have to manually check them out as we did in Recipe 5-2. The HEAD reference points to the master branch—we know this, thanks to an asterisk in front of master in the above output. But you can verify it with either of two commands:

```
$ cat HEAD
$ git symbolic-ref HEAD
```

To change the current branch, execute the following command:

```
$ git symbolic-ref HEAD refs/heads/info
```

After this, the command $ git branch outputs:

```
  doc
* info
  master
```

Therefore, we know that the current branch was changed. If you are in doubt, you can always double-check it with the $ git log --oneline -3 command. It will print the i3, i2, and i1 commits.

How It Works

The command to switch a branch in a non-bare repository is:

```
$ git checkout [branch-name]
```

Actually, it performs two operations: it changes the reference stored in HEAD, and it checks out the files. These two operations can also be performed manually:

```
$ git symbolic-ref HEAD refs/heads/branch-name
$ git reset --hard
```

In a bare repository you cannot use the commands, such as $ git checkout or $ git status, that require the working directory. They simply do not make sense. Working in a bare repository you can change the reference stored in HEAD, but you cannot reset the working directory.

Therefore, to change a current branch in a bare repository use the following command:

```
$ git symbolic-ref HEAD refs/heads/branch-name
```

This is a low level command that operates on symbolic references. Used with one parameter, as in $ git symbolic-ref HEAD, the command works as a getter: it outputs the reference. When two parameters are used, it acts as a setter: the symbolic reference passed as the first parameter is set to the value passed as a second parameter.

It is worth remembering that the current branch in a clone will be the branch that was current in the original repository at the time the $ git clone command was issued. This is true that no matter if the original repository was bare or non-bare. You can change this using the additional parameter -b passed to clone. The commands:

```
$ git clone -b doc 05-01 05-13-doc-nonbare
$ git clone --bare -b doc 05-01 05-13-doc-bare
```

would create new clones with the HEAD pointing to refs/heads/doc.

Summary

The content of this chapter is a solid base that we will need in the chapters to follow—merging and rebasing in particular. To recap, we learned:

- To create, delete, and rename branches

- To switch branches

- To commit in a current branch

- To display the history of a given branch or all branches—both with the $ git log and $ gitk commands

That's the ABC—the first step to use branches. The recipe concerning creation and switching of branches gave you detailed information about the way git stores branches and the information concerning which branch is current. You know two formats git uses to store branches—loose and packed. You also know how to change from one to the other.

Deleting branches, on the other hand, required the introduction of two terms: merged and not merged branch. These terms are very important—they will be utilized at length in the chapters on merging and rebasing. When in doubt, consult Figures 5-15, 5-16, and 5-17 for help.

We also considered branching in clones, which gave us two classifications:

- Remote branches

- Local branches

Local branches are further classified into three different types:

- Ordinary local branches

- Local tracking branches

- Remote tracking branches

You learned to create all types of local branches and thanks to the -vv parameter of the $ git branch command, you should easily classify all the branches in your repository—even if this classification is still a little vague. Remember, that commands can be restricted to the work only on branches of a given type. For example deleting branches with $ git branch -d or $ git branch -D works only for local branches. These commands don't work for remote branches.

At the very beginning of the branching tour it is easier to switch branches in a clear state. That is not compulsory, however. Once you practiced the basics, you will need to switch to a branch while keeping the repository dirty. I've dissected this task into two separate recipes: unconflicted and conflicted case. The unconflicted case can result in committing in a wrong branch. This problem is addressed by cherry-picking and reset commands. Conflicted case of branch switching is a perfect place to introduce stashing—a method of storing your dirty state.

The next aspect of branching is related to bare and non-bare classification. While learning to switch branches in bare repositories, we dissected the same operation in non-bare repositories into a symbolic reference update and a reset of the working directory. It gave you a deeper insight into some commands, such as checkout. They operate on the working directory and thus cannot be executed in bare repositories.

Finally, you learned new methods to identify revisions:

- Symbolic reference HEAD

- Branch names

- Ancestor references

- Stash references

The ancestor references can be used together with all other methods, as in:

```
HEAD~
master~2
stash@{4}~5
```

And remember, do not use the detached HEAD state to commit your work. Always use branches for that.

CHAPTER 6

■ ■ ■

Merging Branches

The commands to create and switch branches allow you to fork the project into independent development lines. You can create branches, for example, to start new features in your application or to implement fixes. Sooner or later you will finish a feature or a fix and then in all probability, you will want to incorporate your efforts into the main line of development. The process of joining separate branches can be done using two different techniques. The first one is realized with the **$ git merge** command. It is the subject of this chapter. The second is done with the **$ git rebase** command. We will postpone this as it is the subject of the next chapter.

Maybe you have noticed that the term **merging** is not totally new. We have already used it in Recipe 5-7 to denote the process of joining changes in the working directory with the branch we switched to. There, the merge was done during checkout. The result was left in the working directory to be committed. Here in this chapter, we consider merging different branches together. The result of the merging branches will be stored and committed, that is, in one of the branches. We will perform merging in clean recipes that contain no uncommitted or untracked files. After the recipe, the repository will be in a clean state again.

Here, you will fully appreciate the aliases `simple-commit` and `clone-with-branches`. They will take you to the higher level of abstraction. Instead of using $ `git add` and $ `git commit`, together with $ `echo foo > bar`, we will create a series of commits with $ `git simple-commit`. Thus, you will be able to concentrate on merging. The aliases work in such a way that conflicts do not occur. This is a simplified setting, not a real-life scenario, of course. But I prefer to separate merging and resolving conflicts into two separate steps. Conflicts will be discussed in-depth in Chapter 9.

This chapter reflects the way I usually teach branching and merging. I strongly believe that a key point while learning the git branching model is to grasp the way this operation transforms the graph of revisions. Once you understand how to create a graph with a predefined structure, merging becomes easy and straightforward.

This chapter covers three cases of merging:

- A fast-forward
- Merging of two diverged branches
- Merging of multiple diverged branches

To practice these merges we will need to create:

- A repository with two branches, one of them has to be merged in the other
- A repository with two diverged branches
- And a repository with multiple diverged branches

All of these repositories will be created in separate recipes making it easier to repeat every case a number of times, if necessary. Anytime you want to perform a merge again, just clone a starting repository and execute the commands that merge branches. Working this way, you can, for example, test and analyze how diverse options of the $ `git merge` command influences its behavior.

In addition, this chapter explains:

- How to undo the merge operation
- How to force a fast-forward to be realized as a typical merge using the `--no-ff` switch
- How to make sure that a merge is a fast-forward with the `--ff-only` switch
- How to use n-th parent references

6-1. Implementing a new feature in a branch
Problem

Your repository is clean and contains only one branch named `master`. The branch consists of three revisions. The starting point for this recipe is shown in Figure 6-1. You want to implement a new feature of your application. Because you are not sure whether the solution will be a good one, you decide to use a new branch named `feature`. The result you want to achieve is shown in Figure 6-2.

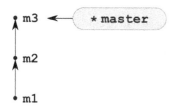

Figure 6-1. *The starting point for Recipe 6-1*

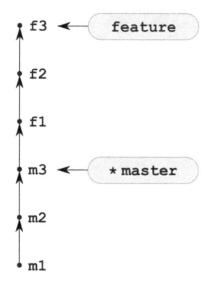

Figure 6-2. *Finished Recipe 6-1*

Solution

Start the command line and create a new repository:

```
$ cd git-recipes
$ git init 06-01
$ cd 06-01
```

Next, create three commits in the master branch with:

```
$ git simple-commit m1 m2 m3
```

Your repository now looks like Figure 6-1. Create a new branch named feature containing three new commits:

```
$ git checkout -b feature
$ git simple-commit f1 f2 f3
```

Finish the recipe checking out the master branch with the $ git checkout master command. Now, the repository looks like Figure 6-2.

How It Works

This recipe uses commands already known. It presents the best approach to implement new features in your application. Whenever you start to work on a new topic, do it in a dedicated branch. Note that the repository shown in Figure 6-2 can be also drawn as in Figure 6-3. The revisions don't have to form a straight line. The recipe is insensitive with regard to the number of commits in the branches. The master branch can include 100 commits and the feature branch only one commit, for example. The only important aspect of this repository is that the master branch is fully merged in the feature branch.

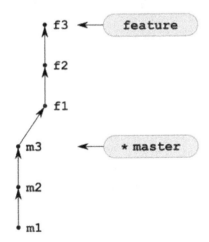

Figure 6-3. *The alternative graphical representation of Figure 6-2*

6-2. Fast-forwarding branches
Problem

You have finished the work on the Recipe 6-1 and have decided that your work in the feature branch should be merged into the master branch. You want to create the repository shown in Figure 6-4.

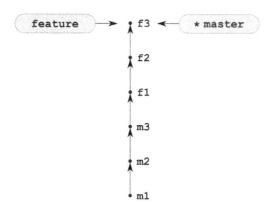

Figure 6-4. *The result of merging the feature branch into the master branch*

Solution

Clone the repository from Recipe 6-1 with branches:

```
$ cd git-recipes
$ git clone-with-branches 06-01 06-02
$ cd 06-02
```

Right now you are on the master branch. Merge the feature branch into the master branch with the $ git merge feature command. The command will print the information that this operation was carried on as a fast-forward. When you finish, the master branch contains all the files created in master branch as well as three files from feature branch. The $ ls command will print six filenames: f1.txt, f2.txt, f3.txt, m1.txt, m2.txt, and m3.txt.

How It Works

This recipe presents the simplest example of merging branches. There are two branches master and feature, and the current branch is master. A very important fact is that all the revisions in the master branch are contained in the feature branch. We say that the master branch is merged into the feature branch. This relation was defined in Recipe 5-9.

In settings such as in Figure 6-2, the command $ git merge feature issued in the master branch just moves the master pointer to the place referenced by the feature branch. This operation is called **fast-forward**. It is the least complicated example of joining two development histories. The resulting repository contains two branches pointing to exactly the same commit. Notice that during fast-forward no new commits are created.

Keep in mind that the history will contain no information at all that we used the $ git merge command. The name of the feature branch can disappear from the history. This can be regarded as a drawback. We will circumvent this drawback in Recipe 6-6.

You also can try to merge the master branch into the feature branch. What would happen in that case? Because the master branch is already merged into feature branch the commands:

```
$ git checkout feature
$ git merge master
```

will only print a short info: Already up-to-date. The repository doesn't change.

6-3. Undoing fast-forward
Problem

You have completed the fast-forward operation presented in Recipe 6-2, and you are not satisfied with it. You want to undo the merge. In other words, you want to transform the repository shown in Figure 6-4 back into the form presented in Figure 6-2.

Solution

Clone the repository 06-02 with the cp command:

```
$ cd git-recipes
$ cp -R 06-02 06-03
$ cd 06-03
```

The easiest solution to undo merging is to use reflog. Thanks to using the cp command for cloning the reflog is not empty, as it would have been if you had used the $ git clone command. The command $ git reflog prints the results similar to:

```
0deae94 HEAD@{0}: merge feature: Fast-forward
757d501 HEAD@{1}: checkout: moving from feature to master
0deae94 HEAD@{2}: checkout: moving from feature to feature
0deae94 HEAD@{3}: clone: from c:/git-recipes/06-01
```

You can undo the merge using $ git reset --hard HEAD@{1}.

How It Works

In the case of merges, the reflog entry HEAD@{1} right after the $ git merge command points to your current branch as it was just before the merge. Passing this as a parameter to $ git reset --hard you will undo the merge. Even if your reflog is empty, you can still undo the merge using the SHA-1 name, as in $ git reset --hard 757d501.

6-4. Developing in parallel diverged branches
Problem

You have just created a branch that contains a new feature of your application. The repository looks like the one shown in Figure 6-2. This is a starting point for Recipe 6-4. You are not sure that your work on the feature branch is finished, however. You are not sure that it is ready for a merge. Meanwhile, you want to continue your work in the master branch. You want to switch to the master branch and create some new revisions. The repository after this recipe should look like Figure 6-5.

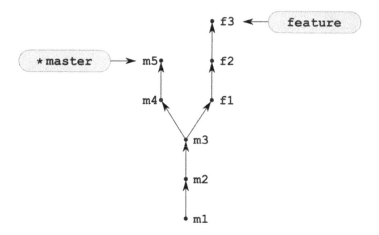

Figure 6-5. *The repository obtained after Recipe 6-4*

Solution

Clone the repository from Recipe 6-1 with branches:

```
$ cd git-recipes
$ git clone-with-branches 06-01 06-04
$ cd 06-04
```

and create two new revisions with:

```
$ git simple-commit m4 m5
```

How It Works

This recipe underlines the fact that the work in different branches can continue **in parallel**. In that case we say that the two branches master and feature **diverge**. The exact moment in time when commits m4 and f1 were created is not important, the illustrations will usually show them at the same level, as in Figure 6-5. In practice, they are always created at different moments. Therefore the commands that visualize a graph of revisions, such as $ git --oneline --graph --decorate --all or $ gitk --all&, always present them at different levels, as in Figure 6-6. The revisions m4 and m5 were created later and therefore they will appear above revisions f1, f2, and f3.

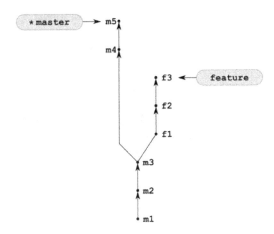

Figure 6-6. *The commits m4 and m5 were created later than the commits f1, f2, f3 and therefore they are drawn above*

The command $ gitk --all & presents the repository from Figure 6-6 in Figure 6-7.

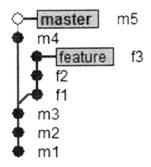

Figure 6-7. *The repository from Recipe 6-4 visualized with the gitk application*

Keep in mind that it is not possible to do a fast-forward merge in the repository shown in Figure 6-5. You can check it using the additional parameter --ff-only of the $ git merge command. This parameter sets an additional condition on git: perform a merge but only if it is a fast-forward case. The command:

```
$ git merge --ff-only feature
```

executed in the master branch can be interpreted as the following conditional statement written in pseudo-code:

```
if (the merge of feature into master is a fast-forward) {
    $ git merge feature
}
```

The command $ git merge --ff-only feature executed in the repository shown in Figure 6-5 will fail producing the output:

```
fatal: Not possible to fast-forward, aborting.
```

Using the `--ff-only` switch you can make sure that your merge operation is always carried out as a fast-forward. If the merging cannot be finished as a fast-forward, it is aborted. To perform a merge of diverged branches as a fast-forward we will use the $ `git rebase` command. This, among others, will be a subject for the next chapter.

6-5. Merging diverged branches

Problem

You want to merge the branches shown in Figure 6-5. The feature branch is to be merged into the master branch. The repository you want to obtain is presented in Figure 6-8. Figure 6-8 underlines the order in which revisions m4, m5 and f1, f2, f3 were created. In this recipe, this order is not important, therefore Figure 6-8 could also be drawn as in Figure 6-9.

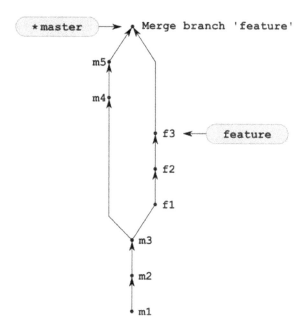

Figure 6-8. *The repository obtained after the diverged branches are merged*

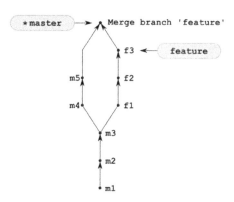

Figure 6-9. *Alternative visual representation of the repository shown in Figure 6-8*

Solution

Clone the repository from Recipe 6-4 with branches:

```
$ cd git-recipes
$ git clone-with-branches 06-04 06-05
$ cd 06-05
```

and merge branches with the $ git merge feature command.

How It Works

In cases where fast-forward is not possible the $ git merge command creates an additional revision, called **merge commit**. This commit differs from the commits you have created so far because it contains more than one parent. It joins two or more different revisions. This gives us the opportunity to classify every commit as either a **non-merge commit** or a **merge commit**. A **merge commit** is a commit that has two or more parents. A **non-merge commit** is a commit with exactly one parent. Obviously, the commit created in this recipe has two parents thus it a merge commit.

When inspecting the history with $ git log or $ gitk, you can filter out both types of commits. The command:

```
$ git log --oneline --merges
```

outputs only merge commits, while

```
$ git log --oneline --no-merges
```

prints only non-merge commits. You also can set the expected minimal and maximal number of parents with:

```
$ git log --oneline --max-parents=X --min-parents=Y
```

where X and Y are arbitrary positive integers.

Git supports references that allow it to pick up any of the parents for a merge commit using the caret (^) sign. The reference [REVISION]^[n] points to the n-th parent of the commit identified with [REVISION]. As for the repository in Figure 6-9, the master^1 points to the revision m5; the master^2 points to the revision f3, as illustrated in Figure 6-10. I will refer to them as **n-th parent references**.

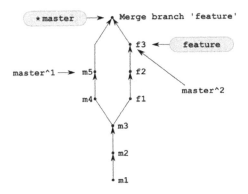

Figure 6-10. *N-th parent references master^1 and master^2*

Remember that the references [REVISION]~, [REVISION]~1, [REVISION]^, and [REVISION]^1 are equivalent. This is because 1 is a default value and ~ always references the first parent in merge commits.

If you want to use the $ git merge command with confidence, you have to remember that **the current branch is the branch you merge into**, and **the branch passed to $ git merge command is the branch to be merged in**. The tip of the branch you merge into (master branch) becomes the first parent of a merge commit and the tip of the branch you merge in (feature branch) becomes the second parent. The branch you merge in doesn't change—it still points to the same revision as before the command. The branch you merge into receives a new commit with comment similar to:

```
Merge branch 'X'
```

where the X is the name of the branch you merged in (feature, in our recipe). You can memorize the above rules, remembering that, when on the master branch, the $ git log --oneline -1 command prints:

```
6fb2 Merge branch 'feature'
```

As you can guess the working directory now contains all the files from both branches. The command $ ls outputs the files: f1.txt, f2.txt, f3.txt, m1.txt, m2.txt, m3.txt, m4.txt, m5.txt.

The merge can be undone exactly as in Recipe 6-3. Only this time you can use not only reflog and SHA-1, but also ancestor and n-th parent references. Assuming that you are in the master branch both the following commands will undo the merge discussed in this recipe:

```
$ git reset --hard master^
$ git reset --hard master~
```

However, if you work in Windows command line, things are complicated. Because the caret is a special character you will have to use it in a special way. The caret is used by Windows shell parser as an escaping character. In Linux shells this role is usually assigned to the backslash (\) character. If you want to use the caret in Windows command line you have to type it twice (^^). Moreover, because on Windows git subcommands are fired through an indirect shell call, the escaping is performed twice. As a result, if you want to use the reference master^2 in Windows command line, you have to type four carets master^^^^2. Of course, this does not apply if you work in bash shell.

The funniest situation like this occurs when you want to use backslash (\) in a regular expression in an SQL statement embedded in a string, such as:

```
$query = "SELECT * FROM paradox WHEARE content REGEXP '\\\\\\\\'";
```

All three languages—RegExp, SQL, and PHP—use the same escaping character, which is a backslash (\). Thus one backslash is encoded as eight backslashes!

6-6. Avoiding a fast-forward merge
Problem

Your repository looks like Figure 6-2. You want to merge the branch feature into the master in such a way that the history looks like Figure 6-11. You want all the revisions from the feature branch to be grouped visually in a bulb.

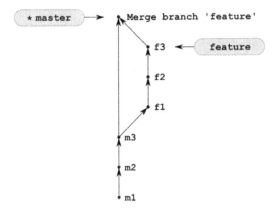

Figure 6-11. *The result of merging the feature branch into the master branch using the --no-ff option*

Solution

Clone the repository from Recipe 6-1 with branches:

```
$ cd git-recipes
$ git clone-with-branches 06-01 06-06
$ cd 06-06
```

and then merge the feature branch with:

```
$ git merge --no-ff feature
```

How It Works

The option `--no-ff` of the `$ git merge` command changes the default behavior forcing the creation of a merge commit even if the merge can be performed as a fast-forward. Working this way you retain the information that the commits f1, f2, and f3 are related with each other. They all deal with the same aspect of development and together constitute a complete piece of work. If, for any reason, you need to revert or copy the whole branch into some other place in history, having commits organized like this will make the operation easier.

6-7. Diverging multiple branches
Problem

You want to create the repository shown in Figure 6-12. It contains five branches that have diverged. Notice that the actual order in which the revisions were created is not important. The figure presents revisions from different branches as created at exactly the same moment, which as we know is not true. You are working alone, and all your revisions are created sequentially, one at the time, not parallel. But the role of the image is to underline, that the procedure described in Recipe 6-7 works well, no matter what the order of your commits.

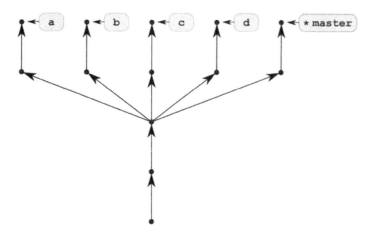

Figure 6-12. *The repository with five divergent branches*

Solution

Clone the repository from Recipe 6-1 with branches:

```
$ cd git-recipes
$ git clone-with-branches 06-01 06-07
$ cd 06-07
```

and create four new branches:

```
$ git branch a
$ git branch b
$ git branch c
$ git branch d
```

Then one by one switch to every branch and create two new commits. The commands are shown in Listing 6-1.

Listing 6-1. The commands to create the diverged branches as shown in Figure 6-9

```
$ git checkout master
$ git simple-commit m4 m5

$ git checkout a
$ git simple-commit a1 a2

$ git checkout b
$ git simple-commit b1 b2

$ git checkout c
$ git simple-commit c1 c2

$ git checkout d
$ git simple-commit d1 d2

$ git checkout master
```

How It Works

The structure of the repository shown in Figure 6-12 can be obtained after the release of a new version for your product, for example. I use the repositories structured like this to add new independent features to frameworks. Once the stable feature of a framework is released, I implement diverse features, such as authorization, database connection, development environment settings, and various extensions in separate branches. Working this way, I can create framework distributions that will be tailored to meet specific requirements. A distribution can contain any of the features implemented in branches. Every feature can be turned on or off, depending on your needs. The distribution is created with merge commands: the branches that you merge will be present in the final distribution.

The repository form Figure 6-12 created with commands from Listing 6-1 would be displayed by the $ git log --oneline --graph --all command as in Figure 6-13.

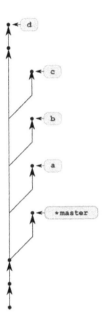

Figure 6-13. *The repository from Figure 6-12 as drawn by the $ git log --oneline --graph --all command*

6-8. Merging multiple branches
Problem

Working in the repository shown in Figure 6-12, you want to merge the four branches a, b, c, and d into the master branch. Your aim is to convert the repository shown in Figure 6-12 into the one presented in Figure 6-14.

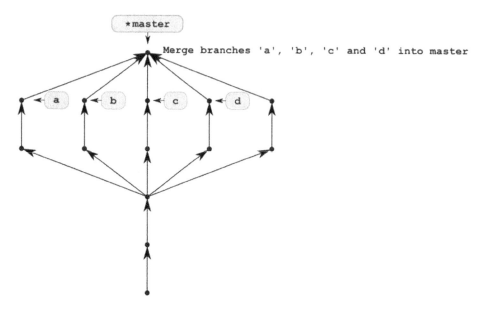

Figure 6-14. *The result of merging branches a, b, c, and d into the master branch*

Solution

Clone the repository from Recipe 6-7 with branches:

```
$ cd git-recipes
$ git clone-with-branches 06-07 06-08
$ cd 06-08
```

and merge four branches into the master branch executing:

```
$ git merge a b c d
```

How It Works

The command `$ git merge a b c d` creates a new commit labeled with `Merge branches 'a', 'b', 'c' and 'd'` into the master. It will be a merge commit created in the current branch. Its five parents will be accessible with the following n-th parent references:

```
master^1
master^2
master^3
master^4
master^5
```

The first parent, `master^1`, points to the same commit as the one pointed to in Figure 6-14 by the `master` branch. The second parent, `master^2`, points to the commit pointed to in Figure 6-14 by a branch. The third parent, `master^3`, points to the commit denoted in Figure 6-14 by b branch. And so on. As you can guess, the order of parents depends on the order of branches passed to by the `$ git merge a b c d` command.

The merging of many branches can be undone in the same way as in Recipe 6-3 or Recipe 6-5. You can use reflog, SHA-1 names, or n-th ancestor reference:

```
$ git reset --hard master^
```

The visual representation of the repository shown in Figure 6-14, as printed by the $ git log command with --graph switch, is presented in Figure 6-15.

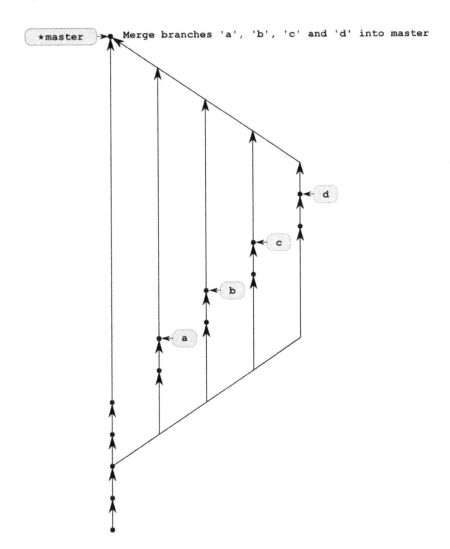

Figure 6-15. *The repository from Recipe 6-8 as drawn by the $ git log with --graph switch command*

There is rarely a need to merge more than two branches. In fact, in many popular projects, such as jQuery, Twitter Bootstrap, Ruby on Rails, Symfony, there are no commits with more than two parents. The only projects that I know of with merges of more than two branches at the same time are git and Linux. Surprisingly, Linux contains commits that have 32 parents! You can verify it using --min-parents=n options of $ git log command, such as:

```
$ git log --oneline --min-parents=32
```

The other complementary parameter, --max-parent=n sets the requirements for the maximal number of parents for commits printed by $ git log.

Of course, the ability to merge numerous branches is not crucial. The operation:

```
$ git merge a b c d
```

can be executed as four different merges each of them concerns only two branches:

```
$ git merge a
$ git merge b
$ git merge c
$ git merge d
```

The only drawback of the above is that the history will contain four merge commits instead of one.

Summary

Now, that you know $ git merge, you can begin to fully appreciate the **git branching model**. Using $ git merge you deal with the **branch you merge into** and the **branch you merge in**. The branch you merge into is your current branch. The branch you merge in is the branch passed to the $ git merge command. If the command $ git branch prints:

```
  bar
* foo
```

then for $ git merge bar we have:

- foo is the branch you merge into

- bar is the branch you merge in

In general, the $ git merge command performs one of two operations: it is either a **fast-forward** or a **merge**.

A **fast-forward**, also denoted by FF, is a process of updating a branch by moving it forward in the graph. It occurs when the branch you merge into is merged in a branch that it is already merged in. In that case no new commits are created. The only result of the command is an updated SHA-1 hash for a branch you merge in (your current branch). Fast-forward is not possible if your branches have diverged.

In the other case, when FF is not possible, the $ git merge command performs a merge by creating a new commit. This new commit is quite special: it has at least two parents. Not surprising, it is called a **merge commit**.

After this chapter you should be able to merge an arbitrary number of branches and, if you are not satisfied with the result, undo the operation. You know how to force a non-fast-forward merge even in cases when the operation would be, by default, carried out as fast-forward. And finally, you know how to use a --ff-only switch to avoid performing non-fast-forward merges.

All of these aspects of merging will be important when we dive into workflows.

CHAPTER 7

Rebasing Branches

You can join two different development histories with the $ git merge and $ git rebase commands. In this chapter we will deal with rebasing. Merging was discussed in the previous chapter.

Generally speaking rebasing is a method for converting divergent branches into linear history. You can think about it as an automatic cherry-picking operation for moving a series of commits from one place on the graph to another. The advantages of using rebasing will become apparent when you start to cooperate with other developers in the same repository. By using the rebasing command you will be able to produce a clean linear history of your project.

We will start with an in-depth explanation of rebasing divergent branches. We will perform this operation using three different approaches:

- With the $ git rebase command

- With the $ git format-patch and $ git am commands

- With the $ git cherry-pick command

This will provide you with a solid background and deep understanding of the way rebasing works.

Then we will proceed with joining disjointed branches using $ git rebase solely (i.e., without the $ git merge command). There you will learn to fast-forward diverged branches with rebasing.

Next we will cover the problem of moving only a part of your new branch. This can be done thanks to the --onto parameter of the $ git rebase command, and it applies to scenarios where your repository contains three or more divergent branches. This setting will also serve as a starting point to the discussion of ranges of commits. Before proceeding with the $ git rebase --onto operation we will cover both the two dots and three dots operators.

The final recipes in this chapter will deal with bulbs. We learned how to create them in Recipe 6-6. Rebasing is much more difficult if you want to preserve the merges.

7-1. Rebasing divergent branches
Problem

You work in a repository with two branches named master and feature. The branches diverged and your repository now looks like Figure 7-1(a). You want to transform the feature branch in such a way that:

- The history is linear (that means that the branches are not divergent anymore).

- The master branch is merged into the feature branch.

- All of the commits that were made in the feature branch are at the very top of the master branch.

The repository you want to achieve is presented in Figure 7-1(b).

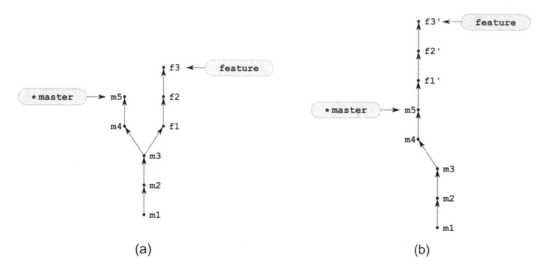

Figure 7-1. *The repository from Recipe 7-1 before rebasing (a) and after rebasing (b)*

Solution

Clone the repository from Recipe 6-4 with branches:

```
$ cd git-recipes
$ git clone-with-branches 06-04 07-01
$ cd 07-01
```

and then follow these steps:

1. Checkout the feature branch with the $ git checkout feature command.

2. Rebase the feature branch onto the master branch with the $ git rebase master command.

3. Checkout the master branch with the $ git checkout master command.

How It Works

The transformation performed by $ git rebase master can be described as applying the changes introduced by the commits from the current branch at the top of another branch. This is depicted in Figure 7-2.

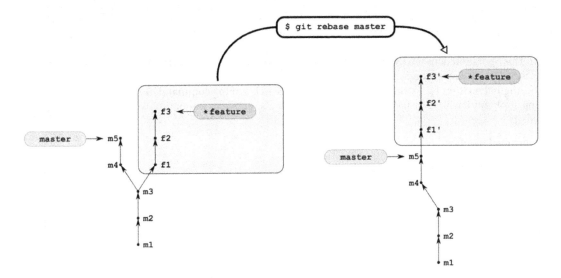

Figure 7-2. *Rebasing "moves" commits from current branch above another branch*

As you already know from Recipe 5-8 there is no way to move revisions from one place to another. All you can do is to create a new revision that will have the same comment and that will introduce the same changes to your files. That's why the revisions in Figures 7-1(b) and 7-2 contain primes. It underlines the fact that these are new revisions with different SHA-1 names.

What happens to the original revisions f1, f2, and f3? Nothing. They are left intact. To be more accurate, rebasing can be depicted as seen in Figure 7-3. The original revisions f1, f2, and f3 are not referred to by any branch anymore—they became dangling revisions. But they remain unchanged in the database. At least as long as you do not expire the reflog and prune the database.

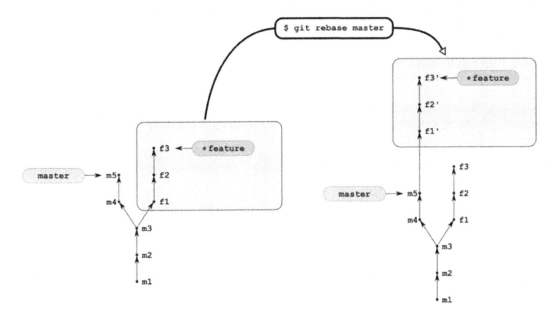

Figure 7-3. *More exact rebasing copies of revisions f1, f2, and f3 into another branch—original revisions are left intact*

The Figure 7-3 contains a hint on how to recover from rebasing. To undo rebasing all you have to do is to change the revision that is pointed to by the `feature` branch. You should remember from the previous chapter that branches are just pointers. You can treat them as stickers: everything can be unstuck from one place and then stuck again in another location. This operation does not modify the database—all revisions remain intact. If you modify the `feature` branch in such a way that it points to the `f3` revision again, the rebasing will be undone.

Let's find the original revision `f3`. As always—you can use the `$ git reflog` command. But this time its output can be misleading. Probably it will be easier to explore reflog with the `$ git log` command. We want to get the list of all the commits that:

- Are included in reflog
- Have comments containing `f3` string

The appropriate command is presented in Listing 7-1. The format defined with the `--pretty` parameter prints shortened hashes (`%h` placeholder), comments (`%s` placeholder), and commit dates (`%cd` placeholder). Every commit can appear in reflog many times. Actually, every checkout will store a new reference to the commit in reflog. Thanks to piped `sort` and `uniq` commands, the output produced by the command from Listing 7-1 will contain every commit exactly once.

Listing 7-1. The command to list all the reflog commits with comments containing f3

```
$ git log --walk-reflogs --grep=f3 --pretty="%h %s %cd" | sort | uniq
```

When you find the correct commit, you can change the `feature` branch using the `$ git reset --hard [SHA-1]` command. If your repository is clean this command can be regarded as a way to move your current branch to arbitrary revision. The same effect can be also accomplished with two separate commands:

```
$ git branch -D feature
$ git checkout -b feature [SHA-1]
```

The first command deletes the `feature` branch; the second creates a new `feature` branch pointing to the desired revision. You can combine both above commands into one:

```
$ git checkout -B feature [SHA-1]
```

The switch `-b` is a safe one: it creates a branch only if the repository doesn't already contain such a branch. If the branch exists, `$ git checkout -b` fails. The switch `-B` forces the `$ git checkout` command to override the existing branch.

Okay, we know how rebasing converts the structure of the graph of revisions. But what happens to the files? In this sense, the result of rebasing produces exactly the same results as merging. Both commands:

```
# current branch is feature
$ git rebase master
$ git merge master
```

result in exactly the same contents of the working directory. The working directory contains files from both branches: `feature` and `master`.

In general, the rebasing depicted in Figures 7-2 and 7-3 operates on two branches; therefore the command expects two parameters:

```
$ git rebase a b
```

If you skip the second parameter, HEAD will be used. Thus the commands:

```
$ git rebase a
$ git rebase a HEAD
```

are equivalent. To rebase the feature branch onto the master branch, as in this recipe, you can:

- Change the current branch to feature and use one parameter for rebase as in:

  ```
  $ git checkout feature
  ```

  ```
  $ git rebase master
  ```

- Use two parameters for rebasing—your current branch is not important then:

  ```
  $ git rebase master feature
  ```

Whichever is the case, feature is the current branch after successful rebasing.

7-2. Manually rebasing divergent branches
Problem

To get a deeper insight into rebasing, you want to perform the same transformation as in Recipe 7-1 without using the $ git rebase command. In this recipe you would like to split rebasing into two operations: creating patches and applying them. Working this way, the patches can be created by one developer, emailed, and then applied by another developer.

Solution

Clone the repository from Recipe 6-4 with branches:

```
$ cd git-recipes
$ git clone-with-branches 06-04 07-02
$ cd 07-02
```

and then follow these steps:

1. Checkout the feature branch with $ git checkout feature

2. Generate patches for revisions f1, f2, and f3 with:

   ```
   $ git format-patch --ignore-if-in-upstream master
   ```

3. Enter the detached HEAD state with HEAD pointing to the same revision as the master branch. You will achieve this executing: $ git checkout `git rev-parse master`

4. Apply patches with $ git am *.patch

5. Move the feature branch to your current revision using $ git checkout -B feature

6. Remove the patches with $ rm *.patch

How It Works

The feature branch contains three commits f1, f2, and f3 that are not included in the master branch. You can check it with:

```
$ git log --oneline master..feature
```

The output will present three commits:

```
0deae94 f3
c1cab03 f2
3df8f34 f1
```

The parameter master..feature specifies a set of commits. You can treat it as a subtraction operator:

```
feature - master
```

or more precisely:

```
revisions included in feature - revisions included in master
```

That's how you can discover which set of commits were or will be moved during rebase to some other location. The command:

```
$ git log --oneline master..feature
```

issued before rebasing will print the commits that will be moved. When issued after rebasing it will print the commits that were moved.

Now we want to produce the patches for these three commits. A patch is a text file that describes precisely the changeset to be introduced in your project files. When issued in the feature branch, the command:

```
$ git format-patch --ignore-if-in-upstream master
```

produces three text files named 0001-f1.patch, 0002-f2.patch, and 0003-f3.patch. The first file is a patch for the revision f1. The second file is a patch for the revision f2. And the third file is a patch for the revision f3. The parameter --ignore-if-in-upstream guarantees that only the patches for commits that were not already merged in the master branch are generated. This option becomes necessary when you want to generate patches numerous times for a lot of branches.

All generated files are new and untracked, as proved by the $ git status -s command:

```
?? 0001-f1.patch
?? 0002-f2.patch
?? 0003-f3.patch
```

In Recipe 5-6 you learned that new untracked files do not influence the checkout command. You know that a current branch can be switched—untracked files will remain unchanged. That's exactly what we want to do because we want to apply the patches to the master branch. However, because the master branch should remain unchanged in the resulting repository, we will use detached HEAD state.

This recipe gives you more detailed, practical knowledge about detached HEAD state. I warned you to avoid it so you may ask why introduce it in git at all. The reason behind a detached HEAD state is that some commands, such as rebase, change the graph of revisions. To preserve the original branches, it is necessary to perform these operations in a detached HEAD state. If something goes wrong, you can easily return to the state before the operation because the original branches are not changed.

Okay, right now we need to enter a detached HEAD state in which HEAD points to the same revision as the master branch. How to produce the SHA-1 name of the revision pointed to by the master branch? You can do this using the $ git rev-parse command:

```
$ git rev-parse master
```

The above command converts a symbolic reference, such as HEAD, HEAD~, feature, info^2, into a SHA-1 name. Using a back-tick operator to pass the result of the $ git rev-parse as a parameter to checkout you will enter the desired detached HEAD state. The complete command is shown in Listing 7-2. Your repository now looks like Figure 7-4.

Listing 7-2. Using rev-parse to enter a detached HEAD state with HEAD pointing to master

```
$ git checkout `git rev-parse master`
```

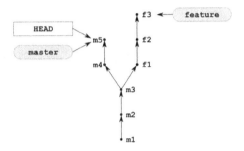

Figure 7-4. *The repository from Figure 7-1(a) after the command from Listing 7-2*

When the repository looks like Figure 7-4, we apply the patches stored in the files with the .patch suffix:

```
$ git am *.patch
```

The above command reproduces the commits f1, f2, and f3 using the HEAD pointer as a parent. The repository now looks like Figure 7-5.

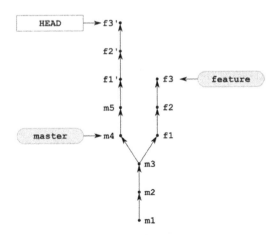

Figure 7-5. *The repository from Figure 7-4 after applying patches with the $ git am *.patch command*

The last step is to now change the `feature` branch. We want it to point to our current revision. We can use `$ git checkout` command for this. However, the command `$ git checkout -b feature` will not work. The reason is quite obvious: `feature` branch already exists. Still, we can force the checkout using the `-B` switch:

```
$ git checkout -B feature
```

The updated repository is shown in Figure 7-6. The commits `f1`, `f2`, and `f3` are still available in the database as dangling revisions, but they are not show in the figure.

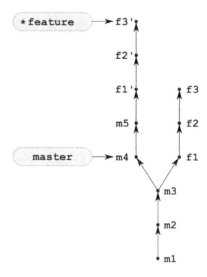

Figure 7-6. *The repository from Figure 7-5 after the $ git checkout -B feature*

We do not need the patches any more. Remove them with the `$ rm *.patch` command.

Using cherry-pick for rebase

You can achieve similar results using the `$ git cherry-pick` command

1. Enter the detached HEAD state: `$ git checkout \`git rev-parse master\``

2. Reapply the revision `f1` in HEAD with the `$ git cherry-pick feature~2`

3. Reapply the revision `f2` in HEAD with the `$ git cherry-pick feature~1`

4. Reapply the revision `f3` in HEAD with the `$ git cherry-pick feature`

5. Move the `feature` branch to your current revision using `$ git checkout -B feature`

The main drawback of the above solution is that here you have to know which revisions you want to reapply. The command `$ git format-patch` takes this burden off of your shoulders! Also `$ git cherry-pick` doesn't create patches. To email patches you will have to generate them with the `$ git format-patch` command.

■ **Hint** The main reason behind Recipe 7-2 is to provide you with deeper understanding how $ git rebase works. Do not rebase your branches using $ git format-patch, $ git am, or $ git cherry-pick unless you want to email patches to someone else. Use the $ git rebase command instead. The analysis included in Recipe 7-2 will help you to understand the internals of rebasing. Depending on your workflow, rebasing may be necessary every time you want to publish your work.

7-3. Joining divergent branches into linear history
Problem

You work in a repository with two divergent branches named master and feature, as shown in Figure 7-7(a). You want to merge the feature branch into the master branch in such a way that the resulting history is linear, that is, it doesn't contain merge commits. The starting point for this recipe is shown in Figure 7-7(a). The repository you want to obtain is presented in Figure 7-7(b).

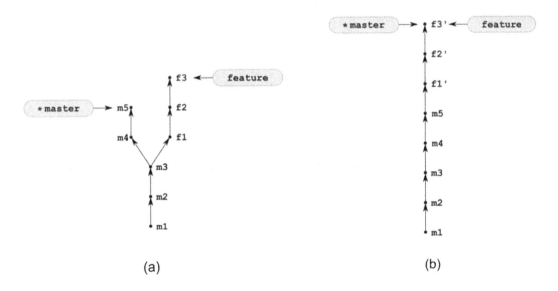

(a)   (b)

Figure 7-7. *The starting point and the result of joining divergent branches into linear history*

Solution

Clone the repository from Recipe 6-4 with branches:

```
$ cd git-recipes
$ git clone-with-branches 06-04 07-03
$ cd 07-03
```

and then follow the steps:

1. Rebase the feature branch onto the master branch with $ git rebase master feature

2. Rebase the master branch onto the feature branch with $ git rebase feature master

How It Works

We start with the repository shown in Figure 7-7(a). The first step in this recipe performs the operation described in Recipe 7-1. After $ git rebase master feature the repository will look like Figure 7-1(b). We need to fast-forward the master branch to the feature branch. This is exactly the purpose of the second command $ git rebase feature master.

Fast-forwarding can be done with either $ git merge or $ git rebase. Here are the commands to fast-forward the master branch with the $ git merge command:

```
$ git checkout master
$ git merge feature
```

and this is the command to do the same with the $ git rebase command:

```
$ git rebase feature master
```

Fast-forwarding with $ git merge was discussed in Recipe 6-2.

7-4. Diverging three branches
Problem

Your repository contains two divergent branches master and feature, as shown in Figure 7-8(a). First you want to work on some new idea, basing your work on the latest revision in your feature branch. You need to create a new branch called brave-idea and to commit your changes as revisions b1 and b2. Next you want to switch to the feature branch and create three new revisions f4, f5, and f6. The repository you want to achieve is shown in Figure 7-8(b).

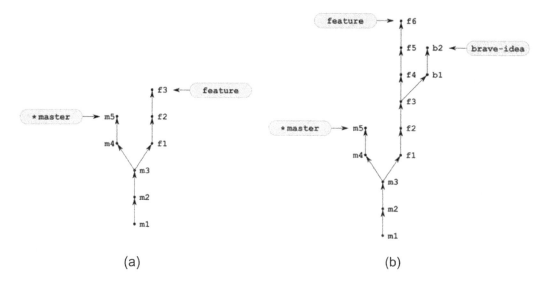

(a)   (b)

Figure 7-8. *By applying Recipe 7-4 for repository (a) you will get repository (b)*

Solution

Clone the repository from Recipe 6-4 with branches:

```
$ cd git-recipes
$ git clone-with-branches 06-04 07-04
$ cd 07-04
```

and then follow the steps:

1. Create and checkout the brave-idea branch with $ git checkout -b brave-idea feature

2. Create two revisions in the brave-idea branch with $ git simple-commit b1 b2

3. Checkout the feature branch with $ git checkout feature

4. Create three revisions in the feature branch with $ git simple-commit f4 f5 f6

5. Change the current branch to master with $ git checkout master

How It Works

This recipe explains how you can create many divergent branches. We only use commands already quite well-known to achieve this: clone, checkout, and simple-commit. That's how you can easily generate a repository with a given structure. This capability is very useful, in case you want to analyze a git command and the impact it has on the graph's structure.

Keep in mind that when you use the $ git log command with --graph option the drawing you get can be a little different. The result of $ git log --oneline --graph --decorate --all for a repository from Figure 7-8(b) is shown in Figure 7-9.

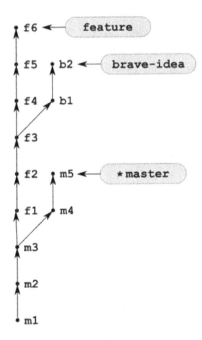

Figure 7-9. *The repository from Figure 7-8(b) as drawn by $ git log --oneline --graph --decorate --all*

Once you create the repository shown in Figure 7-8, many questions regarding the graph of revisions may arise. Such as the following:

- How to find a common ancestor of branches a and b?

- How to find a common ancestor of arbitrary number of branches?

- How to find a difference a - b of two branches, that is, revisions that are included in branch a but excluded from branch b?

- How to find a symmetric difference a Δ b of two branches, that is, revisions that are included in either a or b but not in both?

- How to find revisions included in branches a, b, and c and excluded from d, e, and f?

The common ancestor of two branches is the latest revision included in two branches. For branches feature and brave-idea it is f3. For master and feature it is m3. You can find the common ancestor using:

```
$ git merge-base feature brave-idea
```

If you want to get the common ancestor for more than two branches, use --octopus parameter. The command:

```
$ git merge-base --octopus feature brave-idea master
```

prints the SHA-1 of m3 commit.

The range of commits was already discussed in Recipe 7-2. A special operator .. is interpreted as a difference of branches. The command:

```
$ git log --oneline master..brave-idea
```

prints commits b2, b1, f3, f2, and f1, while:

```
$ git log feature..master
```

outputs revisions m4 and m5.

The set of new commits introduced by two branches is resolved by the ... operator. It is a symmetrical difference of branches. The output of:

```
$ git log feature...brave-idea
```

consists of f6, f5, f4, b2, and b1.

The even more verbose way to specify included and excluded revisions is to use --not operator. The command:

```
$ git log a b c --not d --not e --not f
```

prints the revisions included in a, b, or c and excluded from d, e, and f. This can also be written as:

```
$ git log a b c ^d ^e ^f
```

Using the above syntax you can list new revisions introduced in the `master`, `feature`, and `brave-idea` branches with the command shown in Listing 7-3. This command outputs revisions:

- `f6`, `f5`, `f4`—commits introduced in `feature` branch

- `b2`, `b1`—commits introduced in `brave-idea` branch

- `m5`, `m4`—commits introduced in `master` branch

Listing 7-3. The command to list new commits introduced in the master, feature, and brave-idea branches

```
$ git log --oneline
    master feature brave-idea
    ^`git merge-base master feature`
    ^`git merge-base feature brave-idea`
```

How do we achieve the above result? We include all three branches:

```
master feature brave-idea
```

and then exclude commits available through the common ancestor of the `master` and `feature` branches (it is revision m3):

```
^`git merge-base master feature`
```

And exclude commits available through the common ancestor of the `feature` and `brave-idea` branches (it is revision `f3`):

```
^`git merge-base feature brave-idea`
```

Using shell subcommands defined with back-tick operators, we don't have to copy/paste the SHA-1 names of m3 and f3 as they are embedded.

Exploring the graph of revisions you may also find useful the command that produces the SHA-1 name of a commit with a given comment:

```
$ git log --format="%h" --grep=XXX --all
```

The above command takes into account all branches (`--all` option) and searches for revisions that contain the XXX string. Thanks to the `--format` parameter the output contains only the shortened SHA-1 name.

7-5. Partial rebasing
Problem

You decided that the code introduced in the `brave-idea` branch in the repository shown in Figure 7-10(a) is now ready to be shared with others. Therefore you want to move the revisions b1 and b2 to the `master` branch. The repository you want to achieve is shown in Figure 7-10(b). A situation such as this can happen if during your work on `brave-idea` your original idea evolves and becomes large enough to be treated as independent feature.

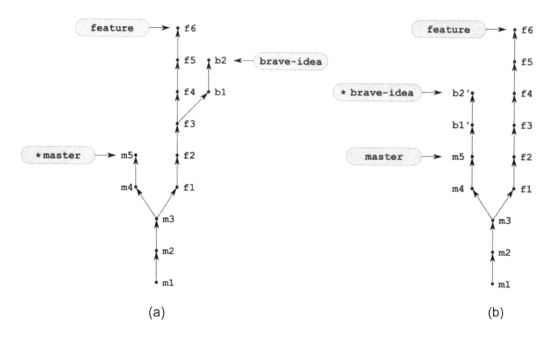

Figure 7-10. *By applying Recipe 7-5 for repository (a) you will get repository (b)*

Solution

Clone the repository from Recipe 7-4 with branches:

```
$ cd git-recipes
$ git clone-with-branches 07-04 07-05
$ cd 07-05
```

and then rebase the brave-idea branch onto the master branch with the command shown in Listing 7-4.

Listing 7-4. The command that transforms the repository shown in Figure 7-10(a) into the state shown in Figure 7-10(b)

```
$ git rebase --onto master feature brave-idea
```

How It Works

The command $ git rebase --onto operates on three branches:

```
$ git rebase --onto a b c
```

The first branch—a—is the branch onto which we will reapply the patches. Two other branches define the set of patches to be reapplied. It will be the set defined by the double dot operator b..c. In other words the command takes the revisions that are included in c but not in b and reapplies them on top of a. If the operation is successful then c is moved and points to the resulting commit.

The command shown in Listing 7-4 can be executed in any branch. The result will always be the same: the commits b1 and b2 will be reapplied as b1' and b2' on top of the master branch. After the operation branch c will be your current branch.

In case you omit the last parameter, your current branch will be rebased. The following commands are equivalent:

```
$ git rebase --onto foo bar
$ git rebase --onto foo bar HEAD
```

We can say that the command from Listing 7-4 is equivalent to two commands:

```
$ git checkout brave-idea
$ git rebase --onto master feature
```

7-6. Creating bulbs for divergent branches

Problem

You repository looks like Figure 7-11(a). You want to merge the changes introduced in the feature branch back into the master branch in such a way that reapplied revisions f1', f2', and f3' form a bulb above the revision from the master branch. The repository you wish to achieve is shown in Figure 7-11(b).

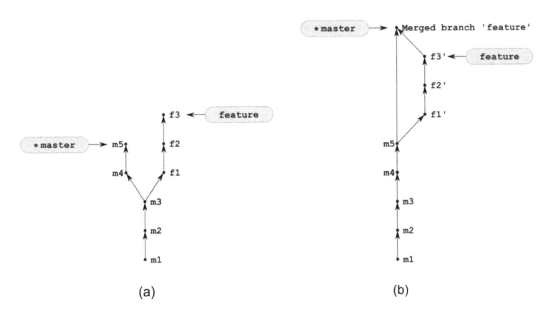

Figure 7-11. *The repository you will obtain after applying Recipe 7-6 to the repository from Figure 6-5*

Solution

Clone the repository from Recipe 6-4 with branches:

```
$ cd git-recipes
$ git clone-with-branches 06-04 07-06
$ cd 07-06
```

and then follow these steps:

1. Rebase the feature branch onto the master branch with $ git rebase master feature

2. Switch to the master branch with $ git checkout master

3. Merge the feature branch into the master branch with $ git merge --no-ff feature

How It Works

Recipe 7-6 consists of two steps:

- First we used Recipe 7-1 to transform the repository shown in Figure 7-1.

- Next we used Recipe 6-6 to perform a merge that forms a bulb.

7-7. Creating bulbs in subbranches
Problem

You repository looks like Figure 7-12(a). You want to merge the brave-idea branch back into the feature branch as a bulb. The repository you wish to achieve is shown in Figure 7-12(b).

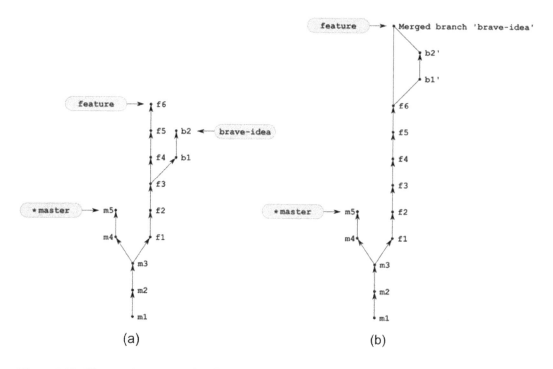

Figure 7-12. *The repositories considered in Recipe 7-7*

Solution

Clone the repository from Recipe 7-4 with branches:

```
$ cd git-recipes
$ git clone-with-branches 07-04 07-07
$ cd 07-07
```

and then follow these steps:

1. Rebase the brave-idea branch onto the feature branch with $ git rebase feature brave-idea

2. Switch to the feature branch with $ git checkout feature

3. Merge the brave-idea branch into the feature branch with $ git merge --no-ff brave-idea

4. Delete the brave-idea branch with $ git branch -d brave-idea

5. Checkout the master branch with $ git checkout master

How It Works

Recipe 7-7 shows how to apply Recipe 7-6 for the feature and brave-idea branches. You may consider it superfluous but the resulting repository is necessary for the next recipes.

7-8. Rebasing branches with bulbs

Problem

Your repository now looks like Figure 7-12(b). You want to rebase the feature branch onto the master branch.

Solution

Clone the repository from Recipe 7-7 with branches:

```
$ cd git-recipes
$ git clone-with-branches 07-07 07-08
$ cd 07-08
```

and then rebase the feature branch onto the master branch with $ git rebase master feature. You will obtain the repository shown in Figure 7-13. Notice that the feature branch doesn't contain the merge branch 'brave-idea' revision any longer.

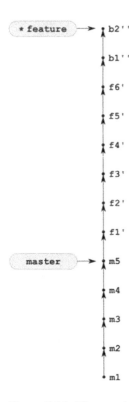

Figure 7-13. *The repository from Figure 7-12 after $ git rebase master feature*

How It Works

As you can see in Figure 7-13, rebasing operates only on non-merge commits. All merge commits are lost. Rebasing always produces a straight line of commits, without bulbs or merges. In the case of branches with bulbs it doesn't necessarily have to be what you expect. If you want to preserve merges and bulbs you cannot use a simple rebase command. You have to move whole branches and then reproduce the merge commits.

Take a good look at Figure 7-13. The commits b1 and b2 are denoted with two primes b1'' and b2''. Double primes underline the fact that these are new commits. They introduce the same changes as b1' and b2' in Figure 7-12 and as b1 and b2 in Figure 7-8 but their SHA-1 names are different.

7-9. Preserving merges during rebase
Problem

Your repository looks like Figure 7-14(a). You want to rebase the feature branch onto the master branch preserving bulbs. The repository you want to achieve is shown in Figure 7-14(b).

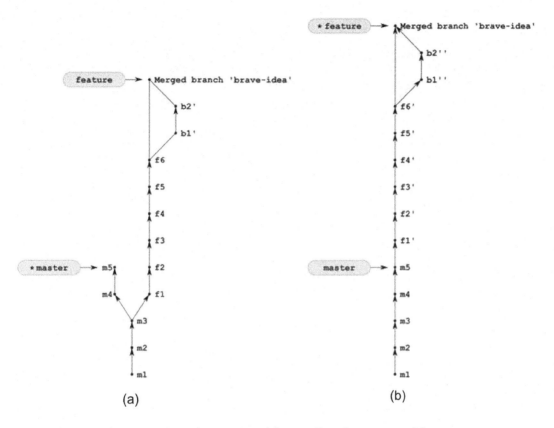

Figure 7-14. *By applying Recipe 7-9 to repository (a) you will get the repository (b)*

Solution

Clone the repository from Recipe 7-7 with branches:

```
$ cd git-recipes
$ git clone-with-branches 07-07 07-09
$ cd 07-09
```

and then perform the rebase with the --preserve-merges parameter:

```
$ git rebase --preserve-merges master feature
```

How It Works

The parameter --preserve-merges forces git to preserve merges during rebasing.

Summary

This chapter introduced the concept of **rebasing**—the operation to reproduce a sequence of commits from one branch at the top of another. You can treat it as a tool to transform divergent branches into linear history. The syntax of rebasing allows you to rebase one complete branch on top of another. You can do this with:

```
$ git rebase dest src
```

where src is the branch you want to take commits from and dest is the branch where the commits will be reapplied. After this operation src will be the current branch.

You can also perform a partial rebase with:

```
$ git rebase --onto dest part src
```

Here again dest is the branch where commits will be reapplied. The set of commits to be moved is defined by part and src branches. The operation moves the commits that are included in src and excluded from the part branch. You can memorize it as the difference (src - part) reapplied at dest.

In both cases final src branch can be omitted. If that is the case then the current branch will be used. The commands:

```
$ git rebase dest
$ git rebase dest HEAD
```

are equivalent exactly as are the following commands:

```
$ git rebase --onto dest part
$ git rebase --onto dest part HEAD
```

In this chapter, for the first time, we intentionally worked in detached HEAD state. The off-branch state can be regarded as the means to perform operations such as rebasing in an atomic way. The operation is performed in a detached HEAD state. When successfully finished we then adjust the branches as needed. Otherwise the branches are not modified and the operation can be cancelled. More on this appears in chapter 9 during the discussion of conflicts.

Remember that by default, rebasing skips merge commits. If you want you can preserve them using the --preserve-merges option.

In this chapter, as an aside you also learned how to find the common ancestor of two branches with the $ git merge-base command, and how to specify ranges commits. Ranges of commits can be defined with two special operators .. and ... or in a more verbose manner.

When you type a..b, it is a set of commits included in b but excluded from a. You can think of it as a difference (b - a).

Three dots c...d specify the **symmetric difference**, that is, the set of two groups of commits:

- Those available in c but not in d

- And those available in d but not in c

This can be regarded as (c - d) + (d - c).

The more verbose syntax uses --not operator, shortened as ^ to exclude a branch. The ranges:

```
a b c ^d ^e ^f
a b c --not d --not e --not f
```

include commits available in a, b, and c and exclude commits available in d, e, and f.

CHAPTER 8

■ ■ ■

Modifying the History

This chapter deals with the diverse commands that modify the structure of the revision graph. Sometimes you will need to merge three different revisions into one revision. At other times you may need the opposite operation: splitting a single commit into many separate commits. Whatever the case may be, keep in mind that git revisions are permanent. They never change. Once you have created a revision, there is no way to modify it. All you can do is to throw it away using the method presented in Recipes 3-12 and 5-4. Therefore, whenever I say something like "let's modify a revision," the operation I have in mind is to create a new revision that will resemble the original one. The original revision remains unchanged in the git database. It can be inaccessible through symbolic references other than reflog, but it is still there. Until the next database purging, that is.

If any of the operations produce results that you find unsatisfactory, you can always return to the previous state. All you need is the name of the revision that contains the correct snapshot. You can use reflog to find this name, but you can also create a temporary branch that will preserve the reference to the desired revisions. Because the revisions do not change, you don't need to worry about the consequences of modifying the revisions. Whatever you do, you will never change the revisions that are already stored in the database. Committing, rebasing, and merging only produce new revisions—these operations do not modify the existing revisions. It's impossible to modify a revision.

This was a real breakthrough for me in my study of git. Once I learned how to restructure the graph of revisions and how to undo various operations, I gained the confidence that allowed me to freely use the tool.

8-1. Amending the most recent revision
Problem

You have just committed a set of changes into the repository and a minute later you realized that there are some additional modifications that should have been incorporated into the previous revision. You do not want to create yet another commit; you would prefer to modify an existing revision by adding some extra changes.

Solution

Create a new repository:

```
$ cd git-recipes
$ git init 08-01
$ cd 08-01
```

and then follow these steps:

1. Create the file lorem.txt with $ echo lorem > lorem.txt

2. Stage the file with $ git add lorem.txt

3. Commit the file with $ git commit -m "lorem"

The repository contains one revision labeled lorem. Listing 8-1 presents the output of the $ git log --pretty=fuller command.

Listing 8-1. The original revision that we wish to modify

```
commit 5a786865f21b5c1725e56c2bf60f6516ce736b9b
Author:     Włodzimierz Gajda <gajdaw@gajdaw.pl>
AuthorDate: Thu Aug 22 07:02:00 2013 +0200
Commit:     Włodzimierz Gajda <gajdaw@gajdaw.pl>
CommitDate: Thu Aug 22 07:02:00 2013 +0200

    Lorem
```

Now you realized that the text stored in a lorem.txt file should be capitalized and extended. To get a deeper insight into git's internals we will amend the revision under different user name.

Modify the user.name and user.email configuration settings stored locally in this particular repository. You can achieve this with:

```
$ git config --local user.name "John Doe"
$ git config --local user.email john@example.net
```

Finally amend the revision following these steps:

1. Modify the contents of lorem.txt with $ echo Lorem Ipsum Dolor > lorem.txt

2. Stage the file with $ git add lorem.txt

3. Commit the file with $ git commit --amend -m "Lorem Ipsum Dolor"

The history still contains only one revision. The command $ git log --pretty=fuller prints the output shown in Listing 8-2.

Listing 8-2. The commit created by $ git commit --amend command

```
commit f63bce5e17a3ba02b0dbee13bb56ceabfd622ce7
Author:     Włodzimierz Gajda <gajdaw@gajdaw.pl>
AuthorDate: Thu Aug 22 07:02:00 2013 +0200
Commit:     John Doe <john@example.net>
CommitDate: Thu Aug 22 07:07:45 2013 +0200

    Lorem Ipsum Dolor
```

Both revisions, the original and amended, are available through reflog. The command $ git reflog outputs:

```
f63bce5 HEAD@{0}: commit (amend): Lorem Ipsum Dolor
5a78686 HEAD@{1}: commit (initial): lorem
```

Therefore, you can always undo what you amended with $ git reset --hard HEAD@{1}.

How It Works

The parameter --amend of the $ git commit command allows you to modify the most recent revision in the history. The command $ git commit --amend:

- Takes the most recent commit from the history (in Recipe 8-1 it is the commit named 5a78; the file lorem.txt contains lorem; the commit is shown in Listing 8-1)

- Takes the current state of the staging area (in Recipe 8-1 it is the staged file lorem.txt with Lorem Ipsum Dolor)

- And combines them into a new revision (in Recipe 8-1 it is the commit named f63b; the commit is shown in Listing 8-2)

This new revision (f63b) replaces the original revision (5a78) in the history.

Technically speaking the command doesn't modify a revision. It creates a new commit. You can find the names of both commits using the $ git reflog command. The original commit remains dangling in the git database until it is finally deleted by a garbage collection operation.

Hint Remember—git revisions are permanent! It is not possible to change any information stored in a commit and preserve the same SHA-1. The $ git commit --amend command creates a brand new revision and then updates the master branch to point to the new revision.

Why did we change the user.name and user.email configuration in this recipe? It will help you to understand the way git handles dates and assigns authorship. Every commit contains four attributes: Author, AuthorDate, Commit, and CommitDate. They store:

- Author—the name of the author

- AuthorDate—the date when the commit originally was made

- Commit—the name of the committer

- CommitDate—the date when the commit was introduced in the history

When you create the commit for the first time both Author and Commit will be set to your name. The dates stored in AuthorDate and CommitDate will be the same. This situation is shown in Listing 8-1.

What happens if you modify the commit with the --amend option? Git preserves the original Author and AuthorDate fields and sets new values for the Commit and CommitDate fields. This is shown in Listing 8-2. The same rules apply when you cherry-pick or rebase your commits.

Hint Git doesn't care about the last modification dates of your files. Git tracks contents—the last modification dates of your files do not influence your revisions in any way. Every commit stored in the database contains AuthorDate and CommitDate. These dates are set when you commit, rebase, or cherrypick. The last modification dates of the files are set when you check out the files. This is done when you switch branches, for example.

A careful reader will notice that the authorship of changes introduced by $ git commit --amend is wrongly attributed to the original author. In Recipe 8-1 two words Ipsum and Dolor were authored by the user John Doe but are attributed to Włodzimierz Gajda. In practice this never happens, however, because you are not allowed to amend commits authored by other developers. You can cherry-pick or rebase them, but then the authorship is attributed correctly.

8-2. Removing *n* most recent revisions

Problem

You want to remove from your current branch the two most recent revisions. The transformation you want to achieve is depicted in the Figure 8-1.

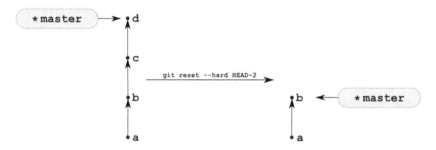

Figure 8-1. *Removing two most recent revisions*

Solution

Create a new repository containing revisions a, b, c, and d:

```
$ cd git-recipes
$ git init 08-02
$ cd 08-02
$ git simple-commit a b c d
```

Your repository now contains four revisions. All of them are included in the master branch. To remove the two most recent revisions use the command $ `git reset --hard HEAD~2`. Now the $ `git log --oneline` command returns only two revisions: a and b. Revisions c and d are removed from the history.

■ **Hint**   You can use this recipe to remove any number of most recent commits. The command $ `git reset --hard` HEAD~13 will remove the last 13 commits.

How It Works

The reference HEAD~2 points to the revision b in Figure 8-1. You can also use the SHA-1 of the revision b to achieve the same result. Assuming that the name of revision b is a1b2c3d4 the following commands are equivalent:

```
$ git reset --hard HEAD~2
$ git reset --hard a1b2c3d4  # SHA-1 of revision b
```

As you already know, git commands usually do not remove objects from the database. Therefore, the operation performed in Recipe 8-2 can be more accurately depicted in Figure 8-2. The revisions c and d remain available in the database until all their symbolic references in reflog have been cleared and database has been pruned. To undo the operation you can always use reflog.

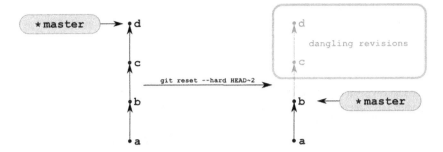

Figure 8-2. *The revisions c and d remain dangling until they are purged with git gc*

■ **Hint**   The commands discussed in Recipe 8-2 were used in Recipe 3-5 to check out the desired revision.

8-3. Squashing many revisions into one revision
Problem

Your repository contains quite a few revisions. You want to squash the last three revisions into one revision. The operation you want to perform is depicted in Figure 8-3.

Figure 8-3. *Squashing the last three revisions*

Solution

Create a new repository containing revisions a, b, c, and d:

```
$ cd git-recipes
$ git init 08-03
$ cd 08-03
$ git simple-commit a b c d
```

Your repository now contains four revisions and the working directory contains four files. You can check it with the $ git log and $ ls command, of course. If you want to verify which files are included in last revision use the following command:

```
$ git show --name-only HEAD
```

It will print the information that the last revision has the comment d, which includes one file named d.txt. In similar way you can list the files included in any previous revisions:

```
$ git show --name-only HEAD~
$ git show --name-only HEAD~2
```

Let's squash the last three commits into a single revision. To do this run the following command:

```
$ git rebase -i HEAD~3
```

The switch -i of the rebase command turns on the interactive mode. The command will start the vim editor with the contents shown in Listing 8-3. Change the contents of the editor—type the commands shown in Listing 8-4. You should change the words *pick* that appear before second and third commit into *fixup*.

Listing 8-3. The contents of vim right after $ git rebase -i HEAD~3

```
pick f2136a0 b
pick a36ee90 c
pick 46c002f d

# Rebase d344a8a..46c002f onto d344a8a
#
# Commands:
#  p, pick = use commit
#  r, reword = use commit, but edit the commit message
#  e, edit = use commit, but stop for amending
#  s, squash = use commit, but meld into previous commit
#  f, fixup = like "squash", but discard this commit's log message
#  x, exec = run command (the rest of the line) using shell
```

Listing 8-4. The contents of vim that you have to type right after $ git rebase -i HEAD~3

```
pick f2136a0 b
fixup a36ee90 c
fixup 46c002f d
```

After you have typed the contents of the Listing 8-4, close the editor. Then git will perform the operation. After this check the history of the repository with:

```
$ git log --oneline
```

This command will print only two commits a and b. According to the $ ls command the working directory still contains four files. The command:

```
$ git show --name-only HEAD
```

proves that the last commit now contains three files b.txt, c.txt, and d.txt.

How It Works

During interactive rebasing git treats the contents you type in the editor as a list of subcommands. The Listing 8-4, for example, contains three subcommands. One of them is:

```
fixup a36ee90 c
```

It has the meaning: "perform fixup operation on revision a36ee90c." Here is the complete list of available subcommands for interactive rebasing:

- pick—the commit will appear in the resulting history
- reword—the commit will be used, but git will allow modification of its comment
- edit—the commit will be used, but git will allow modification (add and remove files)
- squash—the commit will be squashed into the previous one and git will allow modification of the comment of the resulting commit
- fixup—the same as squash, but this time git will not allow modification of the comment of the resulting revision (the comment of the first revision will be used)
- exec—this command allows you to perform arbitrary shell command

Every subcommand can be abbreviated with its first letter. The commands you type are executed by git one by one in the order they appear in the editor.

So what are the meanings of the commands shown in Listing 8-4? There are three of them: the first is a pick command, the second is a fixup command, and the third is another fixup command. The first command

```
pick f2136a0 b
```

picks the commit b. Thus it will appear in the resulting history. You can think of a pick command as a cherry-pick. The patch defined by the revision f2136a0 is applied. The next command:

```
fixup a36ee90 c
```

squashes the commit c into the previous commit b. The fixup command doesn't allow you to modify the comment for the resulting commit. You will get the commit that incorporates the change sets from commits b and c and is denoted with the original comment of commit b.

The last command:

```
fixup 46c002f d
```

performs one more squashing. This time git squashes commit d into the result of the squashing of c into b. Thus you will end up with a single commit denoted with comment b and incorporating the change sets from commits b, c, and d.

All the operations performed by t he interactive rebasing are stored in the reflog. Now, the command $ git reflog prints the following results:

```
e3fc0e0 HEAD@{0}: rebase -i (finish): returning to refs/heads/master
e3fc0e0 HEAD@{1}: rebase -i (squash): b
5eb1d5a HEAD@{2}: rebase -i (squash): # This is a combination of 2 commits.
f2136a0 HEAD@{3}: checkout: moving from master to f2136a0
46c002f HEAD@{4}: commit: d
a36ee90 HEAD@{5}: commit: c
```

```
f2136a0 HEAD@{6}: commit: b
d344a8a HEAD@{7}: commit (initial): a
```

As you may guess the original revisions remain in the database until they are purged. In case you wanted to undo the rebasing here is the command you would need: $ git reset --hard HEAD@{4}.

The list of files modified in a given revision is printed by the $ git show --name-only [REVISION] command. You can also use $ git log --name-only REVISION~..REVISION or $ git diff --name-only REVISION~..REVISION to achieve similar results. The range REVISION~..REVISION restricts the output of the $ git log and $ git diff commands to only one revision.

8-4. Splitting one revision into many revisions
Problem

The most recent revision in your repository introduced three new files into your working directory. You inadvertently committed all three files only to realize a minute later that every file should be stored in a separate revision. You want to split the most recent revision into three different revisions, each of them pertaining to a single file. Recipe 8-4 performs a reversal of Recipe 8-3.

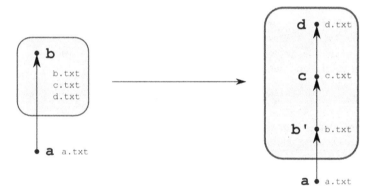

Figure 8-4. *Splitting the most recent revision into many different revisions*

Solution

Create a new repository that will contain two revisions: a and b. The first revision should include one file a.txt and the second revision should include three files: b.txt, c.txt, and d.txt:

```
$ cd git-recipes
$ git init 08-04
$ cd 08-04
$ echo a > a.txt
$ git add -A
$ git commit -m a
$ echo b > b.txt
$ echo c > c.txt
$ echo d > d.txt
$ git add -A
$ git commit -m b
```

Verify that the repository contains two revisions with the $ git log --oneline command and that the last revision really contains three files. The output of the $ git show --name-only command will print three filenames: b.txt, c.txt, and d.txt.

Now, reset your history to revision a, preserving the modifications introduced by revision b in the working directory as the new uncommitted change. You can do this with the $ git reset HEAD~ command. After this command the state of your repository returned by $ git status -sb will be the following:

```
?? b.txt
?? c.txt
?? d.txt
```

As you can see the files are now untracked. You can create three different revisions with:

```
$ git add b.txt
$ git commit -m b

$ git add c.txt
$ git commit -m c

$ git add d.txt
$ git commit -m d
```

The recipe is finished. You can check that the history contains four revisions a, b, c, and d with the $ git log command. Every revision contains a single file. To verify it use the following commands:

```
$ git show --name-only HEAD
$ git show --name-only HEAD~
$ git show --name-only HEAD~2
```

How It Works

To get a deeper insight into the way the $ git reset command transforms your repository you need a thorough understanding of the structure of the repo. The repository consists of:

- The working directory
- The staging area
- The database

The HEAD stored in .git/HEAD points to one of the commits stored in the database.

The working directory can be interpreted as a single snapshot of your project. That's clear. But in the same way you can also treat the staging area and your HEAD pointer as two different snapshots. Thus we can say that in any given point of time your repository operates on three different snapshots:

- The first snapshot—the working directory
- The second snapshot—the staging area
- The third snapshot—the snapshot stored in the revision pointed by HEAD

Let's suppose that you have just created a revision with $ git simple-commit lorem. The repository is clean and the working directory contains a file named lorem.txt storing a string lorem.

When the repository is clean all three snapshots—the working directory, the staging area, and HEAD—are identical. Let's modify the lorem.txt file with $ echo foo > lorem.txt. After this operation the command $ git status -sb prints:

_M lorem.txt

The lorem.txt file stored in the three snapshots contains:

- The first snapshot (the working directory): the file contains foo

- The second snapshot (the staging area): the file contains lorem

- The third snapshot (HEAD): the file contains lorem

Thus _M means that the file in the working directory differs from the file stored in the staging area while at the same time the file stored in the staging area is identical to the file in the revision pointed by HEAD.

The two lettered codes printed by $ git status -sb, such as _M, lets you know the differences between the three snapshots. If the two lettered code is XY then:

- X lets you know the differences between the third snapshot (HEAD) and the second snapshot (the staging area)

- Y lets you know the differences between the second snapshot (the staging area) and the first snapshot (the working directory)

Let's stage the lorem.txt file with $ git add lorem.txt. The output of $ git status -s is following:

M_ lorem.txt

The code is M_ and this time the lorem.txt file stored in the three snapshots contains:

- The first snapshot (the working directory): the file contains foo

- The second snapshot (the staging area): the file contains foo

- The third snapshot (HEAD): the file contains lorem

Thus M_ means that the file in the working directory is identical as the file in the staging area; the file stored in the staging area differs from the file stored in HEAD.

If you commit this modification with $ git commit then all three snapshots become synchronized again. All of them would contain the file lorem.txt with the foo string.

Once you grasp the idea behind the three snapshots it is easy to understand the way the $ git reset command works. This command changes the three snapshots: HEAD, the staging area, and the working directory. It has three important options --soft, --mixed, --hard that influence its behavior. Their meaning is summarized in Table 8-1.

Table 8-1. *The options --soft, --mixed, --hard of the $ git reset command*

	HEAD	The staging area	The working directory
--soft	Yes	No	No
--mixed (default value)	Yes	Yes	No
--hard	Yes	Yes	Yes

Table 8-1 informs us that --soft option influences only HEAD, --mixed option influences HEAD and the staging area. The third option (--hard) influences all three snapshots: HEAD, the staging area, and the working directory.

The operation we already know quite well is:

```
$ git reset --hard [REVISION]
```

The internals of this operation can be described as:

- Modification of HEAD: update the HEAD so that it points to the [REVISION]

- Modification of the staging area: take the snapshot so that it is now pointed by the HEAD and store it in the staging area

- Modification of the working directory: take the snapshot now pointed by the HEAD and check it out into the working directory

After the command all three snapshots are exactly the same. Your current revision is [REVISION]. Be careful: this command modifies the working directory. As you already know you will lose uncommitted changes!

The second option, --mixed is default. Thus both the following commands are identical:

```
$ git reset --mixed [REVISION]
$ git reset [REVISION]
```

You can treat the $ git reset --mixed operation as the reverse of staging and committing. Here are the internals described in terms of three snapshots:

- Modification of HEAD: update the HEAD so that it points to [REVISION]

- Modification of the staging area: take the snapshot that is now pointed by the HEAD and store it in the staging area

- Do not touch the working area

Right now it is easy to analyze the command presented in this recipe: $ git reset HEAD~. The command is equivalent to $ git reset --mixed HEAD~. It performs two operations:

- Sets the HEAD so that it points to the parent revision

- It takes the snapshot so that it is now pointed by HEAD and stores it in the staging area.

Notice that the working directory is not changed. All your modifications (they were already committed) remain there. The result is exactly as it was before you staged and committed changes. The three files b.txt, c.txt, and d.txt are now displayed as unstaged.

The third option, --soft, only moves the pointer stored in HEAD. It does not modify the staging area or the working directory. If you try to use $ git reset --soft HEAD~ in this recipe, then the state returned by $ git status -sb would be:

```
A_ b.txt
A_ c.txt
A_ d.txt
```

The files are staged. If you want to create a revision that stores only one file you have to unstage some files. To change the c.txt file from A_ into _A you can use the $ git rm --cached c.txt command. The alternative way to perform the $ git reset HEAD~ is to use two commands:

```
$ git reset --soft HEAD~
$ git rm --cached [b-d].txt
```

Even though this solution is worse, I encourage you to try it. Using $ git add and $ git commit you can stage and commit files in two different steps. The commands $ git reset --soft and $ git rm --cached perform the reversed operations: uncommit and unstage.

In this recipe we performed an undo operation on a single commit. Remember that in the same way you can undo arbitrary number of commits with $ git reset HEAD~5.

8-5. Reordering revisions

Problem

Your repository contains a number of revisions. The last three revisions are labeled b, c, and d. They appear in the history in this order: d is the most recent revision, c was created right before d, and b precedes c. You want to reorder the revisions b, c, and d to correspond with Figure 8-5.

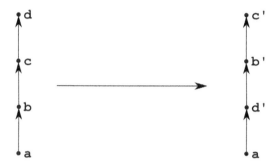

Figure 8-5. *Reordering revisions*

Solution

Create a new repository containing revisions a, b, c, and d:

```
$ cd git-recipes
$ git init 08-05
$ cd 08-05
$ git simple-commit a b c d
```

The command $ git log --oneline now returns the following output:

```
cc595c7    d
7bb0fe3    c
b040c68    b
9dfe77d    a
```

The revisions are ordered a, b, c, d. The oldest is a, and d is the newest.

Now perform interactive rebasing with $ git rebase -i HEAD~3. After this command git will start vim with the contents shown in Listing 8-5. Replace the contents shown in Listing 8-5 with the code presented in Listing 8-6. The change is very slight: the commits are reordered. Then save the file and close the editor.

Listing 8-5. The original contents of vim after $ git rebase -i HEAD~3 (the commits are ordered b, c, d)

```
pick b040c68    b
pick 7bb0fe3    c
pick cc595c7    d
```

Listing 8-6. The contents you should type in the editor during interactive rebasing (the commits are ordered d, b, c)

```
p    cc595c7    d
p    b040c68    b
p    7bb0fe3    c
```

When you save and close the editor git will perform rebasing. After this operation is finished check the order of your revisions with the $ git log command. The output of $ git log -oneline should be the following:

```
7bb0fe3    c
b040c68    b
cc595c7    d
9dfe77d    a
```

The commits are now ordered (from the newest to the oldest)as c, b, d, a.

How It Works

The subcommand pick of interactive rebasing can be abbreviated as p. By changing the order of subcommands in the editor you modify the order in which patches are applied. The rebasing applies the patches according to their order in the editor window. The first subcommand in Listing 8-6, which is p-cc595c7-d, defines the first patch to be applied. Therefore in the resulting history the revision d' will appear right after a.

The original revisions remain in the database and can be accessed through reflog references.

8-6. Removing several revisions
Problem

Your repository contains several revisions. The last five revisions are labeled b through f. You want to remove revisions b, d, and f. The transformation you want to achieve is depicted in Figure 8-6.

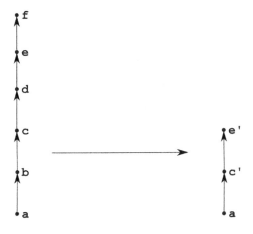

Figure 8-6. *Removing revisions*

Solution

Create a new repository containing revisions a through f:

```
$ cd git-recipes
$ git init 08-06
$ cd 08-06
$ git simple-commit a b c d e f
```

The `$ git log --oneline` command now prints the revisions in the following order:

```
35cba5a     f
4932572     e
bb7f037     d
93b7397     c
9219566     b
17e5231     a
```

You want to remove some commits from the history. The oldest commit you want to remove is b. It is fifth commit in the history (f is the first, e is the second, d is the third, c is the fourth, and b is the fifth). The command you need is `$ git rebase -i HEAD~5`. It is interactive rebasing so git will start the editor. The original subcommands of interactive rebasing are shown in in Listing 8-7. Replace them with the subcommands shown in Listing 8-8. Finally save the file and close the editor.

Listing 8-7. The original subcommands of interactive rebasing in Recipe 8-6

```
pick 9219566 b
pick 93b7397 c
pick bb7f037 d
pick 4932572 e
pick 35cba5a f
```

Listing 8-8. The commands that perform the transformation shown in Figure 8-6

```
pick 93b7397 c
pick 4932572 e
```

When you finish rebasing `$ git log --oneline` should print:

```
4932572     e
93b7397     c
17e5231     a
```

How It Works

If you remove a subcommand pick from the editor, then the corresponding revision will not appear in the history.

8-7. Editing an old revision

Problem

Your repository contains a number of revisions. The third revision in the history is labeled x, and it introduced a single new file x.txt. Now you want to re-edit this revision: it should introduce two new files x.txt and y.txt. You also want to introduce a new revision z right after commit x'. The other revisions should remain unchanged. The transformation you want to achieve is presented in Figure 8-7.

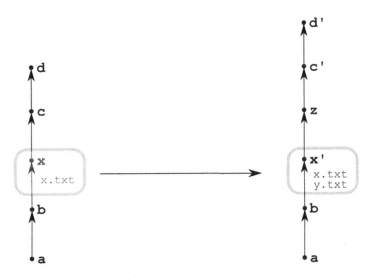

Figure 8-7. *Editing older revisions*

Solution

Create a new repository containing revisions a, b, x, c, d:

```
$ cd git-recipes
$ git init 08-07
$ cd 08-07
$ git simple-commit a b x c d
```

and perform interactive rebasing with $ git rebase -i HEAD~3. The original subcommands of interactive rebasing are shown in Listing 8-9. Replace them with the subcommands shown in Listing 8-10. You are to change the command concerning the revision x from pick into edit. Then save the file and close the editor.

Listing 8-9. The original subcommands of interactive rebasing in Recipe 8-7

```
pick 9aa7b18 x
pick 2455e82 c
pick f8bf7b5 d
```

Listing 8-10. The commands that perform the transformation shown in Figure 8-7

```
edit 9aa7b18 x
pick 2455e82 c
pick f8bf7b5 d
```

The rebasing process stops at the commit x. You can now adjust the x commit with following commands:

```
$ echo y > y.txt
$ git add y.txt
$ git commit --amend --no-edit
```

When the x commit is adjusted, create a new revision z with `$ git simple-commit z`. Finally, finish the rebasing with `$ git rebase --continue`.

How It Works

The interactive rebasing is implemented as an iteration that loops through the commands shown in Listing 8-10. This iteration is performed in a detached HEAD state. When you close the editor containing the subcommands shown in Listing 8-10 git enters detached a HEAD state and performs the iteration.

The first subcommand in Listing 8-10 is `edit 9aa7b18 x`. This command first applies the patch defined by the revision x identified with `9aa7b18` and then the rebasing is paused. You are left in a detached HEAD state right after the patch x. If you want to verify, this run the command `$ git status -sb`. You will see the following output:

```
## HEAD (no branch)
```

It proves that you are now working in a detached HEAD state. The bash command prompt:

```
gajdaw@GAJDAW /c/git-recipes/08-07 (master|REBASE-i 1/3)
```

prints the information that you are performing a rebase operation with three patches and that the first patch was applied.

As you know, git allows you to work in a detached HEAD state with commands such as `$ git add` and `$ git commit`. Thus you can create a new file with `$ echo y > y.txt`, stage it with `$ git add y.txt`, and finally amend the current commit with `$ git commit --amend --no-edit`. That's how the x commit gets modified. If you skip the `--no-edit` option, then git will fire the editor and you will get the chance to modify the comment for revision x'.

Once you finish with the x commit you can proceed with creating revision z. When this is finished you finalize the recipe with the `$ git rebase --continue` command.

It's worth noting that when interactive rebasing is paused you may modify the history with other methods. You can insert additional commits with `$ git commit` or you can remove some commits with `$ git reset`. However, you cannot perform another interactive rebasing until you finish the first one.

You can abort paused rebasing with `$ git rebase --abort`. To undo the operation use reflog.

8-8. Reverting revisions
Problem

Your repository contains any number of revisions. One of the commits introduced a bug in your project. You want to undo the changes introduced by this commit in such a way that the history of the project up to the current HEAD remains unchanged.

The transformation you want to achieve is presented in Figure 8-8. The revision labeled with b should be reverted. The history up to the revision c has to remain unchanged. The operation will be realized by the creation of an additional revision labeled Revert "b". This new commit reverts the changes introduced by b.

Figure 8-8. *Reverting revisions*

Solution

Create a new repository containing revisions a, b, c:

```
$ cd git-recipes
$ git init 08-08
$ cd 08-08
$ git simple-commit a b c
```

and then execute the $ git revert --no-edit HEAD~ command.

How It Works

The command $ git revert [REVISION] creates a new revision that reverts the changes introduced by [REVISION]. The additional parameter --no-edit sets the comment of a new revision to Revert "...". This is the only way to undo the revision that was already included in the public history of your project.

8-9. Reverting merge commit revisions
Problem

You work in your project using two branches: master and feature. The branches diverged and you decided to merge feature branch into the master branch. When you completed merging the feature branch was deleted.

After some time you realized that feature branch introduced a number of bugs and serious problems. Therefore you want to revert the merge of branch feature into the master branch.

The transformation you want to achieve is shown in Figure 8-9.

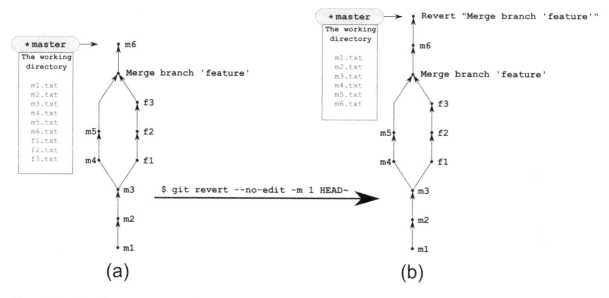

Figure 8-9. *Reverting a merge commit*

Solution

Create the repository shown in Figure 8-9(a) with the following commands:

```
$ cd git-recipes
$ git init 08-09
$ cd 08-09
$ git simple-commit m1 m2 m3
$ git checkout -b feature
$ git simple-commit f1 f2 f3
$ git checkout master
$ git simple-commit m4 m5
$ git merge feature
$ git branch -d feature
$ git simple-commit m6
```

Verify that the history of your repository looks like Figure 8-9(a) with the $ git log --oneline --graph command. You also can list the contents of the working directory with $ ls. The working directory now contains nine files: f1.txt through f3.txt and m1.txt through m6.txt.

When the repository is ready you can revert the merge commit with:

```
$ git revert --no-edit -m 1 HEAD~
```

The command moves the history forward. The repository will now contain a new revision with the comment Revert "Merge branch 'feature'". This revision removes all the changes introduced in commits that you created in feature branch. The working directory now contains only six files m1.txt through m6.txt. The files f1.txt, f2.txt, and f3.txt are gone. You can verify it with the $ ls command.

How It Works

Merge commits have two or more parents. If you revert a merge commit you have to indicate which part of the history should be reverted. The commit labeled as Merge branch 'feature' in Figure 8-9 has two parents:

- The first is the commit m5

- The second parent is the commit f3

Reverting the Merge branch 'feature' commit can lead to a snapshot that is composed of revisions:

m1, m2, m3, m4, m5, m6

or to the snapshot composed of revisions:

m1, m2, m3, f1, f2, f3, m6

The decision is up to you. You make your decision with additional parameter -m passed to the $ git revert command. If you want to keep the history stored under the first parent of the merge commit then use -m 1 parameter, such as:

```
$ git revert --no-edit -m 1 HEAD~
```

The above command will produce the snapshot composed of revisions m1, m2, m3, m4, m5, m6. This case is illustrated in Figure 8-10.

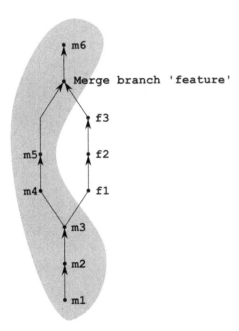

Figure 8-10. *The snapshot obtained with $ git revert --no-edit -m 1 HEAD~*

If you want to keep the history stored under the second parent of the merge commit then use -m 2 parameter, such as:

```
$ git revert --no-edit -m 2 HEAD~
```

This command produces the snapshot consisting of revisions m1, m2, m3, f1, f2, f3, m6. This case is illustrated in Figure 8-11.

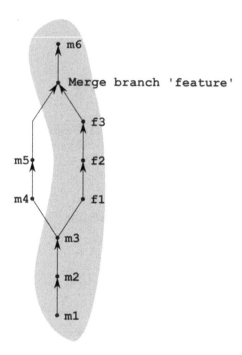

Figure 8-11. *The snapshot obtained with $ git revert --no-edit -m 2 HEAD~*

If you forget to indicate the branch you want to keep, git will refuse to revert the merge commit. The command will fail producing following message:

```
error: Commit XXXXXX is a merge but no -m option was given.
fatal: revert failed
```

8-10. Cherry-picking revisions
Problem

You want to copy a revision from one branch to another. The transformation you have in mind is presented in Figure 8-12. Your master branch contains a revision labeled as m4. You want to copy it to the feature branch.

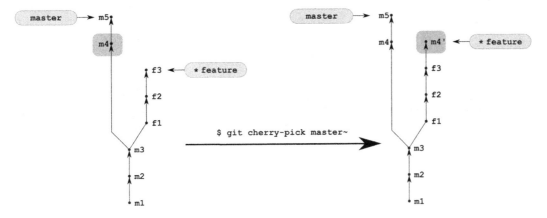

Figure 8-12. *Cherry-picking revisions*

Solution

Clone the repository from Recipe 6-4:

```
$ cd git-recipes
$ git clone-with-branches 06-04 08-10
$ cd 08-10
```

and then go to the feature branch with `$ git checkout feature` and copy revision m4 with `$ git cherry-pick master~`.

How It Works

The `$ git cherry-pick` command applies the patch defined by a revision given as a parameter into your current branch.

8-11. Squashing a branch
Problem

You have just finished the work on a new feature. Your work consists of three commits stored in a dedicated branch. You want to squash these commits and add them as a one new commit on top of your master branch.

This task is presented in Figure 8-13. The feature branch contains the three revisions f1, f2, and f3. You want to squash them into a single revision that will appear in master branch.

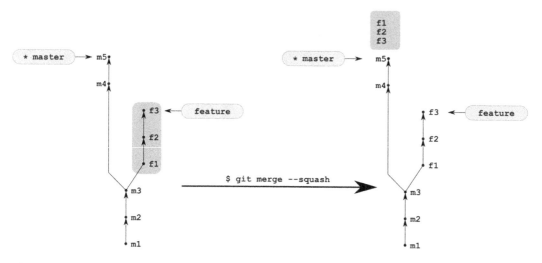

Figure 8-13. *Squashing a branch*

Solution

Clone the repository from Recipe 6-4:

```
$ cd git-recipes
$ git clone-with-branches 06-04 08-11
$ cd 08-11
```

Next squash the feature branch with: $ git merge --squash feature. Finally, commit the change with $ git commit -m "The feature branch was squashed".

How It Works

The operation $ git merge --squash feature modifies the working directory and the staging area of the repository reproducing the changes introduced in the feature branch. Right after this command $ git status -sb prints:

```
A  f1.txt
A  f2.txt
A  f3.txt
```

It means that:

- The working directory contains all the changes from the feature branch
- All the changes are already staged

If you are really satisfied with this modification you can commit them with the $ git commit command.

8-12. Re-using a reverted branch

Problem

Working on your project you create a branch named feature that contains a number of revisions. All the code in the feature branch looks correct and you merge it into the master branch forming a bulb. As it happens the branch has caused a lot of problems. Therefore, you decide to revert a merge commit using the procedure explained in Recipe 8-9.

The work on your project goes on and the master branch moves forward. After some time you want to merge your reverted feature branch again. The operation you want to achieve is shown in Figure 8-14.

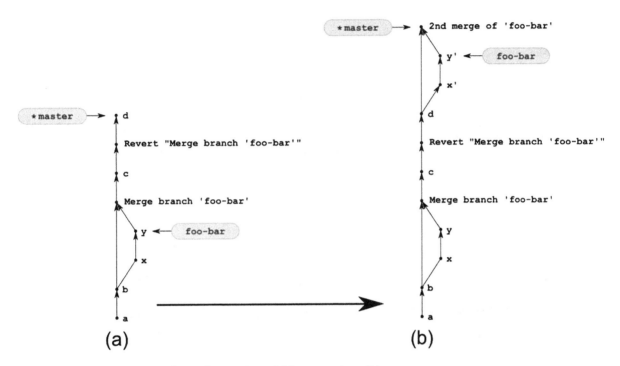

Figure 8-14. *Recipe 8-12 transforms the repository (a) into repository (b)*

Solution

Create a new repository:

```
$ cd git-recipes
$ git init 08-12
$ cd 08-12
```

and create the repository shown in Figure 8-14(a). Use the following commands:

```
$ git simple-commit a b
$ git checkout -b foo-bar
$ git simple-commit x y
$ git checkout master
$ git merge --no-ff foo-bar
```

```
$ git simple-commit c
$ git revert -m 1 --no-edit HEAD~
$ git simple-commit d
```

Using the $ ls command you can verify that the working directory doesn't contain the files x.txt and y.txt. Thus the foo-bar branch was successfully reverted.

The history of your project moved forward. Revision d was created after the revert command. Now you want to remerge foo-bar branch into the master branch again. To do this, run the following commands:

```
$ git format-patch foo-bar~2..foo-bar
$ git checkout -b foo-bar-tmp
$ git am *.patch
$ rm *.patch
$ git branch -M foo-bar-tmp foo-bar
$ git checkout master
$ git merge --no-ff -m "2nd merge of 'foo-bar'" foo-bar
```

The repository should look like Figure 8-14(b). You can verify this with the $ git log --graph --oneline --all --decorate command. The working directory contains the files x.txt and y.txt.

How It Works

When your repository looks like the one in Figure 8-14(a) then the command:

```
$ git rebase master foo-bar
```

will not perform a rebase operation. It will just fast-forward a foo-bar branch to the revision pointed by master branch. If you want to force rebasing you will have to do it manually with the $ git format-patch and $ git am commands.

The revisions in the foo-bar branch are available with a range specifier foo-bar~2..foo-bar. The command:

```
$ git log --oneline foo-bar~2..foo-bar
```

lists two revisions x and y. To create the patches for these revisions we use:

```
$ git format-patch foo-bar~2..foo-bar
```

Next we create a new temporary branch named foo-bar-tmp:

```
$ git checkout -b foo-bar-tmp
```

and apply the patches in it:

```
$ git am *.patch
```

The patches are not needed anymore, thus you can remove them with:

```
$ rm *.patch
```

Then you rename temporary branch foo-bar-tmp the original name foo-bar with:

```
$ git branch -M foo-bar-tmp foo-bar
```

When the branch foo-bar is ready you go to the master branch:

```
$ git checkout master
```

And merge the foo-bar branch again:

```
$ git merge --no-ff -m "2nd merge of 'foo-bar'" foo-bar
```

Summary

Two previous chapters presented merging and rebasing—two operations that complicate the structure of the graph of revisions. Here in chapter 8 we focused on the revision graph even more, considering diverse methods to transform its structure. I'm quite sure that you will find many of the recipes discussed here useful in your daily work.

All recipes presented here underline the nature of revisions. Let me remind you once again: revisions do not change. Once created, they cannot be modified. All you can do is to create new revisions that will—in some respects— resemble originals. This rule forms the basis for various undo operations. If you ever want to undo something in git you have to look for a revision pointed by HEAD before you start the operation. If you know its name, then $ git reset --hard [REVISION] will undo the operation.

The second important thing to remember from this chapter concerns the three areas of the repository:

- The working directory
- The staging area
- And your current branch (i.e. the revision pointed by HEAD)

Each of them defines a snapshot of the files in your project. You can modify the snapshot stored in the working directory using filesystem commands, such as $ rm, $ cp, $ echo foo > bar, and so forth. The snapshot stored in the staging area is modified with git commands, such as $ git add, $ git rm, $ gim mv, and so on. Finally, the snapshot stored in the revision pointed by HEAD can be modified with the $ git commit command.

Using these three snapshots you can interpret the two lettered state codes returned by $ git status -sb as:

- The first letter of the code compares the HEAD snapshot and the staging area:
    - The space denotes that the file stored in the HEAD snapshot and in the staging area are identical
    - Any other character denotes that the file stored in the HEAD snapshot is different than the file in the staging area
- The second letter of the code compares the staging area and the working directory
    - The space denotes that the file stored in the staging area and the file stored in the working directory are identical
    - Any other character denotes that the file stored the staging area differs from the file stored in the working directory

This chapter also clarified the concept of authorship and the way git handles dates. Every commit stores four different attributes: Author, Commit, AuthorDate, and CommitDate. Author and Commit preserve the identity of the person who authored the code, introduced in this commit (Author attribute), and the person who introduced the commit in the projects history (Commit attribute). As you know Author is set when you execute the $ git commit command (without the --amend parameter). When you modify the commit using $ git commit --amend or $ git cherry-pick, $ git rebase, then git changes only the username of the committer—the authorship remains unchanged. Notice that when you squash some commits there is no way to preserve the original authors. The squashed commit will be attributed to the author of the first commit.

The other attributes AuthorDate and CommitDate are timestamps. The first stores the information when the commit was authored, the second when the commit was introduced in the history. Git doesn't care or store any other dates. In particular, git operations are not affected by the modification dates stored in your filesystem. If you:

- Commit at 5:00 p.m.

- Create, edit, and save the file a.txt at 5:10 p.m.

- Create, edit, and save the file b.txt at 5:20 p.m.

- Commit at 5:30 p.m.

then your repository will contain two commits. The first will contain the timestamp 5:00 p.m. The second revision will be denoted as created at 5:30. There is nothing in between. The information that your files were modified at 5:10 and at 5:20 is lost—git doesn't track it.

Four of the presented recipes used interactive rebasing. You should analyze all of them very carefully, especially Recipe 8-7. Even if you do not plan to use it in the way presented. The rebasing will be paused in case of conflicts— that's what makes Recipe 8-7 especially important. Once you know how to edit old revisions with Recipe 8-7, it will be easier for you to resolve conflicts.

■ **Caution**   Be aware that the recipes in this chapter can lead you to serious problems when used to modify the revisions have been shared with others. You can only use the $ git revert command presented in Recipes 8-8 and 8-9 to modify the revisions that have been published. All other recipes can be used only for the revisions that were not sent to the shared repository. Remember: the public history of your repository can only move forward. Otherwise it will be very difficult and cumbersome to synchronize the work within your team.

## CHAPTER 9

Resolving Conflicts

Until now, we mainly have focused on the structure of the graph of revisions. We usually committed using the $ git simple-commit alias; thus, the files we produced were very simple. In fact, almost every file we have created so far contained only one word. Once created, the files were rarely if ever modified. Moreover, the recipes were composed in such a way that we usually used different filenames in different branches. This simplified procedure of committing is a very efficient way of learning the diverse operations on the graph of revision, such as merging and rebasing, for example. However, they do not fully prepare you for working on a team where your colleagues are making changes to the same file. In this chapter we will fill the gap. You will learn how to control the contents of your file up to the point of resolving.

Working with real projects you will sooner or later encounter **conflicts**. They occur when you merge branches that include **different modifications of exactly the same line of a file**. If in some file, for example readme.txt, one developer types the first line as:

Lorem ipsum

and the other developer types:

Dolor sit amet

git will not be able to automatically merge both versions. You will have to manually choose between Lorem ipsum and Dolor sit amet. Because conflicts generally cause much concern and consternation—they are regarded as something to be afraid of—four recipes will explain accurately how to deal with conflicts during merge and rebase for both text and binary files. Once you are acquainted with conflicts, take a good look at the way conflicts are resolved. **In git, a conflict is resolved when you stage a file.** This means that in all four recipes concerning conflicjts the most important job is done by a well-know $ git add command.

9-1. Creating conflicting changes in text files
Problem

You want to create a repository containing two branches that when merged or rebased would produce a conflict in the text files. The repository you want to create is shown in Figure 9-1.

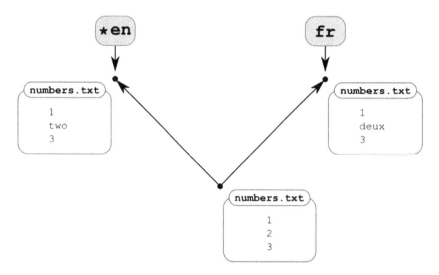

Figure 9-1. *The repository with branches en and fr that will produce a conflict in the text files*

Solution

Create a new repository:

```
$ cd git-recipes
$ git init 09-01
$ cd 09-01
```

and then follow these steps:

1. Create the file numbers.txt with the contents shown in Listing 9-1

    Listing 9-1. The numbers.txt file created in the master branch

    ```
    1
    2
    3
    ```

2. Commit numbers.txt file with $ git snapshot Numbers: 1, 2, 3

3. Create the branch named en with $ git branch en

4. Create the branch named fr with $ git branch fr

5. Create a new commit in the en branch

    a. Switch to the en branch with $ git checkout en

    b. Change the contents of numbers.txt. Replace 2 with two as shown in Listing 9-2

Listing 9-2. The numbers.txt file commited in the en branch

```
1
two
3
```

    c. Commit the change with `$ git snapshot Numbers: two`

6. Create a new commit in the fr branch

    a. Switch to the fr branch with `$ git checkout fr`

    b. Change the contents of numbers.txt. Replace 2 with deux as shown in Listing 9-3

Listing 9-3. The numbers.txt file commited in the fr branch

```
1
deux
3
```

    c. Commit the change with $ git snapshot Numbers: deux

Finish the recipe with `$ git checkout en`.

How It Works

To create a conflicting change you have to modify exactly the same line of a file in two different branches. In this recipe, we modify a line containing the number 2. In the first branch named en, we replace 2 with two, and in the second branch named fr, we replace 2 with deux.

In this situation git is not able to automatically merge or rebase the branches. As you will see the merging and rebasing will be paused, and you will have to manually resolve the conflicts.

9-2. Resolving textual conflict after merging
Problem

You and your colleague are working on the same project. You both appreciate the independence offered by the git branching model. Therefore each of you has created a branch. Unfortunately, while working in different branches, you both edited the same file inserting overlapping changes. Now you want to merge your work with the work of your colleague. During this operation you will face the conflict. You want to resolve the conflict in such a way that everything you and your colleague typed in the file is preserved.

This real-life scenario simplifies to merging the branches en and fr in the repository we created in Recipe 9-1. You want to use a repository created in Recipe 9-1 as a starting point. The result you want to achieve is shown in Figure 9-2. The second line of numbers.txt file should contain the contents shown in Listing 9-4. You want to keep both conflicting words two and deux.

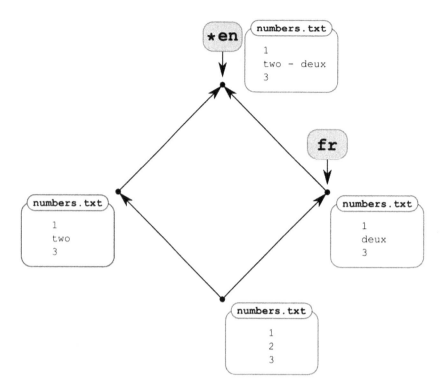

Figure 9-2. *The repository from Recipe 9-1 with merged branches en and fr*

Listing 9-4. The numbers.txt file after merging the en and fr branches

```
1
two - deux
3
```

Solution

Clone the repository from Recipe 9-1:

```
$ cd git-recipes
$ git clone-with-branches 09-01 09-02
$ cd 09-02
$ git checkout en
```

Your current branch now is en. Merge the fr branch into en with $ git merge fr. This time the automatic merge fails with the following message:

```
Auto-merging numbers.txt
CONFLICT (content): Merge conflict in numbers.txt
Automatic merge failed; fix conflicts and then commit the result.
```

As you can see the merging was paused. You have to **fix conflicts and then commit the result.** The output of `$ git status -s` is:

```
UU numbers.txt
```

The conflicted files are labeled with `UU`, which according to `$ git status --help` stands for *updated but unmerged*. The contents of `numbers.txt` right after `$ git merge fr` is shown in Listing 9-5.

Listing 9-5. The contents of the numbers.txt file right after the $ git merge fr command

```
1
<<<<<<< HEAD
two
=======
deux
>>>>>>> fr
3
```

Right now, you have to edit the file and prepare the contents that you regard as the proper solution for the conflict. You can use any editor you like, and you can insert any contents you like. Open the file `numbers.txt` and change it according to Listing 9-6.

Listing 9-6. The contents of numbers.txt file with manually edited contents

```
1
two - deux
3
```

When the file is saved you can verify that its status did not change. The command `$ git status -s` returns the same output as before: `UU numbers.txt`.

Once you have manually resolved the conflict you can change the status of the file from `UU` into `M_`. This is done with the `$ git add numbers.txt` command. Committing the change with the `$ git commit --no-edit` command, you will finish the recipe.

How It Works

When the `$ git merge` command produces a conflict the merging is paused. You are left with a repository in which some files are denoted as `UU`. These files contain conflicts that have to be resolved manually.

Every conflict is denoted with special markers:

```
<<<<<<<
=======
>>>>>>>
```

The first part of the conflict comes from your current branch, which is stored in HEAD. Git informs you that your current branch (which in our recipe is en) contains the word `two`:

```
<<<<<<< HEAD
two
=======
```

The second part of the conflict comes from the fr branch. The conflicting word is deux. This information is shown as:

```
=======
deux
>>>>>>> fr
```

How do you resolve a conflict in git? This is done with a single command $ git add. From now on you need to remember one simple rule: **staging a file resolves a conflict**. In terms of states, we can say that staging a file changes its state from UU into M_. At first, it may be surprising that the content of a file doesn't matter. You can leave the file as shown in Listing 9-5 and commit it with the <<<<<<<, =======, >>>>>>> markers, if you wish. When you edit a file and remove these markers it doesn't mean that you have resolved a conflict. This is done only when you stage a file (with $ git add command, for example).

From time to time you would need to resolve the conflict by using the contents introduced in one branch and ignoring the changes from the other branch. It will be especially important for binary files. You can achieve this with two commands:

```
$ git checkout --ours [filename]
$ git checkout --theirs [filename]
```

The --ours flag means the current branch. This is the en in the recipe. The --theirs flag means the branch passed to the $ git merge command. In this recipe it is the fr branch. In other words the command $ git checkout --ours numbers.txt will produce in the working directory the file shown in Listing 9-2, while the command $ git checkout --theirs numbers.txt—the file shown in Listing 9-3. Notice that these commands do not resolve conflicts. They only restore the contents of the file without changing its state. The restored file remains in UU state.

If you want to produce the file shown in Listing 9-5 you can use:

```
$ git checkout --merge [filename]
```

With the above command you will get a file in which conflicts are denoted with <<<<<<< ours and >>>>>>> theirs labels, as in:

```
1
<<<<<<< ours
two
=======
deux
>>>>>>> theirs
3
```

The above output doesn't contain the original line before the branches en and fr diverged. If that is important to you, use the command:

```
$ git checkout --conflict=diff3 numbers.txt
```

It will create the file with the contents shown in Listing 9-7. This time, the file contains another section tagged base. The base section displays the version stored in a merge base—the commit returned by the $ git merge-base en fr command.

Listing 9-7. The conflict presented in diff3 format

```
<<<<<<< ours
two
||||||| base
2
=======
deux
>>>>>>> theirs
3
```

■ **Hint** In Recipe 5-12 we discussed the command to restore an arbitrary file from an arbitrary revision:
`$ git checkout [REVISION] [filename]`. It can be applied instead of using `--ours` or `--theirs` parameters. In this recipe, the command `$ git checkout en numbers.txt` is equivalent to `$ git checkout --ours numbers.txt` and `$ git checkout fr numbers.txt` is equivalent to `$ git checkout --theirs numbers.txt`.

When you resolve all conflicts you can resume the paused merge with the `$ git commit --no-edit` command. The option `--no-edit` is not mandatory—you can skip it. But it takes the burden of typing or inspecting the commit's message off of your shoulders.

Whenever in doubt, you can always abort the merge in progress with: `$ git merge --abort`. The methods to undo a merge were discussed in chapter 6.

■ **Hint** Resolving a merge conflict consists of three steps: 1) editing a file; 2) staging a file with the `$ git add` command; and 3) finishing the merge with the `$ git commit --no-edit` command.

9-3. Resolving textual conflict after rebasing
Problem

For the repository created in the Recipe 9-1 you want to rebase the branch en onto `fr`. Your aim is to produce the repository shown in Figure 9-3. The conflicting line of `numbers.txt` file should contain the contents shown in Listing 9-8.

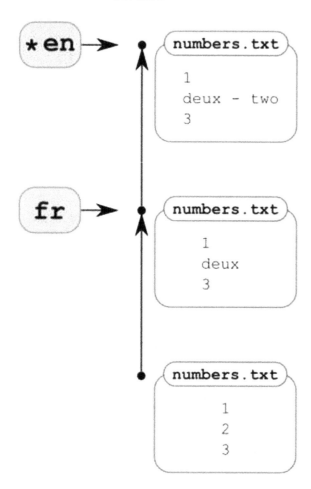

Figure 9-3. *The repository from Recipe 9-1 with the branch en rebased onto fr*

This recipe is a simplified scenario where two developers work in different branches and produce overlapping changes in one of the files. The recipe presents a method to rebase your work onto the work of your colleague.

Listing 9-8. The numbers.txt file you want to keep after rebasing the en branch onto fr

```
1
deux - two
3
```

Solution

Clone the repository from Recipe 9-1:

```
$ cd git-recipes
$ git clone-with-branches 09-01 09-03
$ cd 09-03
```

Rebase the en branch onto the `fr` branch with the `$ git rebase fr en` command. The rebasing will fail with the following message:

```
First, rewinding head to replay your work on top of it...
Applying: Numbers: two
Using index info to reconstruct a base tree...
M       numbers.txt
Falling back to patching base and 3-way merge...
Auto-merging numbers.txt
CONFLICT (content): Merge conflict in numbers.txt
Failed to merge in the changes.
Patch failed at 0001 Numbers: two
The copy of the patch that failed is found in:
   /git-recipes/09-03/.git/rebase-apply/patch

When you have resolved this problem, run "git rebase --continue".
If you prefer to skip this patch, run "git rebase --skip" instead.
To check out the original branch and stop rebasing, run "git rebase --abort".
```

Rebasing was paused in the same manner as in Recipe 8-7. You have to resolve the conflict and then you can continue rebasing.

The output of `$ git status -s` is:

```
UU numbers.txt
```

The conflicting files are labeled in exactly the same way as during the merge with UU. When you open the `numbers.txt` file you will see that the content of the file is changed, however. The `numbers.txt` file right after `$ git rebase fr en` is shown in Listing 9-9.

Listing 9-9. The contents of numbers.txt file right after the $ git rebase fr en command

```
1
<<<<<<< HEAD
deux
=======
two
>>>>>>> Numbers: two
3
```

The rebasing starts with the checkout of the tip commit of the `fr` branch. Thus, the contents presented in HEAD section come from the `fr` branch:

```
<<<<<<< HEAD
deux
=======
```

The first patch applied during rebase is from the commit labeled as Numbers: two. As a result, the second portion of a conflict is formatted as:

```
=======
two
>>>>>>> Numbers: two
```

Right now, you have to edit the file and type in the contents presented in Listing 9-8.

Finally, stage the file with the $ `git add numbers.txt` command. This command will change the state of the file from UU into M_. Finish the recipe proceeding with the paused rebase: $ `git rebase --continue`.

How It Works

If there is a conflict during rebasing, the operation is paused. You have to manually resolve the conflict. The procedure is exactly the same as in the case of a merge conflict: you edit the file and then stage it. The same rule applies here: **staging a file resolves a conflict**.

The four states of numbers.txt file as shown in Listings 9-2, 9-3, 9-7, and 9-9 can be retrieved with the following commands:

```
$ git checkout --ours numbers.txt
$ git checkout --theirs numbers.txt
$ git checkout --merge numbers.txt
$ git checkout --conflict=diff3 numbers.txt
```

But be careful: this time the meaning of --ours and --theirs is reversed: --ours means the fr branch and --theirs means the en branch. That's because the rebasing starts with the checkout of the latest commit in the fr branch.

When all conflicts are resolved you can continue rebasing with $ `git rebase --continue` or you can abort the operation with $ `git rebase --abort`. The undoing of this operation was discussed in chapter 7.

■ **Hint**   Resolving a rebase conflict consists of three steps: 1) editing a file; 2) staging a file with the $ `git add` command; and 3) finishing the rebasing with the $ `git rebase --continue` command.

9-4 Creating conflicting changes in binary files
Problem

You want to create a repository containing two branches that when merged or rebased would produce a conflict in binary files. The repository you want to create is shown in Figure 9-4.

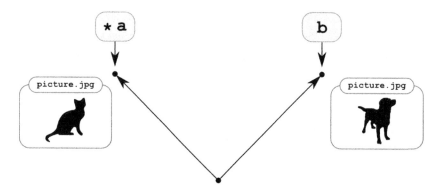

Figure 9-4. *The repository with branches a and b that will produce a binary conflict*

Solution

Create a new repository:

```
$ cd git-recipes
$ git init 09-04
$ cd 09-04
```

and then follow the steps:

1. Create the first revision with the `$ git commit --allow-empty --allow-empty-message -m " "` command. That's how you can produce an empty commit with empty comment.

2. Create a branch named a with `$ git branch a`

3. Create a branch named b with `$ git branch b`

4. Create a new commit in a branch

   a. Switch to a branch with `$ git checkout a`

   b. Create the image displaying a cat and save it in the file named `picture.jpg`

   c. Commit the change with `$ git snapshot Cat`

5. Create a new commit in b branch

   a. Switch to b branch with `$ git checkout b`

   b. Create the image displaying a dog and save it in the file named `picture.jpg`

   c. Commit the change with `$ git snapshot Dog`

   Finish the recipe with the `$ git checkout a` command.

How It Works

This time the repository contains two different images saved in files with the same name. The file stored in the branch named a displays a cat, and the file stored in b branch displays a dog.

Notice that the command `$ git commit --allow-empty --allow-empty-message -m " "` produces the empty commit with the empty message.

9-5. Resolving a binary conflict during merging
Problem

You want to merge branches a and b created in Recipe 9-4 with the `$ git merge` command. You want to obtain the repository shown in Figure 9-5. The repository after the merge should contain the `picture.jpg` file from b branch.

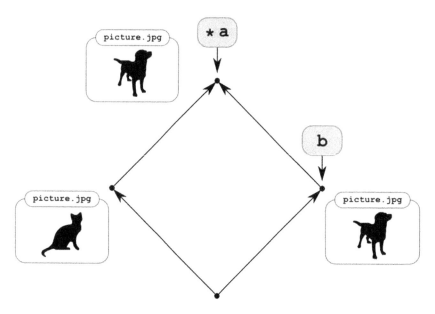

Figure 9-5. *The repository from Recipe 9-4 with the merged branches a and b*

Solution

Clone the repository from Recipe 9-4:

```
$ cd git-recipes
$ git clone-with-branches 09-04 09-05
$ cd 09-05
$ git checkout a
```

Your current branch now is a. Merge b branch into a with the $ git merge b command. As you can guess the merge fails. The message informs you about a binary conflict in the picture.jpg file:

```
warning: Cannot merge binary files: picture.jpg (HEAD vs. b)
Auto-merging picture.jpg
CONFLICT (add/add): Merge conflict in picture.jpg
Automatic merge failed; fix conflicts and then commit the result.
```

The merging is paused and the conflicting binary file is denoted with:

```
AA picture.jpg
```

by the $ git status -s command. You have to choose exactly one version of a file. To choose an image displaying a dog use the $ git checkout --theirs picture.jpg command.

Once you have checked out the appropriate version of a file you can change the status of the file from AA into M_. This is done with the $ git add picture.jpg command. Committing the change with $ git commit --no-edit you will finalize the merging. When merging is finished open your favorite image editor and verify that picture.jpg displays a dog.

How It Works

Binary files cause more trouble-free conflicts than text files. That's because git cannot merge two different binary files into one file. There is no method to produce the merged file that is presented in Figure 9-6. You can only do it using an image editor, such as Gimp, git cannot help you with this. For a binary file you can only request the first or second version of a file. This is done with two commands:

```
$ git checkout --ours [filename]
$ git checkout --theirs [filename]
```

Figure 9-6. *Git cannot merge two separate binary files into one file*

or with:

```
$ git checkout a [filename]
$ git checkout b [filename]
```

Conflicted binary files are denoted with AA. This is another difference as textual conflicts are denoted with UU.

The rest, which is resolving a conflict and finishing a merge, is performed as was done previously with the $ git add and $ git commit --no-edit commands.

9-6. Resolving a binary conflict during rebasing

Problem

While working in the repository created in the Recipe 9-4, you would like to rebase branch a onto b. You want to obtain the repository shown in Figure 9-7. When you finish rebasing, branch a should contain a picture displaying a cat.

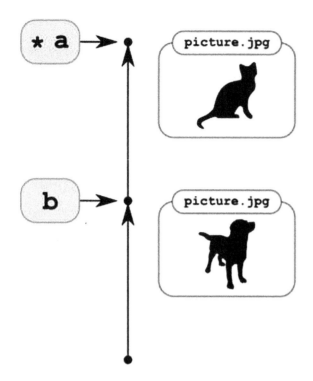

Figure 9-7. *The repository you want to produce in Recipe 9-6*

Solution

Clone the repository from Recipe 9-4:

```
$ cd git-recipes
$ git clone-with-branches 09-04 09-06
$ cd 09-06
```

Rebase branch a onto b with the $ `git rebase b a` command. The rebasing will fail with the following message:

```
First, rewinding head to replay your work on top of it...
Applying: Cat
Using index info to reconstruct a base tree...
Falling back to patching base and 3-way merge...
warning: Cannot merge binary files: picture.jpg (HEAD vs. Cat)
Auto-merging picture.jpg
CONFLICT (add/add): Merge conflict in picture.jpg
Failed to merge in the changes.
Patch failed at 0001 Cat
The copy of the patch that failed is found in:
   c:/git-recipes/09-06/.git/rebase-apply/patch
```

When you have resolved this problem, run "git rebase --continue".
If you prefer to skip this patch, run "git rebase --skip" instead.
To check out the original branch and stop rebasing, run "git rebase --abort".

Rebasing was paused and you have to resolve conflict. The output of $ git status -s is:

AA picture.jpg

To restore an image displaying a cat from branch a use the $ git checkout --theirs picture.jpg command. This time --ours means branch b and --theirs means branch a.

Finish the recipe with the $ git add picture.jpg and $ git rebase --continue commands. Finally open your favorite image editor and verify that picture.jpg displays a cat.

How It Works

The binary conflicts during rebasing are handled almost identically as in Recipe 9-5. The only difference between merging and rebasing is that the roles of --ours and --theirs are reversed. This is summarized in Table 9-1.

Table 9-1. *The roles of --ours and --theirs during merging and rebasing*

The commands	--ours	--theirs
$ git checkout a $ git merge b	a	b
$ git checkout a $ git rebase b	b	a

9-7. Forcing a binary mode during merge
Problem

The starting point for this recipe is the repository created in Recipe 9-1. You want to merge the two branches en and fr in such a way that the two versions of the numbers.txt file are merged in a binary mode.

Solution

Clone the repository from Recipe 9-1:

```
$ cd git-recipes
$ git clone-with-branches 09-01 09-07
$ cd 09-07
$ git checkout en
```

Now create a file named .gitattributes containing the single line numbers.txt binary. You can do it with one command:

```
$ echo "numbers.txt binary" > .gitattributes
```

Commit this new file with

```
$ git snapshot .gitattributes rule to force binary type of numbers.txt
```

Finally, merge the fr branch into en with the $ git merge fr command. This time you will get the message:

```
warning: Cannot merge binary files: numbers.txt (HEAD vs. fr)
Auto-merging numbers.txt
CONFLICT (content): Merge conflict in numbers.txt
Automatic merge failed; fix conflicts and then commit the result.
```

As you can see the numbers.txt files are treated as binary files. The command $ cat numbers.txt prints:

```
1
two
3
```

Thus the two versions of the files were not merged. The working directory contains the version taken from the en branch (which is currently --ours).

How It Works

How does git know which files are binary and which have textual contents? It checks first 8,000 bytes of the file for the occurrence of a NULL byte. If the file contains the byte with the code 0, it is assumed to be a binary file. Otherwise it is treated as text file.

To force a file to be treated as binary you can use the:

```
filename binary
```

rule in the .gitattributes file. Likewise, you can also force a binary file to be treated as a text file with the following rule:

```
filename text
```

In both cases the filename can be replaced with a pattern. Here are two examples: the first forces all files under bindir/ to be treated as binary, the other forces all the files with names ending with .xyz to be treated as text files:

```
bindir/ binary
*.xyz text
```

In general, the syntax of the .gitattributes file allows you to define a list of attributes for every pattern:

```
pattern attribute-1 attribute-2 attribute-3 ...
```

Pattern defines which files should be affected by a rule. Here are four pattern examples:

```
*            # all files
*.txt        # all files ending with .txt
somedir/     # all files under somedir/ directory
readme.txt   # one file readme.txt
```

For every pattern you can apply the arbitrary number of attributes, as in:

```
*.txt          text -merge eol=crlf
```

This line defines a rule that will be used for all the files matching the `*.txt` pattern. The rule consists of three entries:

```
text
-merge
eol=crlf
```

The first entry, which consists of a single word `text`, sets the `text` attribute for all matching files. As a consequence all the `*.txt` files will be regarded as text files, and therefore git will perform an end-of-line normalization on them.

The second entry, which consists of one word `merge` preceded with a dash, unsets the `merge` attribute. It means that all `*.txt` files are to be merged as binary files.

The last rule sets the end-of-line characters that should be used during checkout.

The list of all available attributes is summarized in Table 9-2.

Table 9-2. *The list of available attributes*

Attribute	Description
binary	Turns off three attributes: `diff`, `merge`, `text`
conflict-marker-size	Defines the length of conflicts markers.
delta	Delta compression will not be attempted for blobs that are generated by paths with the attribute delta set to `false`.
diff	This attribute affects the way git performs the `$ git diff` operation for a given file.
encoding	The value of this attribute specifies the character encoding that should be used by GUI tools (e.g., gitk and git-gui) to display the contents of the relevant file.
eol	The attribute defines a line ending to be used during checkout.
export-ignore	Excludes files from archives generated with the `$ git archive` command.
export-subst	Substitutes files with some other files during the `$ git archive` command.
filter	This attribute can be used to perform additional processing during checkout and check-in.
ident	This attribute allows embedding of `$Id$` variables in files. These variables are processed during check-in and checkout.
merge	Defines whether the file can be merged as text files with markers `<<<<<<<`, `=======`, `>>>>>>>` or if it should be treated as a binary file.
text	This attribute governs the end-of-line normalization.
white-space	This attribute allows you to tailor the control of white space errors.

The full description of all the attributes can be obtained with the `$ git attributes --help` command.

Summary

This chapter is a final and necessary step before collaborating with other developers. It gives you accurate answers to following questions:

- What can happen when two people modify exactly the same line of a text file?

- What can happen when two developers change the same binary file storing different contents in them?

- How does git decide which files are binary and which are not?

The first problem, the overlapping changes in a text file, will result in a textual conflict during merge or rebase operations. In both cases, the operation is paused, and you have to resolve all conflicts. When conflicts are resolved you can finish merging using the $ git commit command. To resume paused rebase use the $ git rebase --continue command.

Conflicted text files are denoted as UU by the $ git status -s command. The overlapping parts are marked with <<<<<<<, =======, >>>>>>>. The length of these markers can be adjusted with the conflict-marker-size attribute presented in Table 9.2. You have to manually edit the file and decide what you consider appropriate contents for every conflict. Remember that you do not resolve the conflict by removing the markers <<<<<<<, =======, >>>>>>>. Even if you remove all markers and save the file it is still in an UU state. To change the state of the file from UU to M_ you have to stage the file. This can be done with the $ git add [filename] command.

Binary files also can cause a conflict, but in that case git cannot merge two different binary files into one file. You will be left with the first or second version of a file, depending on whether you used merge or rebase. Conflicted binary files are denoted as AA. The conflict is resolved exactly as in textual case by staging the file with the $ git add [filename] command.

In case of textual conflict the following four commands can be used to generate four versions of conflicted files:

```
$ git checkout --ours [filename]
$ git checkout --theirs [filename]
$ git checkout --merge [filename]
$ git checkout --conflict=diff3 [filename]
```

For binary conflicts only the first two commands can be used.

How does git decide which files are binary and which are text? It browses the first 8,000 bytes of each file. If it finds a NULL byte the file is considered to be binary. Otherwise the file is considered textual. You can also verbosely specify the type for each path using a .gitattributes file. You can regard this file as a means to specify various file properties on the per pattern level.

■ ■ ■

## CHAPTER 10

Remote Repositories and Synchronization

The inherent reason behind all VCS systems is to make the collaboration within a group of developers as seamless as possible. Finally, we have reached the point where we can discuss how to use git for a group work. We will start with the simplest settings where all the repositories are available through local storage.

First you have to learn how to use remotes. We will discuss this in a recipe that shows you exactly what happens when you clone a repository. Then we will dive into recipes that present step-by-step methods on how two or more developers can cooperate. We will consider two important cases:

- First: where a bare repository is shared and accessed by all members

- Second: where two developers cooperate directly, without any additional repository

You can think about the first one as a centralized client/server solution and the other as a peer-to-peer solution. Git is a distributed system that allows you to mingle both approaches.

The easiest way to download new contributions from a central repository is to use the $ git pull command. When used with default settings, this can lead to a very complicated history of your project. I will show you exactly when and why you can expect troubles. This will lead us to improved recipes that will always provide you with a clean history.

The subject of different types of branches that I mentioned in Recipe 5-2 will arise again. This time, we will pursue it to the very end. You will learn all you need to know about remote branches, local tracking branches, and remote tracking branches. Not only will I show you how to list, create, destroy, and synchronize them but also how different commands, such as $ git commit and $ git fetch, affect their state. This chapter will give you a thorough and complete understanding of remote branches, remote tracking branches, and local tracking branches. By acquiring these skills you will be ready to join any team working with git.

10-1. Manual cloning
Problem

You want to get a deeper insight into cloning. One way to achieve this is to manually clone a repository. You want to perform a manual cloning during which every internal git operation, such as the initialization of a new repository and the fetching of revisions from the remote end, are executed with a more specialized command. Proceed with this recipe cloning the https://github.com/creationix/js-git repository. The js-git project is a preliminary JavaScript implementation of git.

Solution

Create a new directory with:

```
$ cd git-recipes
$ mkdir 10-01
$ cd 10-01
```

and then follow these steps:

1. Initialize a new repository with: `$ git init`

2. Add the URL of the remote end: `$ git remote add origin`
   `https://github.com/creationix/js-git.git`

3. Fetch the git database and remote tracking branches from the remote end:
   `$ git fetch --no-tags origin master:refs/remotes/origin/master`

4. Create a local master branch that will point to the same revision as the origin/master
   remote tracking branch: `$ git rev-parse origin/master > .git/refs/heads/master`

5. Set up the master branch as a local tracking branch for the remote tracking branch
   origin/master with: `$ git branch --set-upstream-to=origin/master`

6. Store the information about the default branch in the remote repository locally: `$ git`
   `symbolic-ref refs/remotes/origin/HEAD refs/remotes/origin/master`

7. Checkout the files in the working directory: `$ git checkout`

How It Works

This recipe demystifies the cloning operation. It splits cloning into:

- Initialization

- Definition of a remote

- Downloading the git database and remote tracking branches

- Creating appropriate branches

Git starts a clone, initializing a new empty repository with the `$ git init` command. Right after this command the repository is empty—it doesn't contain any branches. The output of `$ git branch` is empty.

To copy the revisions from an external source we need an URL. This URL is set with the `$ remote add [alias] [URL]` command. The first parameter is the short alias; the second parameter is an URL. Once you define a remote origin with:

```
$ git remote add origin https://github.com/creationix/jz-git.git
```

you can use a short alias origin instead of full URL. The command:

```
$ git fetch --no-tags origin master:refs/remotes/origin/master
```

is equivalent to:

```
$ git fetch --no-tags https://github.com/creationix/js-git.git master:refs/remotes/origin/master
```

Remotes can be listed with the `$ git remote` command. By default this command prints defined aliases. The additional parameter -v turns on the verbose output. The command `$ git remote -v` prints the names and URL for all aliases. The remotes can be removed with the `$ git remote rm [alias]` command.

All the remotes are stored in the `.git/config` file. When you execute: `$ git remote add foo https://example.comnet/bar.git`, git adds the following entry in the `.git/config` file:

```
[remote "foo"]
    url = https://example.comnet/bar.git
    fetch = +refs/heads/*:refs/remotes/foo/*
```

The line:

```
url = https://example.comnet/bar.git
```

stores the URL. The second line:

```
fetch = +refs/heads/*:refs/remotes/foo/*
```

defines a so-called *refspec*. Refspec specifies the way the remote branches (i.e., the branches in the remote repository) are mapped to the remote tracking branches (i.e., local branches stored in the `refs/remotes/foo` directory). The remote repository contains branches in its `.git/refs/heads` directory. We want to copy them in such a way that they do not collide with our ordinary local branches stored locally in `.git/refs/heads`. Therefore we place the remote tracking branches into a separate directory named `.git/refs/remotes/foo`. As long as the aliases used to name the remotes are unique we can be sure that the branches from different remotes will not collide with each other or with our local branches.

You can treat:

```
fetch = +refs/heads/*:refs/remotes/foo/*
```

as 1:1 mapping between two directories: one in the remote repository, the other in the local repository. The above states that all the files in the `.git/refs/heads` directory in the remote end aliased as foo are mapped into the local directory named `.git/refs/remotes/foo`. This mapping is used during the `$ git fetch` and `$ git push` operations. The + character placed at the very beginning of a refspec lets you push the revisions that will override the history stored in the remote repository.

It is important to note that apart from the configuration stored in the `[remote "foo"]` section of the `.git/config` file there is no other dependence between the two repositories. The name of the remote is just an alias that makes your commands shorter. Instead of typing the complete URL you can use the remote's name. Moreover, the remote alias is stored only in the local repository. The remote end doesn't store any information that someone uses its URL in its configuration.

▪ **Hint** Origin is a standard name used by git for the remote repository during a clone operation. There is no magic in it: you can delete an origin remote with `$ git remote rm origin`. And you can create a new origin remote with `$ git remote add origin [URL]`.

Once the remote is defined we can copy the git database from the remote end into the local repository. This is done with the `$ git fetch --no-tags origin master:refs/remotes/origin/master` command. After this command, the repository contains one remote tracking branch. The command `$ git branch -a -vv` prints an output similar to:

```
remotes/origin/master 60478cc Bump version to 0.3.1
```

The parameter `--no-tags` ensures that the tags contained in the remote repository are not copied. The next parameter, `origin`, gives the name of the remote from which we want to copy the revisions. The last parameter `master:refs/remotes/origin/master` is a refspec. It consists of two names separated by a colon:

- `master`—the name of the remote branch in the remote repository aliased as `origin`

- `refs/remotes/origin/master`—the name of the remote tracking branch (it is a local branch in the local repository)

The refspec ensures that the remote `master` branch will be copied into the local `.git/refs/remotes/origin/master` file. After the fetch command, the `.git/objects` directory in the local repository contains the objects copied from the remote repository. You should notice that the `$ git fetch` command creates a local file `.git/refs/remotes/origin/master`. This is a copy of a remote branch. The copy is stored in a local repository as a remote tracking branch. Back in Recipe 5-2 I emphasized that the remote tracking branch is a local branch. This is how remote tracking branches are created: they appear in your repository after the `$ git fetch` command. You can verify this with a `$ git branch -a -vv` command issued right after `$ git fetch`. Even if you remove a remote tracking branch with a `$ git branch -d -r` command, it will be recreated after the next `$ git fetch` command.

The next step is to set up a local `master` branch. As you already know an ordinary local branch is just a text file storing the appropriate SHA-1 name. We want our branch to point to the same revision as the `.git/refs/remotes/origin/master` branch created during fetch operation. The branch stored in `.git/refs/remotes/origin/master` can be referred to as `origin/master`. How do you find the SHA-1 name of the revision pointed by some symbolic reference `origin/master`? We can use the `$ git rev-parse` command for this purpose. Run the command `$ git rev-parse origin/master`. It will print the SHA-1 name of the revision pointed by the `.git/refs/remotes/origin/master` branch. To create an ordinary local branch pointing to the same revision it is sufficient to store the SHA-1 in a text file:

```
$ git rev-parse origin/master > .git/refs/heads/master
```

■ **Hint**   The result of the `$ git rev-parse origin/master > .git/refs/heads/master` command can also be achieved with the `$ cp .git/refs/remotes/origin/master .git/refs/heads/master` command.

The above command creates an ordinary local branch named `master`. The output of the `$ git branch -a -vv` command should be similar to:

```
* master                60478cc Bump version to 0.3.1
  remotes/origin/master 60478cc Bump version to 0.3.1
```

Now we turn an ordinary local branch `master` into a local tracking branch for the remote tracking `origin/master` branch. This is done with:

```
$ git branch --set-upstream-to=origin/master
```

After this, `$ git branch -a -vv` prints:

```
* master                60478cc [origin/master] Bump version to 0.3.1
  remotes/origin/master 60478cc Bump version to 0.3.1
```

Thanks to [origin/master] in the first line we know that master is a local tracking branch for the remote tracking branch origin/master.

The command $ branch --set-upstream-to=origin/master creates the following entry in .git/config file:

```
[branch "master"]
    remote = origin
    merge = refs/heads/master
```

This says that your local master branch is set to track the remote branch stored in refs/heads/master in the repository pointed by origin URL. It is easier to understand the meaning of the above command with the example using a different name for the local and remote branches. Suppose that your local repository contains an ordinary local branch named foo. You want the foo branch to track the bar branch in the remote repository. If you issue the command:

```
$ git branch --set-upstream-to=origin/bar foo
```

then the following configuration entry will be created:

```
[branch "foo"]
    remote = origin
    merge = refs/heads/bar
```

The remote repository pointed by origin contains a file .git/refs/heads/bar. This is the remote branch bar. The local repository contains .git/refs/remotes/origin/bar and .git/refs/heads/foo. The first file .git/refs/remotes/origin/bar is a remote tracking branch and the second file .git/refs/heads/foo is the local tracking branch. The local tracking branch foo is connected with remote tracking branch origin/bar.

■ **Hint** You also can create the master branch that points to origin/master with the $ git branch master origin/master command. I avoided the above command because it not only creates a local master branch but also sets up tracking. I prefer to split both operations. Therefore I used $ git rev-parse and $ git branch --set-upstream-to to perform the two actions separately.

The last step of this procedure is to store the information about the default branch in the remote repository locally:

```
$ git symbolic-ref refs/remotes/origin/HEAD refs/remotes/origin/master
```

This command will create a local file .git/refs/remotes/origin/HEAD. The file will contain a symbolic reference pointing to refs/remotes/origin/master. This is how we know which branch is considered default in the remote end.

Git allows direct manipulation of its configuration with the $ git config command. Therefore the command $ git branch --set-upstream-to=origin/bar issued in the foo branch is equivalent to two commands:

```
$ git config branch.foo.remote origin
$ git config branch.foo.merge refs/heads/bar
```

Using an additional --unset parameter you can also unset the arbitrary option. In Recipe 10-5 we will use:

```
$ git config --unset branch.foo.remote
$ git config --unset branch.foo.merge
```

to unset tracking.

10-2. Coworking with a central repository

Problem

You want to simulate the cooperation of two developers John and Sarah using a central repository. In this case the collaboration will be organized with three repositories:

- `10-02/johns-repo`—a non-bare repository of the first developer
- `10-02/sarahs-repo`—a non-bare repository of the second developer
- `10-02/shared-repo`—a bare repository used to synchronize the work of John and Sara

In this recipe both developers will work using only the `master` branch. You want to analyze what happens when:

- Each developer proceeds with his or her work in the `master` branch
- One developer sends his or her revisions to a shared repo
- The other developer fetches new revisions

■ **Hint**   This recipe shows how to organize a team's work around a central repository. This workflow is similar to the client/server approach used by centralized systems, such as CVS or SVN.

Solution

Create a new directory with:

```
$ cd git-recipes
$ mkdir 10-02
$ cd 10-02
```

The work is initialized by one of the developers. We will assume that it is John who starts the whole project with:

```
# the command issued in git-recipes/10-02 directory
$ git init --bare shared-repo
```

This repository will be used to synchronize John's and Sarah's work.
Next John creates his own repository:

```
# john's commands in git-recipes/10-02 directory
$ git init johns-repo
```

Then he sets his personal data and defines the `origin` remote:

```
# john's commands
$ cd johns-repo
$ git config --local user.name john
$ git config --local user.email john@example.net
$ git remote add origin ../shared-repo
```

The two repositories now look like Figure 10-1. The meta-information user.name, user.email, and remote.origin are not shown in the figure.

johns-repo   shared-repo

Figure 10-1. *The two repositories just after initialization*

Then John creates some revisions in his private repository with:

```
# john's command
$ git simple-commit a1 a2 a3
```

Right now John's repository contains one ordinary branch named master. The output of $ git branch -a -vv would be similar to:

```
* master dc30648 a3
```

The repositories look like Figure 10-2.

johns-repo   shared-repo

Figure 10-2. *The state of the repositories after John's a1, a2, a3 commits*

John sends his a1, a2, and a3 revisions to the shared-repo repository with:

```
# john's command
$ git push -u origin master
```

The command creates a new branch in the remote shared-repo repository. The new remote branch is named master. Thanks to the -u parameter the above command creates a remote tracking branch origin/master in johns-repo. You can verify it with the $ git branch -a -vv command. The output would be similar to:

```
* master                dc30648 [origin/master] a3
  remotes/origin/master dc30648 a3
```

As you can see John's repository contains a local tracking branch master and a remote tracking branch origin/master. We can say that the -u parameter converted the ordinary local branch named master into a local tracking branch. The repositories now look like Figure 10-3.

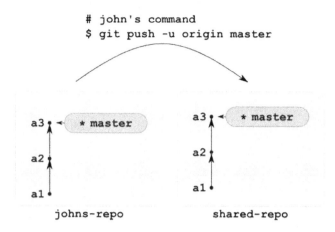

Figure 10-3. *The effect of $ git push -u origin master issued by John*

Next Sarah joins the project. She clones shared-repo with:

```
# sarah's commands
# executed in git-recipes/10-02
$ git clone shared-repo sarahs-repo
$ cd sarahs-repo
```

Because Sarah used the $ git clone command her master branch was set to track the remote master branch. The three repositories now look like Figure 10-4.

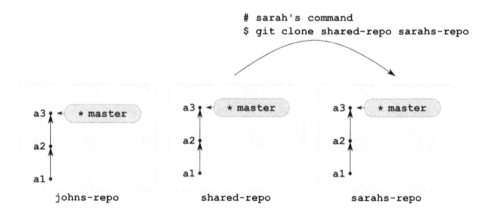

Figure 10-4. *The effect of $ git clone shared-repo sarahs-repo issued by Sarah*

Now it is Sarah's turn to contribute to the project. She creates two revisions b1 and b2:

```
# sarah's command
$ git simple-commit b1 b2
```

The repositories now look like Figure 10-5.

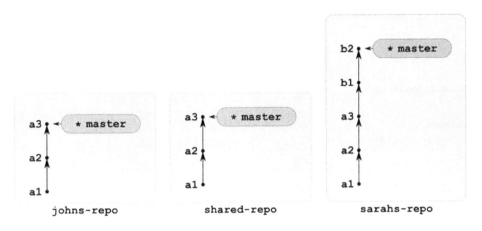

Figure 10-5. *The state of the repositories after Sara has created the b1 and b2 commits*

In the next step Sarah sends her revisions to the shared-repo with:

```
# sarah's command
$ git push origin master
```

Notice that Sarah doesn't need to use -u. She initialized her repository with the $ git clone command thus the tracking for a master branch was initialized automatically. John initialized his repository with $ git init. That is why he needed to use -u when he pushed for the first time. The result of Sarah's push command is shown in Figure 10-6.

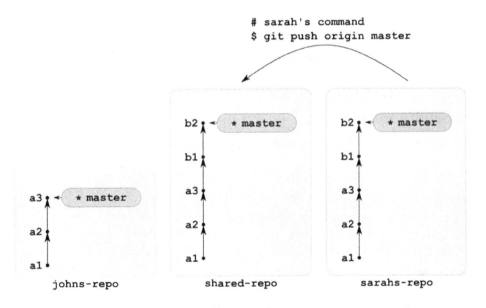

Figure 10-6. *The repositories after Sarah's $ git push -u origin master command*

Now it's John's turn to download Sarah's revisions. He runs:

```
# john's command
$ git pull origin master
```

This leads to the state shown in Figure 10-7.

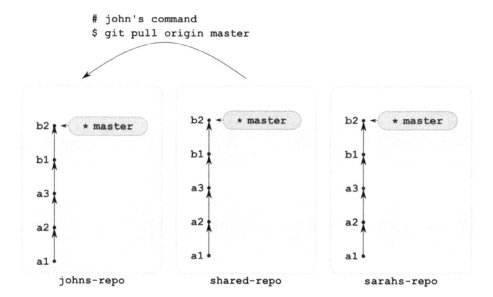

Figure 10-7. *The repositories after John's $ git pull origin master command*

The above schema can be repeated an arbitrary number of times. Nothing special happens until John's and Sarah's master branches diverge. Let's analyze a case such as this.

Diverging John's and Sarah's work

This time both John and Sarah work independently in their repositories. John creates revisions a4 and a5 while Sarah creates revision b3:

```
# john's command
$ git simple-commit a4 a5
```

```
# sarah's command
$ git simple-commit b3
```

The repositories you'll get are depicted in Figure 10-8.

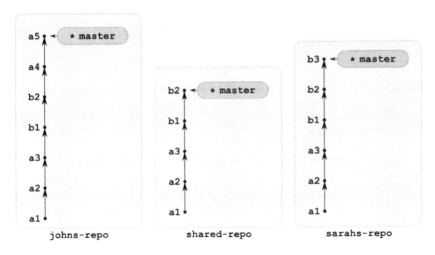

Figure 10-8. *The repositories in which John's and Sarah's branches diverged*

Now both John and Sarah want to push their revisions into the shared-repo. Let's assume that Sarah was the first to execute the $ git push command. After:

```
# sarah's command
$ git push origin master
```

The repositories look like Figure 10-9.

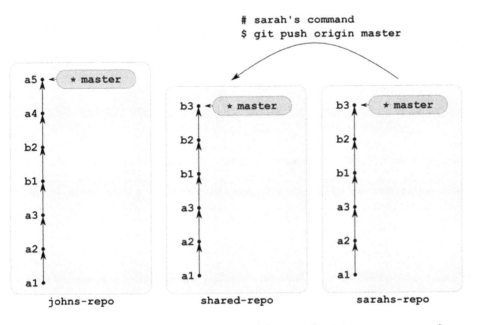

Figure 10-9. *The repositories after Sarah's successful $ git push origin master command*

Now John wants to send his work to shared-repo with:

```
# john's command
$ git push origin master
```

Git refuses to push his commits because johns-repo was out of date. The output of the above command contains the following message:

```
! [rejected]        master -> master (fetch first)
```

Git informs John that his push was rejected and that he has to fetch the missing revisions first. To update his local master branch, John runs the following command:

```
# john's command
$ git pull origin master
```

The pull command fetched Sarah's b3 revision and performed a merge operation. Now the repositories look like Figure 10-10.

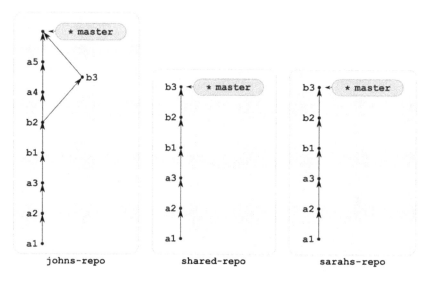

Figure 10-10. *The repositories after John's $ git pull origin master command*

John's $ `git pull origin master` command updated his repository with latest revision by Sarah, so John can now push his work into shared-repo with:

```
# john's command
$ git push origin master
```

Notice that John doesn't need the -u parameter when he pushes anymore as the tracking was already defined by John's first call to $ `git push -u`. The repositories look like Figure 10-11.

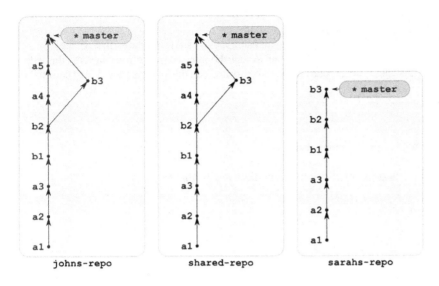

Figure 10-11. *The repositories after John's successful $ git push origin master command*

Finally, Sarah pulls John's work using:

```
# sarah's command
$ git pull origin master
```

The resulting repositories are shown in Figure 10-12.

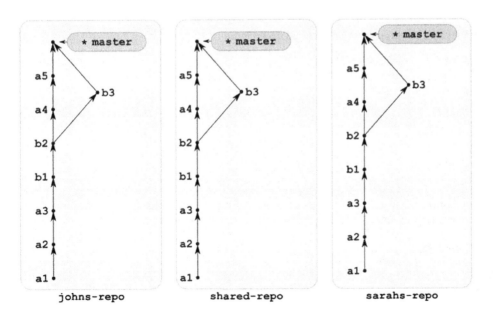

Figure 10-12. *The final state of the repositories from Recipe 10-2*

How It Works

Before we dive into the commands that were used to update the three repositories, let's start with the analysis of the contents of all three repositories shown in Figure 10-12. They all contain exactly the same commits. You can verify this with the $ git log command. Enter the git-recipes/10-02/johns-repo directory and run the following $ git log command:

```
$ cd git-recipes/10-02/johns-repo
$ git log --oneline
```

You will obtain an output similar to the one shown in Listing 10-1.

Listing 10-1. The output of $ git log --oneline executed in johns-repo from Figure 10-12

```
515710e Merge branch 'master' of ../shared-repo
596e379 b3
5d11316 a5
2f46c63 a4
82d0a6b b2
6075835 b1
73e4416 a3
44fc529 a2
c8e56d1 a1
```

Repeat similar commands for Sarah's repository:

```
$ cd git-recipes/10-02/sarahs-repo
$ git log --oneline
```

The above command will print the output shown in Listing 10-2.

Listing 10-2. The output of $ git log --oneline run in sarahs-repo from Figure 10-12

```
515710e Merge branch 'master' of ../shared-repo
596e379 b3
5d11316 a5
2f46c63 a4
82d0a6b b2
6075835 b1
73e4416 a3
44fc529 a2
c8e56d1 a1
```

Although the actual SHA-1 printed on your screen will be different you should notice that both outputs are exactly the same. As you can guess the output of $ git log executed in shared-repo from Figure 10-12:

```
$ cd git-recipes/10-02/shared-repo
$ git log --oneline
```

also will be identical. The three databases stored in: johns-repo/.git/objects, sarahs-repo/.git/objects, and shared-repo/.git/objects contain exactly the same objects. This is proved by the fact that the SHA-1 names returned by $ git log in all three repositories are the same.

In other words when you send or receive revisions with $ git push or $ git pull, git copies the database entries between the repositories. This is contrary to the $ git rebase, $ git cherry-pick, and $ git commit --amend commands. When you work in your local repository there is no method to copy the existing revision—all you can do is to create a new database object with a new SHA-1 name. On the other hand, during the $ git push and $ git pull commands the revisions are copied not recommitted. The copied object has the same SHA-1 as the original.

In this recipe we used two commands to send and receive revisions to and from the remote repository:

- $ git push—sends the revisions from local to remote
- $ git pull—downloads the revisions from remote to local and then merges them with appropriate branch

These commands were used with the two parameters:

```
$ git push origin master
$ git pull origin master
```

In both cases origin is the name of the remote and master is the name of the local branch.

The first command, $ git push origin master, sends the local branch to the remote repository. To be more accurate, we can say that the command sends the missing revisions from the local repository to the remote end and then updates the branches (remote branch and remote tracking branch—we will discuss this soon).

When John executes $ git push origin master for repositories in Figure 10-2, first git copies three revisions a1, a2, a3 from the database in johns-repo to the database in shared-repo, and then updates the branches.

By default, git restricts the $ git push operation to fast-forward cases. This means that $ git push succeeds only when the remote branch can be fast-forwarded with your work. This is the case when John changes the state from Figure 10-2 into the state shown in Figure 10-3. The repository shared-repo in Figure 10-2 is empty; therefore it can safely receive the three commits a1, a2, and a3. The same will happen when Sara changes repositories from Figure 10-5 into the repositories shown in Figure 10-6. The repository shared-repo shown in Figure 10-5 contains the revisions a1, a2, and a3. It doesn't contain the revisions b1 and b2, which are ahead of a3 in sarahs-repo. The master branch in shared-repo can be fast-forwarded with the b1 and b2 revisions, therefore the operation succeeds.

The situation shown in Figure 10-9 is much more complicated. The master branches in the shared repository and in John's repository have diverged. John's contains a4 and a5 and the shared repository contains b3. Thus $ git push origin master executed by John in the repository shown in Figure 10-9 fails. Git prints the information that John needs to fetch the revisions from the remote repository first.

When used with -u parameter, the $ git push command stores the information about tracking. The command:

```
$ git push -u origin master
```

executed by John when he pushed his a1, a2, and a3 revisions created in John's repository the remote tracking branch remotes/origin/master. The master branch was set as a local tracking branch for origin/master branch. You need this parameter only in the very first call to $ git push.

The new command used in this repository is $ git pull origin master. This command copies the revisions from the remote repository pointed by origin. The revisions are copied from the remote master branch and then merged with the current master branch in the local repository. If the operation can be performed as a fast-forward then there is no merge commit. This is the case when you changed the state shown in Figure 10-6 into a state shown in Figure 10-7. When local and remote branches diverged, then the command generates a merge commit. That's why we have the merge commits shown at the top of Listings 10-1 and 10-2. The merge commit appeared in johns-repo when you changed its state shown in Figure 10-9 into the state shown in Figure 10-10.

How committing affects tracking branches

We again analyze how tracking branches change during a commit from the perspective of Sarah's repo. Right after
`$ git clone shared-repo sarahs-repo` the repositories shared-repo and sarahs-repo look like Figure 10-13.

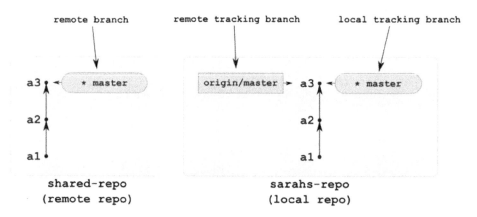

Figure 10-13. *Both shared-repo and sarahs-repo right after cloning*

We are watching this situation from Sarah's perspective. Thus sarahs-repo is the local repository, and shared-repo is the remote repository, as labeled in Figure 10-13. The figure presents three types of branches: remote branch, local tracking branch, and remote tracking branch. Sarah's repository doesn't contain any ordinary local branches. When Sarah clones the repository, the `$ git clone` command automatically creates two local branches for her: master and origin/master. The first is a local tracking branch; the second is a remote tracking branch. You can verify this with the `$ git branch -a -vv` command. The output would contain two important lines:

```
* master                36c7205 [origin/master] a3
  remotes/origin/master 36c7205 a3
```

The first line says that the master is a local tracking branch for origin/master branch. The second line says that origin/master is a remote branch.

When Sarah commits with `$ git simple-commit b1 b2` she moves her master branch (i.e., local tracking branch) forward. The state of the branches after `$ git simple-commit b1 b2` is shown in Figure 10-14.

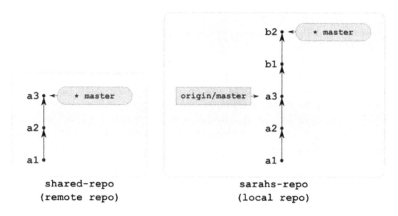

Figure 10-14. *The state of the branches after $ git simple-commit b1 b2 executed in sarahs-repo shown in Figure 10-13*

You can verify the state of Sarah's repository with the $ git log --oneline --decorate command. The output:

```
b019 (HEAD, master) b2
978f b1
66ad (origin/master, origin/HEAD) a3
91d5 a2
b189 a1
```

contains the labels master and origin/master that point to the appropriate revisions. Short abbreviated information about the state of the branches also can be achieved with the $ git status -sb command. When executed in sarahs-repo in Figure 10-14, this command would produce the following output:

```
## master...origin/master [ahead 2]
```

This informs you that your local tracking branch contains two revisions that have not been included in the remote tracking branch. In other words: the local tracking branch master is two revisions ahead of the remote tracking branch origin/master.

As you can see the commit operation moves only the local tracking branch forward. The remote tracking branch and remote branch are left intact.

How pushing affects the tracking branches

How do we update the remote branch master in shared-repo and the remote tracking branch origin/master in Sarah's repository? This is done when Sarah pushes her commits with the $ git push origin master command. This command changes the state of the two repositories as shown in Figure 10-15. Figure 10-15 presents the results of executing $ git push origin master in sarahs-repo in the state shown in Figure 10-14.

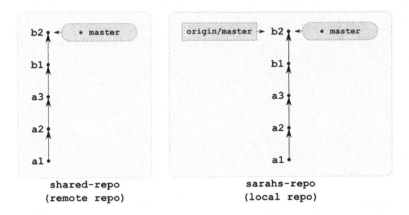

Figure 10-15. *The state of the repositories from Figure 10-14 after the $ git push origin master command executed in sarahs-repo*

You should notice that to decide which revisions should be sent, git has to find only the difference between the two branches master and origin/master in Sarah's repository. Thanks to the two dots discussed in Recipe 7-2 this can be done with the $ git log --oneline origin/master..master command. This command prints the list of revisions that are included in the master and excluded from origin/master.

■ **Hint** Please remember that remote tracking branches, such as origin/master, can be used in git commits in the same manner as ordinary local branches. For example, the command $ git branch foo origin/master~3 creates a new ordinary local branch named foo that points to the same revision as the grand-grand parent of origin/master.

To summarize, pushing updates the branches in the following way:

- In the local repository remote—the tracking branch is updated to the most recent revision in the local tracking branch

- In the remote repository—the remote branch is updated to the most recent revision in the local tracking branch

What happens if the push operation fails? If John executes $ git push origin master in his repository as shown in Figure 10-9, then the push is rejected with the following message:

```
! [rejected]        master -> master (fetch first)
```

and all the branches remain unchanged.

How pulling affects tracking branches

This time we are watching the change from John's perspective. Therefore johns-repo is the local repository and shared-repo is the remote repository.

When you pull from the remote repository, then your local tracking branch and remote tracking branch are updated. The remote branch remains unchanged. The first case (without a merge) is depicted in Figures 10-16 and 10-17. Figure 10-16 presents the state just before a pull operation. The shared repository contains two revisions b1 and b2 that are not included in johns-repo. The pull operation brings these revisions into johns-repo and updates the branches to the state shown in Figure 10-17.

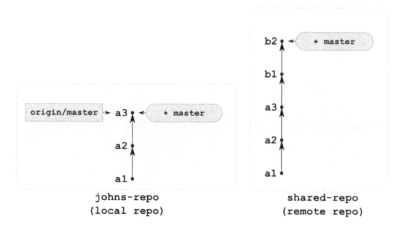

Figure 10-16. *John's repository before the $ git pull origin master command*

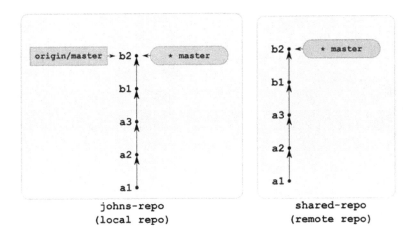

johns-repo
(local repo)

shared-repo
(remote repo)

Figure 10-17. *John's repository after the $ git pull origin master command executed in johns-repo as shown in Figure 10-16*

Figures 10-18 and 10-19 illustrate the second case. This is a fast-forward operation. If a merge occurs during $ git pull origin master, the local tracking branch master and the remote tracking branch origin/master change in exactly the same manner. They will point to the auto-generated merge commit, as shown in Figures 10-18 and 10-19.

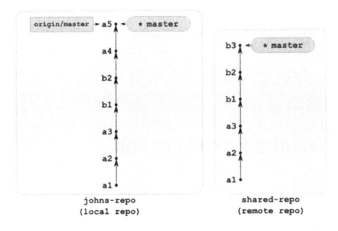

johns-repo
(local repo)

shared-repo
(remote repo)

Figure 10-18. *The master branches in shared-repo and johns-repo diverged*

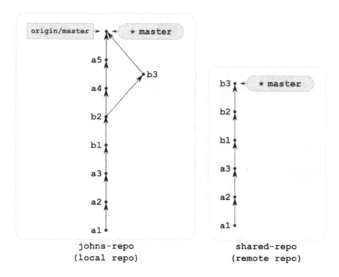

Figure 10-19. *The result of $ git pull origin master issued in johns-repo shown in Figure 10-18*

To summarize, the pull operation updates the local tracking branch and remote tracking branch and leaves the remote branch unchanged.

■ **Hint**   Remember: A remote branch is a branch in the remote repository. A remote tracking branch is a local branch that is used as a link between your work and the contents of the remote repository. All types of branches are clearly presented in Figure 5-7.

10-3. Generating (n-1) merge commits for one commit
Problem

You want to check what the history may look like if the project is realized by n developers using Recipe 10-2. To do this you need to simulate the work of three developers: John, Sarah, and Peter. You have to commit in three different repositories: johns-repo, sarahs-repo, peters-repo in parallel. Then you will need to synchronize all the repositories. As you will see, the history generated by the $ git pull commands will contain a large number of superfluous merge commits. In the worst case scenario one commit can generate up to n-1 merge commits, where n is the number of developers involved.

Solution

Create a new directory with:

```
$ cd git-recipes
$ mkdir 10-03
$ cd 10-03
```

and then initialize a project with:

```
# the command issued in git-recipes/10-03 directory
$ git init --bare shared-repo
```

Next, John initializes his repository, creates an initial commit, and pushes it to the shared-repo:

```
# commands issued in git-recipes/10-03 directory
$ git clone shared-repo johns-repo
$ cd johns-repo
$ git simple-commit "Initial commit"
$ git push -u origin master
```

Then the two other developers create their repositories with:

```
# commands issued in git-recipes/10-03 directory
$ git clone shared-repo sarahs-repo
$ git clone shared-repo peters-repo
```

Now, all of the developers are ready to commit. In this recipe all of the developers work in parallel. Every one of them creates his or her commits:

```
# command issued in johns-repo
$ git simple-commit "The first commit by John"
```

```
# command issued in sarahs-repo
$ git simple-commit "The first commit by Sara"
```

```
# command issued in peters-repo
$ git simple-commit "The first commit by Peter"
```

Now, they want to share their work.

John is the first to push his changes to the central repository:

```
# command issued in johns-repo
$ git push origin master
```

and then Sarah and Peter pull their work:

```
# command issued in sarahs-repo
$ git pull --edit origin master
```

```
# command issued in peters-repo
$ git pull --edit origin master
```

They both enter the merge message. Sarah types "Sarah merges...", and Peter types "Peter merges...".
Now, Sarah pushes her work with:

```
# command issued in sarahs-repo
$ git push origin master
```

and then Peter tries to push:

```
# command issued in peters-repo
$ git push origin master
```

This push is rejected, so Peter merges the latest changes in shared-repo:

```
# command issued in peters-repo
$ git pull --edit origin master
```

Peter types the message for a merge commit as "Peter merges again..." and then he pushes his work with:

```
# command issued in peters-repo
$ git push origin master
```

The recipe is finished when John and Sara both pull the changes made by Peter:

```
# command issued in johns-repo
$ git pull origin master
```

```
# command issued in sarahs-repo
$ git pull origin master
```

Now, all four repositories contain the history presented in Listing 10-3. The listing shows the output of the $ git log --graph --oneline command executed in any of the four repositories.

Listing 10-3. The history created in Recipe 10-3

```
*   901f9b1 Peter merges again...
|\
| *   70984f8 Sarah merges...
| |\
| * | ebf6fff The first commit by Sarah
* | |   192af3a Peter merges...
|\ \ \
| | | /
| |/|
| * | 4721211 The first commit by John
| |/
* | 4314f0a The first commit by Peter
|/
* ebb21d1 Initial commit
```

How It Works

The purpose of this recipe is very simple: I want to convince you that the solution presented in Recipe 10-2 is not a pattern you should follow. The history created with the $ git pull origin master command will be very difficult to read. Recipe 10-3 shows you that if a group of n developers work in parallel and every developer creates exactly one commit, then the commit made by the first developer will generate n-1 merge commits.

In our recipe the commit "The first commit by John" generated two merges:

```
70984f8 Sarah merges...
192af3a Peter merges...
```

It is easy to realize that if the group consisted of n developers we would get n-1 merge commits.

Take a look at Listing 10-3. The history shown was generated by only three commits: one per developer. If your team consists of greater number of developers who commit regularly then the command $ git pull origin master will produce a very complicated graph of revisions with an enormous number of superfluous merge commits.

▪ **Hint**   If you consider a clean history important you should treat Recipe 10-2 as a pattern not to be followed.

10-4. Keeping the history linear
Problem

You want to organize the work of your team consisting of an arbitrary number of developers. Every developer will use his or her own repository. They will share their work using a central repository. The setting is identical to Recipe 10-2.

This time you want to define a workflow that will guarantee a linear structure of the master branch in all repositories. Merge commits are not allowed and should not appear in any repository.

To keep the history linear all team members need to rebase their work on top of the updated remote tracking branch.

Solution

Create a new directory with:

```
$ cd git-recipes
$ mkdir 10-04
$ cd 10-04
```

and then initialize a project with:

```
# the command issued in git-recipes/10-04 directory
$ git init --bare shared-repo
```

Now John initializes his repository, creates an initial commit, and pushes it to shared-repo:

```
# commands issued in git-recipes/10-04 directory
$ git clone shared-repo johns-repo
$ cd johns-repo
$ git simple-commit i1 i2
$ git push -u origin master
```

Then the next developer, Mark, joins the team:

```
# commands issued in git-recipes/10-04 directory
$ git clone shared-repo marks-repo
```

Right now johns-repo, shared-repo, and marks-repo contain the same commits i1 and i2. The $ git status -sb command prints only the name of the current branch master. All repositories are clean and the branches are synchronized. The state of all repositories is shown in Figure 10-20.

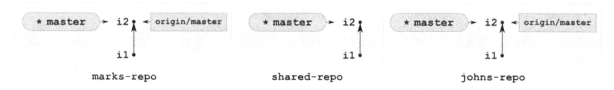

Figure 10-20. *Initial state of all three repositories in Recipe 10-4*

John and Mark work in parallel

John and Mark are working in parallel. John creates three commits j1, j2, j3 and Mark creates two commits m1, m2:

```
# command issued in johns-repo
$ git simple-commit j1 j2 j3

# command issued in marks-repo
$ git simple-commit m1 m2
```

Right now, the command executed in John's repo:

```
# command issued in johns-repo
$ git status -sb
```

prints the following information:

```
## master...origin/master [ahead 3]
```

It means that John's master branch contains three revisions that are not included in his origin/master tracking branch. The same command executed in Mark's repository:

```
# command issued in marks-repo
$ git status -sb
```

outputs:

```
## master...origin/master [ahead 2]
```

The master branch in marks-repo contains two revisions that are not included in Mark's origin/master tracking branch.

The state of all three repositories is shown in Figure 10-21.

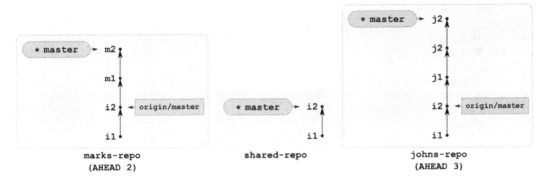

Figure 10-21. *The state in which John's master branch is ahead three, and Mark's master branch is ahead two*

John successfully uploads his work to the shared repository

Now the developers want to share their work. John is the first to push his changes to the central repository:

```
# command issued in johns-repo
$ git push origin master
```

John's command succeeds. When John runs $ git status -sb again the output doesn't contain [ahead: 3] anymore. His master branch is fully synchronized with his origin/master branch right now.

Mark resolves the problem of divergent branches

The shared repository has changed because John has uploaded his revisions. But Mark doesn't know about it. His command $ git status -sb returns exactly the same information as before: [ahead 2]. Keep in mind that this information concerns only Mark's local branches. They have not updated as of yet. Mark's repository and shared repository now look like Figure 10-22. Mark doesn't have John's revisions j1, j2, and j3 in his repository.

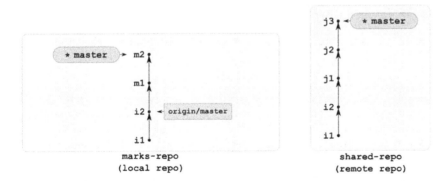

Figure 10-22. *John has successfully pushed his j1, j2, j3 revisions to the shared repo and therefore Mark can not push his m1, m2 revisions*

Mark wants to push his work with:

```
# command issued in marks-repo
$ git push -u origin master
```

but this operation is rejected because the push is not a fast-forward.

Mark needs to update his master branch. He first fetches the latest revisions from the shared repository:

```
# command issued in marks-repo
$ git fetch origin
```

To check the state of his repository Mark runs the $ git status -sb command. It prints:

```
## master...origin/master [ahead 2, behind 3]
```

Now Mark knows that his master and origin/master master branches have diverged. The [ahead 2] informs him that Marks's master branch contains two revisions that are not included in his origin/master branch. The [behind 3] is printed because Mark's master branch misses the three revisions included in his origin/master branch.

Using $ git log --graph --all --oneline --decorate Mark can visualize that his master branch and his origin/master branch diverged. The state of Mark's repository and the shared repositories is presented in Figure 10-23.

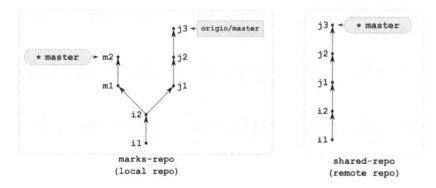

Figure 10-23. *The state of Mark's repo after $ git fetch origin*

To keep the history linear Mark rebases his master branch on top of his origin/master branch fetched from shared repository:

```
# command issued in marks-repo
$ git rebase origin/master master
```

Now the history of Mark's master branch is linear and his rebased revisions m1', m2', and m3' are on top. Mark wants to be sure so he runs either the $ git log --graph --oneline --decorate or $ gitk --all & command. The state of the repositories is shown in Figure 10-24.

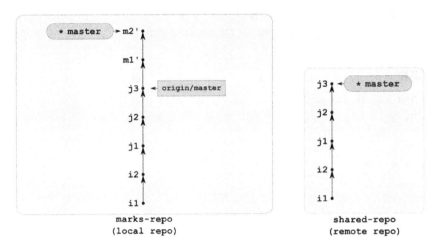

Figure 10-24. *Mark's repo after $ git rebase origin/master master*

The command $ `git status -sb` executed in marks-repo as shown in Figure 10-24 prints:

```
## master...origin/master [ahead 2]
```

The behind message disappeared because Mark's master branch now includes all revisions from his origin/master branch.

When in the [ahead 3] state Mark can push his work to shared repository:

```
# command issued in marks-repo
$ git push -u origin master
```

This time push is accepted. It transforms the shared repository as shown in Figure 10-25.

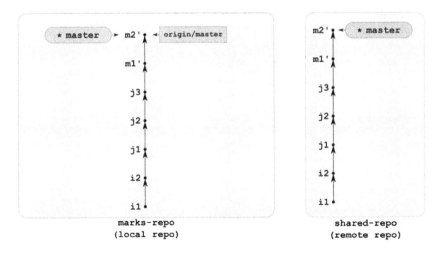

Figure 10-25. *The marks-repo and shared-repo after a successful $ git push -u origin master executed by Mark*

Mark's work is done. There is no ahead or behind message in the output of $ git status -sb. It means that the master and origin/master branches in Mark's repo are synchronized.

John downloads Mark's work

Right now John's repo and the shared repo look like Figure 10-26.

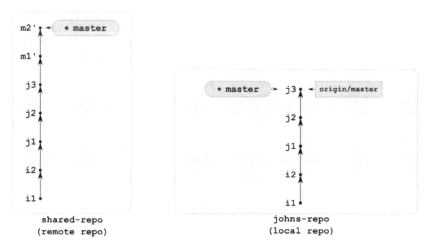

Figure 10-26. *Shared-repo and johns-repo before John's $ git fetch command*

Mark's work can be fetched by John with the following command:

```
# command issued in johns-repo
$ git fetch
```

This command will transform the repositories shown in Figure 10-26 into the form shown in Figure 10-27.

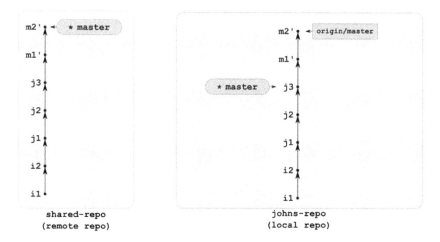

Figure 10-27. *John's repo after his $ git fetch command*

When John's repository is in the state shown in Figure 10-27, then the $ git status -sb command prints:

```
## master...origin/master [behind 2]
```

Therefore, John's master branch misses two revisions included in his origin/master branch. John can fast-forward his branch with the following command:

```
# command issued in johns-repo
$ git rebase
```

The repository shown in Figure 10-27 is transformed with John's $ git rebase command into the state shown in Figure 10-28. The history of all repositories is linear.

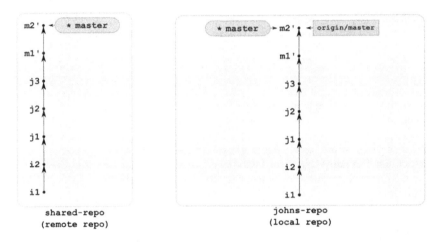

Figure 10-28. *John's repo after his $ git rebase command*

How It Works

Git fetch command performs two operations:

- It copies the objects from a remote database to a local one.
- It updates remote tracking branches.

It doesn't update the local tracking branches, however. There are two interesting cases:

- When after the command $ git fetch is run, local branches can be updated in a fast-forward mode.
- When after the command $ git fetch is run, local branches are diverged.

When executed in the repository johns-repo shown in Figure 10-26, the $ git fetch command would give the effect shown in Figure 10-27. This is a fast-forward case. In this case the $ git status -sb command prints:

```
## master...origin/master [behind 2]
```

This means that the local tracking branch master misses two revisions that are included in the remote tracking branch origin/master.

The case of diverged branches is shown in Figure 10-23. The command $ git fetch executed in marks-repo shown in Figure 10-22 produces the result shown in Figure 10-23. This time the output of $ git status -sb would be:

```
## master...origin/master [ahead 2, behind 3]
```

Therefore, the local tracking branch is two revisions ahead and three revisions behind the remote tracking branch.

Rebasing the local tracking branch onto the remote tracking branch

Remote tracking branches, such as origin/master, are local branches. They can be used in the same manner as ordinary local branches. Therefore, to keep a history linear we can use the $ git rebase command as discussed in Recipe 7-1. The command $ git rebase origin/master master issued in marks-repo from Figure 10-23 will produce the effect shown in Figure 10-24.

If you set tracking for the master branch then the command $ git rebase origin/master master can be simplified to:

```
$ git rebase
```

It performs the rebasing of your current local tracking branch on top of its remote tracking branch.

You also can use the $ git pull command to achieve the same result. By default the command $ git pull is executed as $ git fetch followed by $ git merge. Although changing this behavior you could use the -r flag or configuration settings. The command $ git pull -r is equivalent to $ git fetch followed by $ git rebase.

Remember that the $ git fetch command updates your local database and remote tracking branches. It never influences your local tracking branches or your ordinary local branches. Therefore, you can safely run $ git fetch at any time. It will never cause you any trouble.

Messages [ahead x] and [behind y]

As you have already seen the relation between the local tracking branch and the remote tracking branch can be checked with the $ git status -sb command. In a case where the local tracking branch and the remote tracking branch point to different revisions, the output of this command contains sections [ahead N, behind M], as in:

```
## master...origin/master [ahead 2]
## master...origin/master [behind 2]
## master...origin/master [ahead 2, behind 1]
```

The [ahead 2] message indicates that the local tracking branch is two revisions ahead of the remote tracking branch. This is a state you will obtain after committing in the local tracking branch.

The [behind 2] message indicates you that your local tracking branch is behind the remote tracking branch. Your local tracking branch misses two revisions available in remote tracking branch. You are in this state when some member of your team pushes his or her commits to the shared repository and you download them to your repository with the $ git fetch command.

The final message, [ahead 2, behind 1] means that the local tracking branch and the remote tracking branch have diverged. The local tracking branch contains two revisions that are not in the remote tracking branch and at the same time it has missed one revision contained in the remote tracking branch. You obtained this state after the $ git commit and $ git fetch commands, assuming that someone pushed to the shared repository.

Accessing remote branches

Remember that the $ git status -sb and $ git branch -a -vv commands only work with your local branches. These are: ordinary local branches, local tracking branches, and remote tracking branches. The commands $ git status and $ git branch do not access the remote branches in the remote repository. The remote branches are only transferred to your repository during $ git fetch. Therefore, if you want to inspect the remote end you will need to run $ git fetch followed by $ git status -sb or $ git branch -a -vv. But no matter how fast you are, the result of $ git status -sb or $ git branch -a -vv can be outdated in the sense that someone could have pushed to the remote repository after you fetched and before you executed $ git status -sb or $ git branch -a -vv.

Why tracking branches matter

You should have noticed that $ git status -sb always compares the local tracking branch and the remote tracking branch. This comparison is performed for your current branch. To get the [ahead N, behind M] output of $ git status -sb, you need to define the tracking for your current branch. If there are no [branch"..."] entries in your configuration file .git/config, such as:

```
[branch "master"]
    remote = origin
    merge = refs/heads/master
```

then git doesn't know which branches to compare. The output of $ git status -sb would not contain [ahead N, behind M] information.

When you clone a repository, git automatically configures tracking for your master branch. Git also sets the tracking when you pass to checkout command the name of the remote branch—as $ git checkout doc in Recipe 5-2. Otherwise, you have to set up tracking manually. Here are some different solutions to achieve it:

- $ git branch --set-upstream-to=origin/master command (as shown in the hint in Recipe 10-1)

- $ git push -u origin master command (as shown in the hint in Recipe 10-2)

- $ git config branch commands (as shown in the hint in Recipe 10-1)

- Manually editing the .git/config file

Once set, the tracking information can be used to simplify many commands. If you are currently on the master branch that was set to track the origin/master branch, then the three commands $ git rebase, $ git rebase origin/master, and $ git rebase origin/master master are equivalent.

Basically, there are two reasons to define tracking branches:

- The $ git status -sb command can be used together with $ git fetch to ascertain if your branch is synchronized with the remote branch.

- Many commands can be simplified as missing parameters—as in $ git rebase—to default to tracking branches.

10-5. Coworking without a central repository
Problem

You want to simulate the cooperation of two developers John and Sarah without a central repository. In this case the coworking will be organized with two repositories:

- 10-05/johns-repo—a non-bare repository of the first developer

- 10-05/sarahs-repo—a non-bare repository of the second developer

Both developers will commit within their master branches. John will use the sarah branch to fetch Sarah's work and Sarah will use the john branch to fetch John's work.

▪ **Hint** This recipe underlines the distributed nature of git where everyone can cooperate with each other.

Solution

Create a new directory with:

```
$ cd git-recipes
$ mkdir 10-05
$ cd 10-05
```

The work is initialized by one of the developers. Let it be John. He initializes his repository:

```
# john's commands in git-recipes/10-05 directory
$ git init johns-repo
```

Then he sets his personal data:

```
# john's commands
$ cd johns-repo
$ git config --local user.name john
$ git config --local user.email john@example.net
```

and commits:

```
# john's command
$ git simple-commit j1 j2 j3
```

Now Sarah enters the project. She clones johns-repo and configures her personal information:

```
# sarah's commands
# executed in git-recipes/10-05
$ git clone johns-repo sarahs-repo
$ cd sarahs-repo
$ git config --local user.name sarah
$ git config --local user.email sarah@example.net
```

Next Sarah contributes to the project with two revisions s1 and s2:

```
# sarah's command
$ git simple-commit s1 s2
```

When the commits are ready to be fetched, Sarah emails John about her s1 s2 revisions. To get them John needs to set up the remote repository and the local tracking branch. John runs:

```
# john's command
$ git remote add origin ../sarahs-repo
```

Then, he fetches the remote branches from Sarah's repository as remote tracking branches into his repository with $ git fetch. The command creates the origin/master remote tracking branch that is not related in any way to the local master branch in John's repository. You can check it with $ git branch -a -vv. The line concerning his master branch doesn't contain the [origin/master] part. It looks like:

```
* master            abc123f s2
```

It proves that it is still an ordinary branch because the local tracking branches contain [origin/master], as in:

```
* master            abc123f [origin/master] s2
```

Next John creates an ordinary local branch named sarah with:

```
# john's command run in 10-05/johns-repo
$ git branch sarah
```

and he configures his sarah branch as a local tracking branch for the origin/master branch:

```
# john's command
$ git branch --set-upstream-to=origin/master sarah
```

To check the code written by Sarah in s1 and s2 revisions, John goes to the sarah branch with:

```
# john's command
$ git checkout sarah
```

The branch doesn't contain s1 and s2 revisions yet, as proved by:

```
# john's command
$ git status -sb
```

The output informs you that his current branch (sarah) is two commits behind its remote tracking branch (which is origin/master). John updates his sarah branch with:

```
# john's command
$ git rebase
```

Now the sarah branch in John's repository contains s1 and s2 revisions. John can analyze Sarah's contributions. When he decides that these modifications are okay, he can merge them into his own work with:

```
# john's commands
$ git checkout master
$ git rebase sarah
```

Now it is time for John to author some more revisions. He runs $ git simple-commit j4 j5 j6. Then he emails Sarah about his work.

It's Sarah's turn to download the code contributed by John in revisions j4, j5, and j6. She began her work with the $ git clone command, thus her repository already contains the .git/config entry that sets her master branch as the local tracking branch for origin/master remote tracking branch. You can check it with $ git branch -a -vv command. It outputs:

```
* master                40695ac [origin/master] s2
  remotes/origin/master 604549f j3
```

The fragment [origin/master] says that the master branch is a local tracking branch for origin/master remote tracking branch. To remove this relation Sarah runs:

```
# sarah's command
$ git config --unset branch.master.remote
$ git config --unset branch.master.merge
```

After the above commands the $ git branch -a -vv outputs:

```
* master                40695ac s2
  remotes/origin/master 604549f j3
```

Although her repository still contains the remote tracking branch named origin/master, her local master branch is not connected with it. The two $ git config --unset commands turned her local tracking branch named master into an ordinary local branch. That's good.

Now Sarah wants to create her local tracking branch named john to be connected with John's master branch. She runs:

```
# sarah's command
$ git branch john
$ git branch --set-upstream-to=origin/master john
```

Then she fetches from John's repository with $ git fetch. The command fetches all the missing revisions from the master branch in John's repo as well as a new remote tracking branch remotes/origin/sarah. Sarah doesn't need John's origin/sarah branch, but there is no way to avoid it.

Next Sarah switches to the john branch and checks its status:

```
# sarah's command
$ git checkout john
$ git status -sb
```

The output says that the current branch (john) is three commits behind the remote tracking branch (which is origin/master). She updates her john branch with:

```
$ git rebase
```

She inspects John's revisions j4, j5, j6. Then she merges John's work into her master branch:

```
$ git rebase john master
```

How does John update his project?

To download and merge all of Sarah's code John runs following commands:

```
$ git fetch
$ git checkout sarah
$ git rebase
$ git rebase sarah master
```

How does a developer contribute to the project?

Every developer contributes by committing in his or her master branch:

```
$ git checkout master
$ git simple-commit x y z
```

How does Sarah download John's contributions?

She follows the procedure *How does John update his project?* using the john branch name instead of sarah:

```
$ git fetch
$ git checkout john
$ git rebase
$ git rebase john master
```

How It Works

This recipe emphasizes the distributed nature of git. As you can see, every repository can be used as a source of revisions. You can fetch from every repository you have access to. Git doesn't restrict fetch to some special central repositories, as in shared-repo in Recipe 10-2, stored on a server. The push operation is restricted by default to bare repositories, but we can also circumvent this restriction. It will be done in Recipe 10-10.

If you follow the recipe carefully, you will notice that the $ git fetch operation creates remote tracking branches for all the branches in the remote repository. When you finish the recipe, John's repository contains following branches (as returned by $ git branch -a -vv):

```
* master               542d21a z
  sarah                bacddd0 [origin/master] j6
  remotes/origin/john  bacddd0 j6
  remotes/origin/master bacddd0 j6
```

There are two remote branches origin/master and origin/john. The second is a remote tracking branch for the remote john branch created by Sarah in sarahs-repo. John doesn't need or use it, but it is created anyway. As a conclusion remember that $ git fetch fetches all of the remote branches and stores them as remote tracking branches.

This procedure also showed you that you can convert a local tracking branch named some-branch into ordinary local branches with:

```
$ git config --unset branch.some-branch.remote
$ git config --unset branch.some-branch.merge
```

10-6. Working with remote branches
Problem

You and your colleagues want to use a shared repository with many branches, not just a master branch. It will give you the opportunity to restructure the team into small groups working on separate features. To work on a specific feature named foo of your project you want to create a remote branch named foo stored in shared repository. Developers who work on the foo feature should use the foo remote branch to share their work.

This recipe provides you with all the commands you will need to work with remote branches. You will learn how to:

- Create a remote branch with the identical name as the local branch

- Create a remote branch with a different name than local branch

- Remove a remote branch

- Update your repository to reflect the changes in the remote branches

Solution

Create a new directory and initialize a shared repository:

```
$ cd git-recipes
$ mkdir 10-06
$ cd 10-06
$ git init --bare shared-repo
```

Next create a repository for John, create an initial revision, and send it to the shared-repo:

```
$ git clone shared-repo johns-repo
$ cd johns-repo
$ git simple-commit "Initial commit"
$ git push -u origin master
```

Then create a repository for Sarah:

```
$ git clone shared-repo sarahs-repo
```

Let's assume that John is the leader. He is responsible for setting tasks for all team members. He decides that some of the team's members (including Sarah) will work on documentation. The work will be done in a branch named doc. For this purpose, John creates in his repository a new ordinary local branch named doc:

```
# john's command
$ git branch doc
```

Then John makes the branch available for other developers. He pushes his doc branch into shared-repo with:

```
# john's command
$ git push -u origin doc
```

The -u the above command sets the tracking in johns-repo for the doc branch. After the above command, shared-repo contains the doc branch. You can verify it running:

```
# shared-repo's command
$ git branch
```

Next, John wants to start the work on a specific unit test. He creates an ordinary local branch named test:

```
# john's command
$ git branch test
```

He is aware that this name may already be in use by many team members for their own private work that not related to unit tests in any way. Therefore John decides that the remote branch should be named special-unit-tests. He pushes his local test branch under the name special-unit-tests with the following command:

```
# john's command
$ git push -u origin test:special-unit-test
```

The above command creates a remote branch named special-unit-test in the remote repository aliased by origin. Check it with:

```
# shared-repo's command
$ git branch
```

Let's suppose that Sarah is assigned to work on documentation and tests. She fetches from the remote with:

```
# sarah's command
$ git fetch
```

This command creates remote tracking branches origin/doc and origin/special-unit-tests in sarahs-repo.

Some time has passed and the work in the doc and special-unit-tests remote branches has passed smoothly. The members used Recipe 10-4 to synchronize their work.

John downloaded the most recent revisions from doc branch. He decides that the group work is finished. The remote doc branch should be deleted. John deletes remote doc branch with:

```
# john's command
$ git push origin :doc
```

The above command performed the following operations:

- It deleted doc branch in shared-repo.

- It deleted remote the tracking branch origin/doc in johns-repo.

- It didn't convert the local tracking branch doc in johns-repo into ordinary local branch, however. The doc branch in johns-repo is still tracking a nonexistent origin/doc remote tracking branch. You can verify this with the $ git branch -avv command.

■ **Hint** What is the difference between a local tracking branch and an ordinary local branch? You can commit in both of them, of course. But a local tracking branch is connected to a remote tracking branch; therefore, you can use $ git status -sb to check if a local tracking branch is ahead or behind of a corresponding remote tracking branch.

Therefore, shared-repo doesn't contain the doc branch anymore. The command $ git branch executed in shared-repo prints two branches: master and special-unit-tests. In John's repository, however, the branch doc still exists—it is an ordinary local branch.

Sarah updates her remote branches with:

```
# sarah's command
$ git fetch
```

However, the above command doesn't remove the remote tracking branch origin/doc for a nonexistent remote branch doc in shared-repo. If Sarah wants to update her repository in such a way that it reflects deleted remote branches she needs the following command:

```
# sarah's command
$ git remote prune origin
```

The above command deletes the remote tracking branch origin/doc in Sarah's repository. This operation can be performed automatically during fetch with an additional -p flag:

```
# sarah's command
$ git fetch -p
```

Now the work on doc branch is finished. There is no remote branch doc in the shared repository or in any other member's repository other than John's. John is the leader and he is responsible for the integration of the doc branch into the master branch. He can use any method that was discussed in chapters 6 and 7. For example, he can merge the doc branch into the master branch in such a way that it forms a bulb. The exact procedure was presented in Recipe 7-6. Once he integrates the doc branch into the master branch John pushes the master branch containing the doc branch into the shared repository. This is done exactly as in Recipe 10-4 and maybe (if John needs to rebase the bulb) with Recipe 7-9.

John can restrict the access to remote branches using gitolite, as discussed in Recipe 11-10.

How It Works

The command:

```
$ git push [remote-name] [branch-name]
```

creates the remote branch named `branch-name` in the repository aliased by `remote-name`. To succeed, the branch `branch-name` has to exist in the repository where you are working. It doesn't have to be your current branch, however. If you want to push your current branch you can use:

```
$ git push [remote-name] HEAD
```

Used for an ordinary local branch without -u, as in:

```
$ git push origin doc
```

the command performs three actions:

- It creates a remote tracking branch `origin/doc` in the local repository.

- It creates a remote branch `doc` in remote repository.

- It sends the revisions required revisions from local database to the remote database.

If you use the -u flag then the ordinary local branch `doc` is converted into a local tracking branch for the remote tracking branch `origin/doc`.

This is how you can create a remote branch with the same name as one of your local branches. If you want to create a remote branch with different name then your local branch use the following syntax:

```
$ git push [remote-name] [local-branch-name]:[remote-branch-name]
```

The command:

```
$ git push origin foo:bar
```

sends the local branch named `foo` and stores it at the remote end under the `bar` name. The above command:

- Creates the remote branch `bar` in the remote repository

- Creates the remote tracking branch `origin/foo` in local repository

- Sets the local branch `foo` as a local tracking branch for the remote tracking branch `origin/foo`

If you want to remove a remote branch use:

```
$ git push [remote-name] :[remote-branch-to-remove]
```

as in:

```
$ git push origin :foo
```

The above command:

- Deletes the remote branch `foo` in `origin`

- Deletes the remote tracking branch `origin/foo` in your local repository

- It doesn't delete your local tracking branch `foo`.

- It doesn't convert the local tracking branch `foo` into an ordinary local branch; your local `foo` branch still tracks a nonexistent `origin/foo` branch.

You can delete your local branch with:

```
$ git branch -d foo
```

or you can change it into an ordinary local branch with:

```
$ git config --unset branch.foo.remote
$ git config --unset branch.foo.merge
```

Every time you run $ `git fetch` all the remote branches are copied into your repository as remote tracking branches. But if you remove a remote branch, then this change doesn't propagate among other developers, by default. Every developer can remove stale remote tracking branches with:

```
$ git remote prune origin
```

The above command removes all remote tracking branches for nonexistent remote branches. The same can be done during fetching with:

```
$ git fetch -p
```

The above command performs two operations:

```
$ git fetch
$ git remote prune
```

10-7. Using remote branches for contributions
Problem

You work as one of developers in a large project. To synchronize the work, the whole team uses a shared repository with remote branches. In this recipe we will use the following settings:

- 10-07/leaders-repo—a non-bare repository of a project's leader
- 10-07/johns-repo—your non-bare repository
- 10-07/shared-repo—a bare repository used for synchronization

You are responsible for the work on a new web interface. You plan to share your work with the team using a branch named new-web-interface. In particular, you want to:

- Create a local branch named new-web-interface
- Commit in your local branch new-web-interface
- Push your local new-web-interface to a shared repository to be review by the project leader

Solution

Create a new directory and initialize a leader's repository:

```
$ cd git-recipes
$ mkdir 10-07
$ cd 10-07
```

```
$ git init leaders-repo
$ cd leaders-repo
$ git simple-commit "Initial commit"
```

Next create a shared repository:

```
# command issued in git-recipes/10-07 directory
$ git clone --bare leaders-repo shared-repo
```

The leader needs to add the origin alias in his or her repository:

```
# command issued by leader in 10-07/leaders-repo directory
$ git remote add origin ../shared-repo
```

At this point you join the team:

```
# command issued in git-recipes/10-07 directory
$ git clone shared-repo johns-repo
```

Because we will copy the three repositories created in this recipe, John needs to redefine his origin to use relative path:

```
# command issued in 10-07/johns-repo directory
$ git remote rm origin
$ git remote add origin ../shared-repo
```

To contribute to the project follow the procedure (all the commands should be issued in 10-07/johns-repo):

1. Create the branch for your contributions: `$ git checkout -b new-web-interface`

2. Commit in your new-web-interface branch: `$ git simple-commit a b c`

3. Send the branch to the shared repository: `$ git push -u origin new-web-interface`

Now your contributions are stored in the remote branch new-web-interface in the remote repository shared-repo.

How It Works

This recipe presents a much more convenient solution for organizing the cooperation of project members then working in a master branch. By using a dedicated remote branch for a task, you gain more flexibility in setting groups within your team. You also can inspect the code before merging it into the master branch.

10-8. Accepting contributions
Problem

You are a leader of a project. A member of your team pushed some code to the shared repository using the new-web-interface branch. You are to inspect the contributed code. In this recipe we suppose that the code is correct and you (you are the leader, remember) accept it.

In this recipe we are using the scenario from Recipe 10-7. You act as a leader working in leaders-repo.

Solution

Copy the all the repositories from Recipe 10-7:

```
$ cd git-recipes
$ cp -R 10-07 10-08
$ cd 10-08
```

Now you are a leader and you inspect the contributions in the `new-web-interface` branch (all the commands should be issued in `10-08/leaders-repo`):

1. You fetch the contributions: `$ git fetch`

2. You checkout the remote branch `$ git checkout new-web-interface`

3. You inspect the files with the arbitrary commands and tools, for example, `$ ls`, `$ cat a.txt`, `vi b.txt`

4. You inspect the revisions with arbitrary commands, for example, `$ git log --oneline`, `$ git log --oneline --name-only HEAD~3..HEAD`

5. You decide that the code is correct and should be merged into `master` branch.

6. You checkout the `master` branch: `$ git checkout master`

7. You merge the work into the `master` with `$ git merge new-web-interface`

8. You publish the work to all of the other team members: `$ git push origin master`

How It Works

The integration of `new-web-interface` branch into the main development line in master branch consists of two steps. First the leader has to fetch the work done in `new-web-interface`. This is done with the `$ git fetch` and `$ git checkout new-web-interface` commands. After these two commands, the leader has a local branch named `new-web-interface`.

Because `new-web-interface` is a local branch, the integration can be done with arbitrary methods discussed in chapters 6 and 7. Here we used the simple `$ git merge` command. It can be also done with `$ git merge --no-ff` or `$ git rebase` as well.

Once the `new-web-interface` branch was integrated into the `master` it can be made public. To do this, the leader pushes the `master` branch into the `shared-repo`.

10-9. Appending commits to a remote branch
Problem

You are a developer who has already pushed his work to the `new-web-interface` branch in the shared repository. The leader has asked you to make some improvements. You are to make some new commits in the `new-web-interface` branch.

In this recipe we are using the scenario from Recipe 10-7. You act as a developer working in `johns-repo`.

Solution

Copy the all the repositories from Recipe 10-7:

```
$ cd git-recipes
$ cp -R 10-07 10-09
$ cd 10-09
```

How can a leader download the first version of your work?

To download the first version of your work, the leader updates his repository with (the commands should be run in 10-09/leaders-repo):

- He fetches your revisions: $ git fetch.

- He goes to the new-web-interface branch: $ git checkout new-web-interface.

How can a developer append commits to a remote branch?

To add new commits follow these steps (the commands should be run in 10-09/johns-repo):

1. Go to new-web-interface branch: $ git checkout new-web-interface

2. Create the new commits: $ git simple-commit n1 n2 n3 n4 n5

3. Publish your work: $ git push origin new-web-interface

How can a leader download the latest revisions from a remote branch?

The leader updates his repository with (the commands should be run in 10-09/leaders-repo):

1. He fetches your revisions: $ git fetch

2. He goes to the new-web-interface branch: $ git checkout new-web-interface

3. He updates the new-web-interface branch: $ git rebase origin/new-web-interface

Now he can inspect your new modifications and accept them (as in Recipe 10-8) or ask for new improvements (as in Recipe 10-9). Because the leader created his local new-web-interface branch with $ git checkout new-web-interface command, the tracking was set up for the branch. As a consequence he can use: $ git rebase while on new-web-interface to update this branch.

How It Works

The branch you use for contributions can be used by you and other members of your team for a longer period of time. You can iteratively commit and ask for code review. This can be repeated many times. The recipe explains how the leader can update his repository with the latest changes in the new-web-interface branch.

Of course these same procedures:

- Appending new commits to a remote branch

- Downloading the most recent commits from remote branch

can be performed by every member. Thus you can use the new-web-interface branch as a way to collaborate with others while working on a given feature.

10-10. Rewriting history with $ git push -f

Problem

You are a member of a team. You pushed your work to a remote branch named new-web-interface. Your work was rejected many times. You were asked to make corrections again and again. As a result the remote branch new-web-interface contains a large number of commits. You are in charge of the new-web-interface remote branch. The leader asked you to squash all the commits in this branch into a single commit before he can finally merge it.

In this recipe we are using the scenario from Recipe 10-7. You act as a developer working in johns-repo.

Solution

Copy the all the repositories from Recipe 10-7:

```
$ cd git-recipes
$ cp -R 10-07 10-10
$ cd 10-10
```

Now you are a developer working in new-web-interface in 10-10/johns-repo:

Your local new-web-interface branch contains three revisions a, b, and c. You want to squash them and update the remote branch.

Here is the procedure that you have to follow (all the commands are to be executed in 10-10/johns-repo):

1. Go to the new-web-interface branch: $ git checkout new-web-interface

2. Your new-web-interface branch contains three revisions a, b, and c. You can check it with $ git log --oneline.

3. The revisions a, b, c are not merged into the master branch yet. You can check it with: $ git log --oneline master..new-web-interface

4. Squash your three commits with: $ git rebase -i HEAD~3. Use the following interactive rebasing subcommands:

    ```
    reword XXXXXXX a
    fixup  XXXXXXX b
    fixup  XXXXXXX c
    ```

    Set the comment for the new revision to be abc. The details of interactive rebasing are described in Recipe 8-3.

5. Your new-web-interface branch contains a new revisions abc. You can check it with $ git log --oneline.

6. The revision abc is not merged into the master branch yet. You can check it with: $ git log --oneline master..new-web-interface

7. Republish your work with : $ git push -f origin new-web-interface

How It Works

The command $ git push -f origin new-web-interface forces git to update the remote branch new-web-interface even if it causes the history to be rewritten. By default $ git push succeeds only for fast-forward updates. If you know what you are doing you can use -f flag to force the transfer.

Git allows you to configure a repository that rejects all non-fast-forward updates with $ git push, even when the -f flag is used. You can achieve this by setting the receive.denyNonFastForwards to true. If you run:

```
$ git config receive.denyNonFastForwards true
```

in shared-repo, then you will forbid all pushes that change the history.

■ **Hint** Other options that concern pushing can be found in $ git config --help manual. Many of them start with the receive prefix.

10-11. Finishing the work on the remote branch
Problem

You are a member of a team. You pushed your work to the remote branch named new-web-interface. This branch was integrated into the master branch and is no longer used. You are asked by the leader to remove the remote branch new-web-interface. You want to remove your local branch as well.

In this recipe we are using the scenario from Recipe 10-8. You act as a developer working in johns-repo.

Solution

Copy the all the repositories from Recipe 10-8:

```
$ cd git-recipes
$ cp -R 10-08 10-11
$ cd 10-11
```

Now you are working as John. All the commands should be run in 10-11/johns-repo:

1. You update your project with $ git fetch.

2. Go to the master branch: $ git checkout master

3. Update your master branch with $ git rebase origin/master

4. Check for branches that can safely be removed: $ git branch --merged. The output should include—among others—new-web-interface branch. This means that the new-web-interface branch can be safely removed. The command $ git branch --merged is a safety check: if the branch new-web-interface is not printed by this then it is not safe to delete the branch.

5. Remove the remote branch new-web-interface in shared-repo as well as your local tracking branch origin/new-web-interface with $ git push origin :new-web-interface

6. Finally remove your new-web-interface branch with: $ git branch -d new-web-interface

How It Works

The one strange thing that happens in this recipe was already mentioned in Recipe 10-6. After you delete the remote branch in step 5 with:

```
$ git push origin :new-web-interface
```

The `$ git branch -a -vv` command prints:

```
* master                 59de3b0 [origin/master] z
  new-web-interface            59de3b0 [origin/new-web-interface] z
  remotes/origin/HEAD    -> origin/master
  remotes/origin/master 59de3b0 z
```

This means that the `new-web-interface` branch is still the local tracking branch. It tracks the `origin/new-web-interface` branch that doesn't exist anymore. We solve this discrepancy by removing the `new-web-interface` branch completely in step 6.

10-12. Pushing to non-bare repositories
Problem

You work in a repository that was cloned from a non-bare repository. You want to push to the original repository even though it is not a bare repository. In this recipe we will use two repositories:

- `johns-repo`—a non-bare repository you commit into
- `public-repo`—a non-bare repository you push to

Solution

Create a new directory with:

```
$ cd git-recipes
$ mkdir 10-12
$ cd 10-12
```

Initialize johns-repository with:

```
# commands issued in git-recipes/10-12 directory
$ git init johns-repo
$ cd johns-repo
$ git simple-commit "Initial commit"
```

Next, clone `johns-repo` to get `public-repo`:

```
# command issued in git-recipes/10-12 directory
$ git clone johns-repo public-repo
```

To allow pushes into public-repo, which is a non-bare repository, change its configuration with:

```
# command issued in public-repo directory
$ git config receive.denyCurrentBranch ignore
$ git config core.worktree ../
```

Then rename the file public-repo/.git/hooks/post-update.sample to public-repo/.git/hooks/post-update. You can do this with:

```
# command issued in public-repo directory
$ mv .git/hooks/post-update.sample .git/hooks/post-update
```

Change the contents of public-repo/.git/hooks/post-update as shown in Listing 10-4.

Listing 10-4. The contents of public-repo/.git/hooks/post-update

```
#!/bin/sh
exec git reset --hard
```

The configuration of public-repo is finished. Now go to johns-repo and add the remote:

```
# command issued in johns-repo
$ git remote add origin ../public-repo
```

Create three commits in johns-repo with:

```
# command issued in johns-repo
$ git simple-commit one two three
```

and push them to public-repo with $ git push origin master.

If you now list the files in public-repo with $ ls, you will notice that its working directory contains the one.txt, two.txt, and three.txt files. This proves that the push operation transferred the latest state of johns-repo to public-repo.

How It Works

Pushing to a non-bare remote repository causes problems because of the working directory. Suppose you and you colleague work in the master branch and you both create a file named lorem.txt. If you commit your file and push it to your colleagues repository what should happen to his working directory? Should a checkout be performed? If so your friend can lose his work done in lorem.txt.

The first step is to allow a push in such a way that the remote branch is updated. It is done with:

```
$ git config receive.denyCurrentBranch ignore
```

This command allows you to push to a remote repository. The push will upload necessary objects from your repository to a remote database and then it will update the remote branch you are pushing to. The working directory of the remote repository will not be affected.

To perform a checkout in the remote repository we have to configure the path to the working directory. It is done with:

```
$ git config core.worktree ../
```

The last step is to force a checkout when someone pushes to public-repo. This is done with post-update hook. To use a hook you have to create a shell script named public-repo/.git/hooks/post-update. The script should contain a single $ git reset --hard command, as shown in Listing 10-4.

▪ **Hint**   This recipe can be treated as a deployment tool. The public-repo is the repository where no one works. This is a read-only repository accessible through HTTP protocol. The recipe shows how you can publish your works on the web with a simple $ git push command.

Summary

When we discuss synchronization we always consider two repositories: local (the one you issue the command in) and remote (the one available by its URL). To avoid the chore of typing the URL again and again git can store it locally in the .git/config file. The remote URLs are managed with the $ git remote command.

The synchronization of git repositories is implemented on the basis of the graph of revisions. The $ git push command copies the revisions from local repository to the remote end. When you fetch, the revisions are copied from the remote to the local repository. In both cases, the database entries are not changed during the transfer—their SHA-1 remains unchanged. You can regard a set of git repositories as a distributed database where SHA-1 act as primary key. Because SHA-1 hashes are unique we can copy the items between arbitrary repositories without the risk of colliding keys. If the key exists in a destination database it is always regarded as the same object.

To explain this, I created in one of my repositories the following revision:

6c69fa3372f7099836176c8d0f123895adea58f1 Unique commit by gajdaw

The name of this revision is:

6c69fa3372f7099836176c8d0f123895adea58f1

From git's point of view *this name is unique in the whole universe*—in all known git repositories. This is a very strong assumption that makes synchronization of repositories easy. Everyone who wants to synchronize his or her work with mine needs a copy of this commit. When I push, the remote end will receive the following object:

6c69fa3372f7099836176c8d0f123895adea58f1 Unique commit by gajdaw

It will be an exact copy of my revision, with an identical SHA-1 name.

We can say the same fact in yet another way. Every time you analyze a history in any of your repositories, look for this: 6c69fa3372f7099836176c8d0f123895adea58f1 name. Once you find it you can always say: *Oh, I have in my repository the revision committed by Włodzimierz Gajda on September 6th, 2013, for the sake of "Summary" in chapter 10 of his book*. There is no other revision with the same name.

Once you understand how to add and remove remotes and how revisions are copied, the next step to master group work concerns branches. Until now, we concentrated on ordinary local branches. These are your personal local branches that you use for your work. Nobody knows about them. You don't have to consult on your work in these branches with anyone. You can create, modify, and destroy them.

The same rule applies to all repositories—not only yours. Thus we need the rules that allow for both independence and collaboration. These rules are very simple: your local branches are stored in other repositories inside a separate directory named after the remote's name.

When in loose format, your ordinary local branches a and b are stored in:

```
.git/refs/heads/a
.git/refs/heads/b
```

If someone aliases your repository as foo with:

```
$ git remote add foo [URL]
```

and fetches from your repository with $ git fetch foo, then your local branches a and b will be stored in his or her repository in:

```
.git/refs/remotes/foo/a
.git/refs/remotes/foo/b
```

They will not collide with the local branches that are stored in .git/refs/heads. That's the whole trick.

The remote tracking branches stored in .git/refs/remotes, such as .git/refs/remotes/foo/a, can be shortened to foo/a. And you can use them as ordinary pointers to revisions. Whenever you need an SHA-1 of a revision you can use foo/a just as you would use any other method to refer to commits, HEAD, master~5, doc^2, to name a few.

When you consider synchronization, the three important types of branches are:

- Remote branches
- Local tracking branches
- Remote tracking branches

The relationship between them and the way $ git commit, $ git fetch, $ git push influence them is depicted in Figure 10-29.

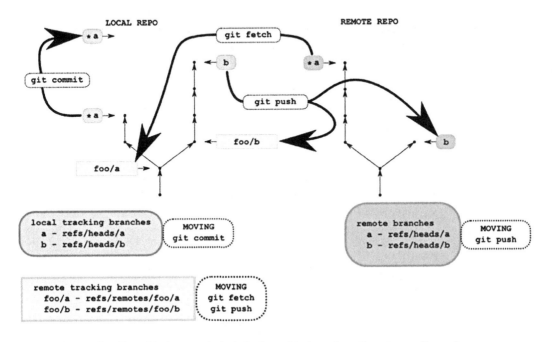

Figure 10-29. *The effect of $ git commit, $ git fetch, and $ git push on three types of branches*

Here is the summary of Figure 10-29:

- When you commit with $ `git commit` you move your local tracking branch forward.

- When you fetch with $ `git fetch` you move your remote tracking branch forward.

- When you push with $ `git push` you move the remote branch and the remote tracking branch forward.

The tracking can be always inspected with the $ `git branch -a -vv` command. The output lists:

- Ordinary local branches as:

  ```
  lorem    a1b2c3f Some commend
  ```

- Local tracking branches as:

  ```
  ipsum    a1b2c3f [origin/ipsum] Some comment
  ```

- Remote tracking branches as:

  ```
  remotes/origin/dolor    a1b2c3f Some comment
  ```

The $ `git branch -a -vv` command doesn't list remote branches. To list remote branches you have to first fetch them with $ `git fetch`. We can say that $ `git branch` is a local command—it doesn't perform a network transfer between your local and remote repositories.

You will find the exact procedures to set and remove tracking in Recipes 10-4 and 10-5. They are quite simple if you understand the role of each type of branches.

The distributed role of git was underlined by recipes that presented team work with and without a central repository. To grasp the idea even further try to run the following command in any of the repositories:

```
$ git fetch --no-tags https://github.com/github/GitPad master:refs/remotes/xyz/pqr
```

The command fetches the `master` branch from the repository `https://github.com/github/GitPad` and stores it in the `.git/refs/remotes/xyz/pqr` file. The operation copies the revisions from the GitPad repository and stores them in your `.git/objects` database. You don't have to define an alias for remote repository if you don't want to. Git doesn't require it. Even without the aliases for remotes defined, git is able to download to your repository the revisions from any repository accessible by some URLs. There is no connection between your repository and GitPad's repository on Github. The mapping between the remote branch master (in GitPad's repository) and the remote tracking branch xyz/pqr (in your repository) is set by refspec:

```
master:refs/remotes/xyz/pqr
```

The part before the colon is the name of the remote branch, the part after the colon is the name of the remote tracking branch. By using the URL and a refspec, you can fetch the arbitrary branch from any repository you wish.

Sometimes I'm asked why at one time we write `origin master` separated with a space and at other time we use a / as a separator. As in:

```
$ git pull origin master
$ git rebase origin/master
```

In the first command `origin` is the name of the remote and `master` is the name of the branch. This is an ordinary local branch or a local tracking branch.

In second command `origin/master` is the name of a remote tracking branch. The syntax of the above commands can be described as:

```
$ git pull [remote] [branch]
$ git rebase [branch]
```

In the second command we use a remote tracking branch `origin/master` as a [branch] parameter.

CHAPTER 11

■ ■ ■

Hosting git Git Repositories

As soon as you and your colleagues learn how to commit, use branches, and work with remotes, you will want to use git as a group. In this chapter, I will show how to set up a virtual host for sharing git repositories with others.

Git can work with ssh, http, https, and git network protocols. To choose the best solution for your needs, you will have to answer two questions:

- Do you want to host repositories with read/write access for authenticated users only (i.e., without anonymous public access)?

- Do you want to host repositories that have anonymous public read-only access?

If you want to host repositories for authenticated users only then ssh is the best choice. If you want to allow anonymous read-only access you can use native git protocol or http. If you need both types of access, anonymous and with authentication, you can combine two or more protocols. For example, you can use ssh to authenticate users and git protocol for anonymous access. Table 11-1 presents the basic properties of ssh, http, https, and git protocols.

Table 11-1. *Properties of ssh, http, https, and git protocols*

Protocol	Read-only access: No authentication required	Read/write access: Authenticated users only
ssh	No	Yes
http	Yes	No
https	Yes	Yes
git	Yes	No

The recipes in this chapter contain detailed tutorials showing how to host repositories over ssh, http, and git. Because I honestly consider ssh the most important solution, we will dive into the details concerning this protocol. I will not only provide you with general information on how ssh authenticates users but also explain the following:

- Generating RSA keys

- Using authorized_keys file

- Configuring ssh with ~/.ssh/config file

Although this knowledge is not strictly related to git but to ssh, I really believe you will need it. As I have already explained, ssh is the best solution for private repositories. The more confident you are with ssh the better.

For those who need to serve repositories with anonymous access, we will use both http and git protocols. If efficiency is one of your concerns then you should use git native protocol.

The phrase "hosting git repository over http" refers to allowing git fetch and git clone operations to be executed through the http connection. Using a web browser for such a repository would be useless: you will get the listing of the working directory and the .git repository. If you want to inspect repositories with a web browser, you need the web application. I will show you two the most popular solutions: gitweb and cgit. Gitweb is a Perl script that was developed by git creators and is included in git sources. Cgit is written in C and it is considered to be the fastest CGI application for git. The other advantage of cgit is that it allows you to append a URL to clone a repository.

The last two recipes concern the problem of privileges. When you host git repositories over ssh the authenticated user gains full access to all the repositories. There is no built-in support either in git or ssh to restrict access. If you want to grant access on:

- A per user basis

- A per repository basis

- A per branch (in general: per reference) basis

you will need gitolite. Gitolite is an additional layer on top of git that is hosted with ssh. This layer allows you to grant or revoke three types of privileges: read, write, and forced write. Every privilege can be assigned for an arbitrary user for an arbitrary repository and for an arbitrary branch.

I planned this book to be a hands-on practical introduction. The recipes concerning hosting git repositories can cause many headaches. Which is the right platform to work with? How to prepare recipes that will work without any flaws on the different systems? How to avoid messing with the system that you currently work on? What if you don't have root access to any machine? To avoid these problems, I decided to use a virtual system. This is, in my opinion, the best way to practice the operating system administration. Therefore you will be able to proceed with the recipes exactly as they are written and if something does go wrong your system will stay untouched. I think that these two advantages alone are sufficient reason to work with a virtual system.

The easiest solution to setting up a virtual machine is to use VirtualBox with Vagrant. The first two recipes in this chapter give you the necessary introduction to this subject.

11-1. Installing VirtualBox and Vagrant
Problem

You want to install VirtualBox and Vagrant on your machine.

Solution

1. Start your web browser, visit `https://www.virtualbox.org/wiki/Downloads` and download VirtualBox 4.2.18 for your platform.

2. Install the VirtualBox 4.2.18 package on your computer. You can leave the default values for all options.

3. Visit `http://downloads.vagrantup.com` and download Vagrant 1.3.1 for your platform.

4. Install Vagrant 1.3.1 on your computer with the default settings.

5. Start the command line and execute

   ```
   $ vagrant --version
   ```

If Vagrant is installed and ready to run, this command will print its version number.

How It Works

Both VirtualBox and Vagrant provide installers that are easy to follow. At the time of writing the latest available versions were 4.2.18 for VirtualBox and 1.3.1 for Vagrant. You can try the recipes with the latest versions available at the time you read this chapter. If the configuration format of Vagrant has changed, you can always switch back to the versions that I used.

11-2. Running virtual Linux
Problem

You want to run virtual Ubuntu Linux on your computer.

Solution

Create a new directory with:

```
# Host OS (e.g., Windows, Linux, OS X)
$ cd git-recipes
$ mkdir 11-02
$ cd 11-02
```

Now initialize a new virtual machine configuration in the current folder:

```
# Host OS (e.g., Windows, Linux, OS X)
$ vagrant init precise32 http://files.vagrantup.com/precise32.box
```

The virtual system is ready to be started. Start the virtual Linux with the following command:

```
# Host OS (e.g., Windows, Linux, OS X)
$ vagrant up
```

When you run this command for the first time it will take a while to complete. That's because Vagrant will download the image file that uses almost 300 MB. The file will be stored within:

```
# Unix-like systems
~/.vagrant.d/boxes/precise32
```

```
# Windows
C:\Users\[username]\.vagrant.d\boxes\precise32
```

This operation is performed only once during the first boot of your virtual system.

When $ vagrant up is finished you will have a fully fledged Linux system running on your machine as one of the applications. The command:

```
# Host OS (e.g., Windows, Linux, OS X)
$ vagrant status
```

outputs the state of the virtual machine as:

```
default                      running (virtualbox)
```

The virtual system doesn't provide a user interface. You can use the ssh session to access and work in this system as you would any other of your other Linux hosts. To open the ssh session to the virtual machine run the following command:

```
# Host OS (e.g., Windows, Linux, OS X)
$ vagrant ssh
```

When the $ vagrant ssh command succeeds, you will have shell access Host repositories:running virtual Linux:shell access to the virtual system. You can, for example, check the system's version with:

```
# Guest OS (Ubuntu 12.04)
$ uname -a
```

or list the logged-in users:

```
# Guest OS (Ubuntu 12.04)
$ who
```

After that you can close the ssh session with:

```
# Guest OS (Ubuntu 12.04)
$ exit
```

and check the status of virtual machine with:

```
# Host OS (e.g., Windows, Linux, OS X)
$ vagrant status
```

As you can see the virtual system is still running. Closing the ssh session doesn't affect the state of the virtual system. Finally, stop the virtual machine with:

```
# Host OS (e.g., Windows, Linux, OS X)
$ vagrant halt
```

This command shuts the system down. When the system is down, the command:

```
# Host OS (e.g., Windows, Linux, OS X)
$ vagrant status
```

prints:

```
default                      poweroff (virtualbox)
```

You can boot it again with the $ vagrant up command.

You have to remember to halt the virtual system in the current recipe before you can proceed with next recipe. If you do not remember, the folder that holds your currently running virtual machine, you can use VirtualBox. Figure 11-1 presents the main window of VirtualBox. Using the Machine/Close/Power off main menu option you can power off every virtual machine available.

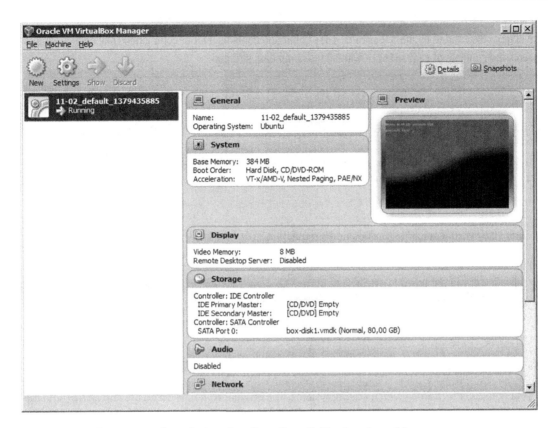

Figure 11-1. *The main window of VirtualBox lists all available virtual machines*

■ **Caution** Before you start to work on the next recipe I advise that you power off the virtual machine from the current recipe. You can use the `$ vagrant halt` command. The reasons why are explained in the Recipe 11-6 in section "What happens if you boot two virtual machines?"

How It Works

The command:

```
$ vagrant init precise32 http://files.vagrantup.com/precise32.box
```

creates a configuration file named Vagrantfile as shown in Listing 11-1.

Listing 11-1. The contents of the default Vagrantfile file without comments

```
VAGRANTFILE_API_VERSION = "2"
Vagrant.configure(VAGRANTFILE_API_VERSION) do |config|
  config.vm.box = "precise32"
  config.vm.box_url = "http://files.vagrantup.com/precise32.box"
end
```

■ **Caution** The original file created by the $ vagrant init command contains a lot of comments. They begin with #. Listing 11-1 presents the contents of Vagrantfile with all the comments stripped.

The entry:

```
config.vm.box_url = "http://files.vagrantup.com/precise32.box"
```

sets the basic box for the virtual system to be http://files.vagrantup.com/precise32.box. The precise32.box file contains Ubuntu 12.04 LTS 32-bit. After running:

```
$ vagrant up
```

you will have Ubuntu 12.04 virtual machine running on your machine.

■ **Hint** A large collection of vagrant boxes is available at http://www.vagrantbox.es. There you will find CentOS, Debian, Gentoo, OpenBSD, among others. By changing the basic box you will change the operating system your virtual machine runs.

Because the virtual system doesn't provide a user interface we will use secure shell (SSH) to gain access to the virtual machine.

Right now, your computer is running two operating systems. The original system is called the *host system,* and the virtual system is called the *guest system*. For example, if you are working in Windows:

- Windows is your host system.

- Ubuntu Linux 12.4 is your guest system.

All the commands issued in previous chapters were executed by the shell of your host operating system. Starting from Recipe 11-2, we will use two command lines: one for the host operating system and the other for the guest operating system. To make the instructions more clear I use the following comments:

```
# Host OS (e.g., Windows, Linux, OS X)
$ command ...
```

```
# Guest OS (Ubuntu 12.04)
$ command ...
```

They explain which command line should be used for every command.

Starting, stopping, and destroying virtual Linux

Vagrant provides the following commands to control the state of your virtual machine:

```
# Host OS (e.g., Windows, Linux, OS X)
$ vagrant status
$ vagrant up
$ vagrant suspend
$ vagrant resume
$ vagrant halt
$ vagrant destroy
```

The first command, $ vagrant status, returns the information about the virtual machine.

The $ vagrant up command boots the virtual machine.

The next command, $ vagrant suspend, saves the system in its current state on your hard drive. When you suspend the virtual system it doesn't consume RAM or processor. The process of waking a suspended system up is done with the $ vagrant resume or $ vagrant up commands.

The $ vagrant halt command shuts the virtual machine down. The next time you bring the virtual machine up with $ vagrant up, the system will be rebooted.

The $ vagrant destroy command removes the virtual machine permanently. The next time you run $ vagrant up the virtual machine will be created from scratch. That means all the files you created during your previous ssh session will be removed.

If you are finished with your virtual system for the moment but you think you may need it in the future, you should use the $ vagrant suspend command. After the $ vagrant suspend command, the virtual system doesn't consume your computer's resources such as RAM or processor. The system is stored on the file system until the next $ vagrant resume or $ vagrant up command. Keep in mind that the process of waking the virtual system that was suspended with $ vagrant suspend is the quickest possible method to bring the virtual system back.

If you want to start over again then use $ vagrant destroy command.

The state of the virtual machine

At any given time the virtual machine can be in one of these following states:

- Not created

- Running

- Saved

- Powered off

The first state is returned by the $ vagrant status command as:

```
default                 not created (virtualbox)
```

The machine is in this state:

- Right after $ vagrant init and before $ vagrant up

- After $ vagrant destroy

The second state is described by the $ vagrant status command as:

```
default                    running (virtualbox)
```

This is the state of the machine after a successful $ vagrant up command.
The next state—denoted as saved—is returned by the $ vagrant status command as:

```
default                    saved (virtualbox)
```

This is the state after the $ vagrant suspend command.
The last state—power off—is returned by the $ vagrant status command as:

```
default                    poweroff (virtualbox)
```

This is the state the virtual machine enters after the $ vagrant halt command.
The state of every virtual machine is clearly indicated by the icons displayed by VirtualBox. The virtual machine visible in Figure 11-1 is denoted with green arrow labeled running.

■ **Hint**   Do not use $ sudo shutdown -h now or any other similar command to power off the virtual system. This command transforms the system from running into not created. The result of $ sudo shutdown -h now is the same as $ vagrant destroy.

Opening the SSH session to a virtual host

You can access the virtual system with SSH using:

```
# Host OS (e.g., Windows, Linux, OS X)
$ vagrant ssh
```

This command runs the ssh client using settings that can be listed with:

```
# Host OS (e.g., Windows, Linux, OS X)
$ vagrant ssh-config
```

You can also use any other ssh client to access the virtual system. It can be a typical ssh client available in your shell. You can run:

```
# Host OS (e.g., Windows, Linux, OS X)
$ ssh -p2222 vagrant@127.0.0.1
```

and use the following credentials:

```
username: vagrant
password: vagrant
```

Right now, you will need to use a password. Later, in Recipe 11-5 I will show you how to avoid typing passwords using RSA keys. There you will also learn how to configure your SSH client.

Accessing root's account

By default, the root's account in your virtual machine is locked. To access it you need to run the $ `sudo su` command. You also can unlock the account with the following procedure:

1. Set a new password for root with:

   ```
   # Guest OS (Ubuntu 12.04)
   $ sudo passwd root
   ```

2. Unlock the root's account with:

   ```
   # Guest OS (Ubuntu 12.04)
   $ sudo passwd -u root
   ```

3. Switch to root's account with:

   ```
   # Guest OS (Ubuntu 12.04)
   $ su
   ```

   You have to run all the above commands within the ssh session, as indicated by # `Guest OS (Ubuntu 12.04)` comments.

Synchronized folders

The folder with the `Vagrantfile` on your host OS (this is `git-recipes/11-02` in Recipe 11-2) is available in your guest OS as `/vagrant`. This means that you can share files among the two systems. The file created in host operating system:

```
# Host OS (e.g., Windows, Linux, OS X)
git-recipes/11-02/lorem.txt
```

is available in guest operating system under the name:

```
# Guest OS (Ubuntu 12.04)
/vagrant/lorem.txt
```

You can verify it with the following procedure:

1. Start the virtual machine with:

   ```
   # Host OS (e.g., Windows, Linux, OS X)
   $ vagrant up
   ```

2. Create the file in the host system with:

   ```
   # Host OS (e.g., Windows, Linux, OS X)
   $ echo lorem > lorem.txt
   ```

3. Open the SSH session with:

   ```
   # Host OS (e.g., Windows, Linux, OS X)
   $ vagrant ssh
   ```

4. List the contents of /vagrant directory with:

```
# Guest OS (Ubuntu 12.04)
$ ls /vagrant
```

As you can see the file /vagrant/lorem.txt is available within the ssh session.

5. Next, check the contents of /vagrant/lorem.txt file with:

```
# Guest OS (Ubuntu 12.04)
$ cat /vagrant/lorem.txt
```

6. Create a file within the ssh session with:

```
# Guest OS (Ubuntu 12.04)
$ echo ipsum > /vagrant/ipsum.txt
```

7. Close the ssh session with:

```
# Guest OS (Ubuntu 12.04)
$ exit
```

8. List the files in the git-recipes/11-02 directory with:

```
# Host OS (e.g., Windows, Linux, OS X)
$ ls
```

The file ipsum.txt is available in your host operating system.

9. Check the content of git-recipes/11-02/ipsum.txt file with:

```
# Host OS (e.g., Windows, Linux, OS X)
$ cat ipsum.txt
```

10. Stop the virtual system with:

```
# Host OS (e.g., Windows, Linux, OS X)
$ vagrant halt
```

As you can see, the two files lorem.txt and ipsum.txt are both available in your host operating system (e.g., Windows) and the guest operating system (i.e., Ubuntu 12.04). This is the easiest way to share the files between the two systems. Later on we will also use the $ scp command to copy the files between both systems.

If you want to synchronize a different folder you can use the following configuration in Vagrantfile:

```
config.vm.synced_folder [HOST-PATH], [GUEST-PATH]
```

The first directory is the path on your host operating system. It can be either absolute or relative to the directory with Vagrantfile but it has to exist during boot up. The second path is on the guest operating system. It has to be absolute. If the guest path doesn't exist during boot up it will be created.

Here are the examples for Windows:

```
config.vm.synced_folder "c:\\some-dir-on\\windows", "/some-dir-on/virtual/ubuntu"
```

and for Linux:

```
config.vm.synced_folder "/some-dir-on/Linux", "/some-dir-on/virtual/ubuntu"
```

11-3. Compiling git on a virtual machine
Problem

You want to compile and install the latest version of git on virtual Ubuntu Linux. The ability to compile git sources is useful when you want:

- To work using the latest git version

- To compile an external application such as cgit that relies on git

- To contribute to a git project

Solution

1. Start the virtual machine:

    ```
    # Host OS (e.g., Windows, Linux, OS X)
    $ cd git-recipes
    $ mkdir 11-03
    $ cd 11-03
    $ vagrant init precise32 http://files.vagrantup.com/precise32.box
    $ vagrant up
    $ vagrant ssh
    ```

2. Install git from a binary package available for Ubuntu:

    ```
    # Guest OS (Ubuntu 12.04)
    $ git --version
    $ sudo apt-get install -y git
    $ git --version
    ```

3. Compile and install git from sources:

    ```
    # Guest OS (Ubuntu 12.04)
    $ sudo apt-get update -y
    $ sudo apt-get install -y make libssl-dev libz-dev gettext libexpat1-dev libcurl4-openssl-dev
    $ git clone --depth 1 git://git.kernel.org/pub/scm/git/git.git
    $ cd git
    $ make prefix=/usr all
    $ sudo make prefix=/usr install
    $ git --version
    ```

4. Finish the recipe:

```
# Guest OS (Ubuntu 12.04)
$ exit

# Host OS (e.g., Windows, Linux, OS X)
$ vagrant halt
```

How It Works

To compile git we need to download its source code, which is—you may guess—available in the git repository. Therefore, we need a git client.

By default, git is not installed on the virtual machine using precise32 box. You can verify it with the $ git --version command. To install it you have to boot the virtual machine and run the $ sudo apt-get install -y git command. This command installs git from a binary package available for Ubuntu. When issued without -y, the $ sudo apt-get install command usually asks for confirmation when additional packages needs to be installed. The -y option forces a yes answer to all these types of questions.

To compile the latest version of git you have to:

- Update the system dependencies. This is done with:

```
$ sudo apt-get update -y
```

- Install all necessary libraries and tools required by git. The command to do this is:

```
$ sudo apt-get install -y make libssl-dev libz-dev gettext libexpat1-dev libcurl4-
openssl-dev
```

- Clone the latest version of git sources using git:

```
$ git clone --depth 1 git://git.kernel.org/pub/scm/git/git.git
```

- And execute the commands that compile the sources and install git:

```
$ cd git
$ make prefix=/usr all
$ sudo make prefix=/usr install
```

When you finish, you will have the latest version of git installed on the virtual machine. You can verify this with:

```
$ git --version
```

■ **Hint**   If you wish you also can generate documentation for the version just installed. You can do this with the following two commands: $ sudo apt-get install -y asciidoc and $ sudo make prefix=/usr install-doc. However, installation of asciidoc will take a lot of time because it installs TeX and LaTeX, among others.

Git sources are hosted at http://git.kernel.org/cgit/git/git.git. You will find many mirrors of this site, for example, https://github.com/git/git. But the latest version is always available at kernel.org and the other sites are just mirrors.

I used the --depth 1 parameter for cloning:

```
$ git clone --depth 1 git://git.kernel.org/pub/scm/git/git.git
```

The above commands create a so-called *shallow repository*. The history of a repository is truncated to a given number of the latest revisions. If you only need a checkout of the latest revision, the shallow clone will do just fine. You can still commit in this repository, but you will have to send your commits as patches as we did in Recipe 7-2. You cannot clone, fetch, or push using a shallow repository. The main advantage of using a shallow repository is that cloning is much faster.

■ **Hint** Please note that the http://git.kernel.org/cgit/git/git.git site is powered by cgit. I will show you how to use cgit to host repositories in Recipe 11-9.

When you finish the recipe do not destroy the virtual machine. If you destroy the virtual machine you will have to repeat the complete procedure, including installation of all packages and cloning the git sources. If you suspend the virtual machine with $ vagrant suspend or power it off with $ vagrant halt, then the next time you boot the machine with $ vagrant up, all the software installed in this recipe will be available.

11-4. Hosting git repositories over ssh
Problem

You want to set up a host that will be used within your company to share git repositories. Your task is:

- To set up a virtual machine for hosting git repositories

- To install the repository created in Recipe 3-1 on a virtual host in such a way that every developer can clone, fetch, and push using this repository

- To check that everything works as expected by committing and pushing to the remote repository stored in the virtual system

---

■ **Hint** With this recipe you can host private git repositories even if you don't have access to the root account. You can use this recipe for virtual shared hosts, for example.

Solution

Start the virtual machine:

```
# Host OS (e.g., Windows, Linux, OS X)
$ cd git-recipes
$ mkdir 11-04
$ cd 11-04
$ vagrant init precise32 http://files.vagrantup.com/precise32.box
$ vagrant up
$ vagrant ssh
```

Install git on the virtual machine:

```
# Guest OS (Ubuntu 12.04)
$ sudo apt-get install -y git
```

The virtual machine is ready. You can close the ssh session:

```
# Guest OS (Ubuntu 12.04)
$ exit
```

Copying a bare repository with scp

Create the bare repository you want to share. We will use the repository created in Recipe 3-1.

```
# Host OS (e.g., Windows, Linux, OS X)
$ cd git-recipes
$ git clone --bare 03-01 03-01.git
```

The bare repository is available in the 03-01.git directory. Copy the bare repository onto your virtual machine with:

```
# Host OS (e.g., Windows, Linux, OS X)
$ scp -P 2222 -r 03-01.git vagrant@127.0.0.1:03-01.git
```

Use the following credentials:

```
username: vagrant
password: vagrant
```

If you want to check that the bare repository was really copied, open the ssh session:

```
# Host OS (e.g., Windows, Linux, OS X)
$ cd git-recipes
$ cd 11-04

$ vagrant ssh
```

and list the files with:

```
# Guest OS (Ubuntu 12.04)
$ ls
```

You will see that the directory /home/vagrant now contains the 03-01.git directory. You can enter this repository and check the log with:

```
# Guest OS (Ubuntu 12.04)
$ cd 03-01.git
$ git log --oneline
```

The $ git log command will print the three revisions that we created in Recipe 3-1.

The repository /vagrant/home/03-01.git on the virtual system is available under the following URL:

```
ssh://vagrant@127.0.0.1:2222/home/vagrant/03-01.git
```

Working with a repository hosted on the virtual machine

Right now you are working as one of the developers. Let's assume that his name is Paul. Clone the repository from the virtual system onto the local Peter's drive:

```
# Host OS (e.g., Windows, Linux, OS X)
$ cd git-recipes

$ mkdir 11-04-pauls-machine
$ cd 11-04-pauls-machine
$ git clone ssh://vagrant@127.0.0.1:2222/home/vagrant/03-01.git
```

Use the credentials:

```
username: vagrant
password: vagrant
```

Now Paul commits into his local repository:

```
# the commands issued in 11-04-pauls-machine/ directory
$ cd 03-01
$ echo one > one.txt
$ git add -A
$ git commit -m "One"
```

Finally Paul pushes his work to the remote repository stored on virtual system:

```
$ git push origin master
```

The credentials he uses are the same as he used previously:

```
username: vagrant
password: vagrant
```

■ **Hint** If you want to access the virtual system over the network, you will need to configure port forwarding, adding the following line to the Vagrantfile: `config.vm.network :forwarded_port, guest: 22, host: 3333`

After adding this line to the Vagrantfile, reload the virtual machine with: `$ vagrant reload`

If the IP address of the machine running the virtual system is 192.168.10.225, then everyone on your local network who knows the credentials of the vagrant account can access the virtual system with: `$ ssh -p3333 vagrant@192.168.10.225`

The following command can be use to clone the repository: `$ git clone ssh://vagrant@192.168.10.225:3333/home/vagrant/03-01.git`

Checking the log of the repository stored on the virtual system

You want to check the history of the bare repository hosted in the virtual system. Open the ssh session:

```
# Host OS (e.g., Windows, Linux, OS X)
# the command should be executed in 11-04 directory
$ vagrant ssh
```

Enter the 03-01.git directory:

```
# Guest OS (Ubuntu 12.04)
$ cd 03-01.git
```

List the history with:

```
# Guest OS (Ubuntu 12.04)
$ git log --oneline
```

The output will include three commits one, two, three created by Paul.
The recipe is finished. Close the ssh session:

```
# Guest OS (Ubuntu 12.04)
$ exit
```

and stop the virtual system:

```
# Host OS (e.g., Windows, Linux, OS X)
```

$ vagrant halt: How It Works

If you want to host git repositories all you need is a host:

- With git client installed

- With ssh access

Virtual box precise32 doesn't contain the git client. To install git we issued the following command within ssh session:

```
$ sudo apt-get install -y git
```

If you now suspend the system with $ vagrant suspend or halt it with $ vagrant halt and boot it up again with $ vagrant up, git client will be available. If, on the other hand, you destroy the virtual machine with $ vagrant destroy, you will have to install git once again.

As you learned in Recipe 2-4, git repositories can be copied with standard commands such as cp, scp, rsync. All you have to do to set up a central shared repository is to copy a bare repository into the virtual system. We access the virtual system using the default account provided by vagrant:

```
username: vagrant
password: vagrant
```

The home directory of `vagrant` user is `/home/vagrant`. The following command:

```
$ scp -P 2222 -r 03-01.git vagrant@127.0.0.1:03-01.git
```

copies the directory `03-01.git` from the local filesystem (i.e., your host operating system) onto the virtual system (i.e., the guest operating system). Thanks to the `-r` option, the operation recurses all subdirectories. The repository `/vagrant/home/03-01.git` on the virtual system is available under the following URL:

```
ssh://vagrant@127.0.0.1:2222/home/vagrant/03-01.git
```

If you want to make it available through the network, remember to configure port forwarding in the Vagrantfile with:

```
config.vm.network :forwarded_port, guest: 22, host: 22
```

then everyone who knows the password to the `vagrant` account can clone, fetch, and push into this repository using this simplified URL:

```
ssh://vagrant@x.x.x.x/home/vagrant/03-01.git
```

where `x.x.x.x` is the IP address of your host.
Using this approach:

- Every developer needs to know the password to the vagrant account.

- Every developer has to type the password to the vagrant account every time he or she clones, fetches, or pushes.

- Every developer has full ssh access to the vagrant account.

- There is no public read-only access to this repository.

- Every developer not only has clone, fetch, push access to one repository but to all other repositories hosted under this vagrant account.

The first three problems will be solved in Recipe 11-5. We will use a git account and RSA keys to do it.
The fourth problem will be solved in Recipes 11-6 and 11-7 in which we will use git and http protocol to host git repositories.
The last problem will be solved in Recipe 11-10 with gitolite.

11-5. Simplifying ssh authorization with authorized_keys
Problem

You want to improve the solution from Recipe 11-4 in a way that:

- Developers don't need the password to the vagrant account anymore

- Developers don't have to type passwords when they clone, fetch, or push

- No one can get ssh access to the host with shared repositories

Solution

Initialize and boot the new virtual machine:

```
# Host OS (e.g., Windows, Linux, OS X)
$ cd git-recipes
$ mkdir 11-05
$ cd 11-05
$ vagrant init precise32 http://files.vagrantup.com/precise32.box
$ vagrant up
$ vagrant ssh
```

Install git on virtual machine:

```
# Guest OS (Ubuntu 12.04)
$ sudo apt-get install -y git
```

Create git user:

```
# Guest OS (Ubuntu 12.04)
$ sudo adduser --disabled-password --shell /usr/bin/git-shell --gecos Git git
```

Initializing a new repository

To create a new repository that can be accessed by all team members, the administrator (i.e., vagrant user) executes the following commands:

```
# Guest OS (Ubuntu 12.04)
# Command executed by vagrant user
$ sudo git init --bare /home/git/lorem.git
$ sudo chown -R git:git /home/git/lorem.git
```

Use the above two commands every time you want to create a new repository shared by your team.

Creating a new account

In this recipe you work as one of the developers. Let his name be Peter. First, we need an account for Peter. This is done by the administrator with the following command:

```
# Guest OS (Ubuntu 12.04)
# Command executed by vagrant user
$ sudo adduser --disabled-password peter --gecos Peter
```

Logging into Peter's account

Log into Peter's account with the following commands:

```
# Guest OS (Ubuntu 12.04)
# Commands executed by vagrant user
$ sudo su - peter
```

When I say that the command should be executed by Peter as in:

```
# Guest OS (Ubuntu 12.04)
# Commands executed by peter user
$ command
```

the three commands:

```
$ whoami
$ pwd
$ hostname
```

should print:

```
Who am i?            peter
Current directory:  /home/peter
Hostname:           precise32
```

Generating keys

This part of the recipe has to be repeated by every member of your organization. Here, we are faking the work by Peter. Log in to Peter's account with (if you haven't done it so far, that is):

```
# Guest OS (Ubuntu 12.04)
# Commands executed by vagrant user
$ sudo su - peter
```

Generate the RSA key pair for Peter and save them in the .ssh directory:

```
# Guest OS (Ubuntu 12.04)
# Commands executed by peter user
$ mkdir .ssh
$ chmod 700 .ssh
$ ssh-keygen -t rsa -C peter@example.net -N "" -f .ssh/id_rsa
```

Hint   Instead of using these three commands:

```
$ mkdir .ssh
$ chmod 700 .ssh
$ ssh-keygen -t rsa -C peter@example.net -N "" -f .ssh/id_rsa
```

You can you a single command:

```
$ ssh-keygen -t rsa -C peter@example.net
```

but you will have to answer some questions. If you do it remember to use the default values for all options (just press ENTER until the command is finished). The meaning of all the options is given in the "How it works section below."

The $ ssh-keygen command generates two files and informs you where they are stored:

```
Your identification has been saved in /home/peter/.ssh/id_rsa.
Your public key has been saved in /home/peter/.ssh/id_rsa.pub.
```

The first contains your private key, and the second file contains your public key. If everything works as expected the command $ ls .ssh/id_rsa* should print the names of two files: .ssh/id_rsa and .ssh/id_rsa.pub.

■ **Caution**　Very often I create virtual systems just for testing, checking, or verifying. The system is used only for a very short time and then destroyed. The remote access to the host is blocked because I do not turn on port forwarding. In these cases I usually use an empty passphrase for imaginary users such as Peter.

Sending public keys to the administrator

Peter has to send his public key to the administrator. Because he works on the same host as the administrator, he can use a simple $ cp command:

```
# Guest OS (Ubuntu 12.04)
# Commands executed by peter user
$ cp /home/peter/.ssh/id_rsa.pub /var/tmp/peter.pub
```

If Peter works on other machine he has to find a way for sending his public key to administrator. He can use email, ftp, removable media (such as flash memory), and so forth.

Peter's work is done for now. You can log him out:

```
# Guest OS (Ubuntu 12.04)
# Command executed by peter user
$ exit
```

Granting SSH access with authorized_keys file

We want to allow Peter access to the git account over SSH. This is done with public key file. I will assume that Peter's public key is stored in /var/tmp/peter.pub.

We want to grant SSH access to the account named git. The configuration file that defines who can open ssh connection to this account is named /home/git/.ssh/authorized_keys.

First, you have to create a /home/git/.ssh/authorized_keys file using the following commands:

```
# Guest OS (Ubuntu 12.04)
# Commands executed by vagrant user
$ sudo su
# mkdir /home/git/.ssh
# touch /home/git/.ssh/authorized_keys
# chown -R git:git /home/git/.ssh
# chmod 700 /home/git/.ssh
# exit
```

To grant access you have to append Peter's key to the /home/git/.ssh/authorized_keys file of the git account. Here is the command that the administrator can use to accomplish this:

```
# Guest OS (Ubuntu 12.04)
# Commands executed by vagrant user
$ sudo sh -c 'cat /var/tmp/peter.pub >> /home/git/.ssh/authorized_keys'
```

■ **Hint**   Instead of one command:

```
$ sudo sh -c 'cat /var/tmp/peter.pub >> /home/git/.ssh/authorized_keys'
```

you can also use two commands:

```
$ sudo su
# cat /var/tmp/peter.pub >> /home/git/.ssh/authorized_keys
```

To revoke the ssh access, the administrator has to remove the line with Peter's public key from the /home/git/.ssh/authorized_keys file of the git account.

Working with remote repository

Peter wants to work in the lorem repository created by the administrator. He wants to:

- Clone the repository

- Create some revisions

- Push his work to the remote repository

First, Peter has to log on to his account:

```
# Guest OS (Ubuntu 12.04)
# Commands executed by vagrant user
$ sudo su - peter
```

Then he configures git:

```
# Guest OS (Ubuntu 12.04)
# Commands executed by peter user
$ git config --global user.name Peter
$ git config --global user.email peter@example.net
```

Now Peter can clone the repository:

```
# Guest OS (Ubuntu 12.04)
# Command executed by peter user
$ git clone ssh://git@localhost/home/git/lorem.git
```

and proceed with his work

```
# Guest OS (Ubuntu 12.04)
# Command executed by peter user
$ cd lorem
$ echo a > a.txt
$ git add -A
$ git commit -m "The first revision by Peter"
```

When the work is finished, Peter pushes his revisions onto the server:

```
# Guest OS (Ubuntu 12.04)
# Command executed by peter user
$ git push -u origin master
```

Peter's work is finished. He closes his session:

```
# Guest OS (Ubuntu 12.04)
# Command executed by peter user
$ exit
```

Administrator checks the log of a repository

The administrator wants to check the log of the bare lorem.git repository stored on the server. He can do this with:

```
# Guest OS (Ubuntu 12.04)
# Command executed by vagrant user
$ cd /home/git/lorem.git
$ git log
```

This command should print the first revision by Peter.

How It Works

In this recipe you will work using three different accounts: vagrant, git, and peter.

The first account, vagrant, is the administrator of your host. It initializes all the repositories and sets the authorization rules.

The second user, git, is a dummy user. It doesn't allow you to open the ssh connection. Its only purpose is to allow other developers to connect with the git repositories using git clone, fetch, and push commands. When a developer, for instance Peter, issues a git command—such as $ git fetch—then Peter's git client will connect to the server using this dummy git account and then will execute some commands using git account privileges. For this to work, the administrator (vagrant user in our example) will have to allow Peter to use the git account on the server. This will be done with the authorized_keys file on the git account.

The last account, peter, is the account you will use to mock the work by someone else. We will use the account on the virtual system but you can also use any other account on any other computers in your organization.

The first account, vagrant, is available by default. Two other accounts, git and peter, are created manually with the $ sudo adduser command.

What does it mean that git is a dummy account? Thanks to the `--shell /usr/bin/git-shell` option of:

```
$ sudo adduser --shell /usr/bin/git-shell --gecos Git git
```

the git account will use `git-shell`. If you try to open the ssh session to the git account with:

```
# Host OS (e.g., Windows, Linux, OS X)
$ ssh -p2222 git@localhost
```

you will see the error message:

```
fatal: Interactive git shell is not enabled.
```

That's how we restrict the access to the git account. Because the account uses the interpreter `/usr/bin/git/git-shell` no one can log into this account using the ssh or the `$ sudo su git` command.

■ **Hint**   You can weaken the restrictions imposed by `git-shell` by creating a directory `~/git-shell-commands`. If this directory contains shell scripts then you will be allowed to open the ssh connection to this account and execute this script. Both the directory and the shell script should have `r` and `x` permission.

Peter's account is an ordinary user account. It is used by one of the developers for his or her daily work. You log on to this account using two methods:

```
# SSH connection to peter's account - first method
# Guest OS (Ubuntu 12.04)
# Commands executed by vagrant user
$ sudo su peter
$ cd
```

or:

```
# SSH connection to peter's account - second method
# Host OS (e.g., Windows, Linux, OS X)
$ ssh -p2222 peter@localhost
```

It doesn't really matter which method you choose.

Every time a new developer wants to join the team the following tasks should be done:

- The developer has to generate his or her RSA keys.

- The developer has to send his public key to the administrator.

- The administrator has to append the developer's public key to the `/home/git/.ssh/authorized_keys` file.

With this method every developer has full access to all repositories available to the git user. You cannot restrict access or define permissions on a per user basis.

There is no public read-only access for any of the repositories.

RSA keys

The command:

```
$ ssh-keygen -t rsa -C peter@example.net
```

generates the private/public key pair for the RSA algorithm. You will be asked two important questions: the path and passphrase. Both are important.

If you already have a pair of keys named ~/.ssh/id_rsa and ~/.ssh/id_rsa.pub then you should not override them. They can be very important to you. If you are not sure do not remove or override these files. Use the keys that you already have.

Assuming that your ~/.ssh/ directory doesn't contain id_rsa and id_rsa.pub, you can use the -f parameter for the ssh-keygen command:

```
$ ssh-keygen -t rsa -C peter@example.net -f .ssh/id_rsa
```

By using this command, you will avoid the question about the path. You can also use a different filename for your keys as in:

```
$ ssh-keygen -t rsa -C peter@example.net -f peter
```

This command will generate two files: peter and peter.pub in the current directory. To use them, you will need the ~/.ssh/config file, as described in the "SSH configuration" section.

The second question asked by the ssh-keygen command is a passphrase. This is a password that protects your private key. You will have to type it every time you run a git push or fetch command.

SSH and authorized_keys

SSH protocol allows you to access your remote account with the ssh client using two different methods of authorization. You can use the password to your account or public/private keys.

The command discussed in Recipe 11-1:

```
$ ssh -p2222 vagrant@127.0.0.1
```

uses the first method. Access is granted if you provide a valid password to the account. This method is straightforward but not convenient because git will ask for your password whenever you push or fetch.

The second method of authorization relies on RSA keys. There are two of them: private and public. Let's assume that your current account is person@local and that your private key is named id_rsa, and your public key is named id_rsa.pub. To allow access to the account foreign@remote from the account person@local you have to:

- Log into the foreign@remote account using the password

- Create a file named ~/.ssh/authorized_keys for the foreign@remote account

- Append the contents of the public key id_rsa.pub from the person@local to the file created in the previous step

The authorized_keys file is a very simple and effective way to allow access to the SSH account. This file can contain an arbitrary number of public keys, each in separate lines.

The first step to master SSH authorization is to use the default ~/.ssh/id_rsa and ~/.ssh/id_rsa.pub files and authorized_keys on the remote host. Sooner or later you will wonder why the keys have to be called ~/.ssh/id_rsa and ~/.ssh/id_rsa.pub. What if I want to use two or more pairs of keys? In that case you will have to change the configuration of your ssh client.

SSH configuration

If you want to use git with SSH protocol you will need a basic knowledge of how to configure your SSH client. The reason is very simple: the git command doesn't know how to parse SSH options. Therefore you cannot pass SSH options to the git command, as such as this:

```
$ git clone --ssh-option ssh://user@host
```

When you run a command such as:

```
$ git clone ssh://git@localhost/home/git/lorem.git
```

git uses your default SSH configuration. And if you want to use a specific SSH option, such as --ssh-option, you have to apply it to your default configuration.

■ **Hint**   Some options, such as a port number, can be handled by the $ git command. You don't need an option for this because the port number can be embedded in the URL: $ git clone ssh://user@host:2222

In general, there is no way to pass SSH options directly to the git command.

The most typical SSH option you will need is the name of the file with your private key. You can pass it to the ssh client as in the following:

```
$ ssh -i /some/path/my-private-key.rsa_id user@host
```

But git command doesn't accept it. The following solution will not work:

```
$ git clone -i /some/path/my-private-key.rsa_id ssh://user@host
```

The configuration of SSH is stored in the ~/.ssh/config file. If this file doesn't exist, then all the options come from the system configuration file named /etc/ssh/ssh_config. Your default keys are named ~/.ssh/id_rsa and ~/.ssh/id_rsa.pub.

If the file ~/.ssh/config exists then its contents override the options used by your ssh clients. The most often used options are shown in Listing 11-2. In fact, Listing 11-2 presents the options used by the $ vagrant ssh command. You can check them with the $ vagrant ssh-config command. That's why you can connect to the virtual machine with only minimal effort (without typing port number or password!).

Listing 11-2. The example contents of ~/.ssh/config file

```
Host localhost
  HostName 127.0.0.1
  User vagrant
  Port 2222
  UserKnownHostsFile /dev/null
```

```
StrictHostKeyChecking no
PasswordAuthentication no
IdentityFile /somewhere/.vagrant.d/insecure_private_key
IdentitiesOnly yes
LogLevel FATAL
```

■ **Hint** To create the file shown in Listing 11-2 you can use the `$ vagrant ssh-config > ~/.ssh/config` command. If you do this, remember to adjust the settings.

If you create the file `~/.ssh/config` shown in Listing 11-2 then the command:

```
$ ssh localhost
```

opens the connection to vagrant@`127.0.0.1` on port 2222 using private key from the `insecure_private_key` file and all the other options from Listing 11-2. The `vagrant` account on the virtual machine has its `~/.ssh/authorized_keys` file with the public key for `insecure_private_key`. That is why you can log onto the virtual machine with ssh without giving the password!

With these settings the command:

```
$ Host OS (Windows, Linux, OS X)
$ git clone localhost:/home/git/lorem.git
```

clones a repository vagrant@`127.0.0.1:/home/vagrant/lorem.git`. As you can see the simple text file `~/.ssh/config` allows you to specify all the options that should be used by git. The options in the `.ssh/config` file can be set on a per host basis.

In summary SSH authorization uses:

- On the client's side:

  - Private key: `~/.ssh/id_rsa`

  - Public key: `~/.ssh/id_rsa.pub`

  - Client's configuration: `~/.ssh/config`

- On the remote side:

  - The list of trusted users: `~/.ssh/authorized_keys`

11-6. Hosting git repositories with git daemon
Problem

You want to set up hosting with public read-only access for all the repositories under the git-recipes directory (i.e., all the repositories you created by following the recipes in this book). By public read-only access we mean that everyone can clone and fetch from your repositories. You want to use git daemon for this recipe.

Solution

Initialize a new virtual machine:

```
# Host OS (e.g., Windows, Linux, OS X)
$ cd git-recipes
$ mkdir 11-06
$ cd 11-06
```

Create the Vagrantfile appropriate for your system: if you work on Windows than change Vagrantfile as shown in Listing 11-3. If you work on a Unix-like system then use the Vagrantfile shown in Listing 11-4.

Listing 11-3. The Vagrantfile in Recipe 11-6 for Windows

```
VAGRANTFILE_API_VERSION = "2"
Vagrant.configure(VAGRANTFILE_API_VERSION) do |config|
  config.vm.box = "precise32"
  config.vm.box_url = "http://files.vagrantup.com/precise32.box"
  config.vm.network :forwarded_port, guest: 9418, host: 9418
  config.vm.synced_folder "c:\\some\\where\\git-recipes", "/pub/git"
end
```

Listing 11-4. The Vagrantfile in Recipe 11-6 for Unix-like systems

```
VAGRANTFILE_API_VERSION = "2"
Vagrant.configure(VAGRANTFILE_API_VERSION) do |config|
  config.vm.box = "precise32"
  config.vm.box_url = "http://files.vagrantup.com/precise32.box"
  config.vm.network :forwarded_port, guest: 9418, host: 9418
  config.vm.synced_folder "/some/where/git-recipes", "/pub/git"
end
```

■ **Hint** In this recipe we do not need to issue $ `vagrant init` because we create the complete Vagrantfile manually.

Boot the virtual machine and open the ssh session:

```
$ vagrant up
$ vagrant ssh
```

Update the system dependencies and install the git and git-daemon-run packages:

```
# Guest OS (Ubuntu 12.04)
$ sudo apt-get update -y
$ sudo apt-get install -y git git-daemon-run
```

The script responsible to start and stop git daemon is saved as /etc/sv/git-daemon/run. Open the editor:

```
$ sudo vi /etc/sv/git-daemon/run
```

And change this script as shown in Listing 11-5. You need to adjust two paths /pub and /pub/git and add the --export-all option. The parameter --export-all allows read-only access for all repositories.

Listing 11-5. Modified script /etc/sv/git-daemon/run

```
#!/bin/sh
exec 2>&1
echo 'git-daemon starting.'
exec chpst -ugitdaemon \
  "$(git --exec-path)"/git-daemon --verbose --reuseaddr \
    --export-all \
    --base-path=/pub /pub/git
```

Now you can restart daemon with

```
# Guest OS (Ubuntu 12.04)
$ sudo sv restart git-daemon
```

The virtual machine is ready. You can close the ssh session:

```
# Guest OS (Ubuntu 12.04)
$ exit
```

Cloning repositories hosted with git daemon

Now git daemon is running and everybody can clone arbitrary repositories stored in the git-recipes directory on your machine.

To clone a non-bare 03-06 repository run:

```
# Host OS (e.g., Windows, Linux, OS X)
$ git clone git://localhost/git/03-06
```

In almost the same manner you can clone a bare repository:

```
# Host OS (e.g., Windows, Linux, OS X)
$ git clone git://localhost/git/03-01.git
```

or even a .git directory of a non-bare repository:

```
# Host OS (e.g., Windows, Linux, OS X)
$ git clone git://localhost/git/03-05/.git
```

If your machine is available as 192.168.10.225, everyone on the network can clone using:

```
$ git clone git://192.168.10.225/git/03-05
```

How It Works

We want to make all the repositories stored in the git-recipes directory on the host system available on the guest system. This is achieved with the `config.vm.synced_folder` configuration entry of `Vagrantfile`. This was already discussed in Recipe 11-2. The second configuration option:

```
config.vm.network :forwarded_port, guest: 9418, host: 9418
```

concerns port forwarding.

Port forwarding

As you already know, when you boot the virtual machine your computer runs two operating systems: the host operating system and the guest operating system. I will assume that your host operating system is Windows and your guest operating system is Ubuntu 12.04. While the following explanation is true whatever your operating systems are these assumptions will help me clarify matters.

The main point you have to understand is that *each of these systems uses its own TCP ports*.

Let's suppose that you work on Windows (i.e., host OS). You start the web browser and you type the address `http://localhost:8080`. The browser will try to connect to the port 8080 on your host operating system (i.e., Windows). If you run the apache server on your Windows machine using the 8080 port, the connection can be successful. Your browser receives a web page served by your host machine.

Let's consider the guest operating system Ubuntu. Suppose that you open the ssh connection to your virtual machine and within your ssh session you run:

```
# Guest OS (Ubuntu 12.04)
$ ftp localhost:8080
```

The ftp will try to open the TCP connection to port 8080 on your guest operating system Ubuntu 12.04. If Ubuntu runs ftp daemon using the 8080 port, your ftp client will receive some ftp output.

In both cases the same port number 8080 was used. But as you can see the same port number can be assigned to different TCP/IP services. If your client runs on the host machine you will connect to the daemon on the host machine. If your client runs on the guest machine you will connect to the daemon on the guest machine.

We can say that both systems are separated.

From the outside world your guest operating system is not accessible at all. If your IP address is 192.168.10.225 and someone on your network tries to access `http://192.168.10.225:8080`, then his request will be sent to the host operating system (i.e., Windows).

How can we connect ports on the host and guest operating systems? This can be done with the `config.vm.network` configuration option in Vagrantfile. The option:

```
config.vm.network :forwarded_port, guest: N, host: M
```

sets the forwarding in such a way that a connection to your host machine on port number M will be served by daemon on the port N working on the guest system. The information about forwarding is printed when your system boots:

```
[default] Forwarding ports...
[default] -- N => M (adapter 1)
```

If you want to serve web pages by apache running on the guest machine you can use the following settings:

```
config.vm.network :forwarded_port, guest: 80, host: 8080
```

With the above settings the addresses `http://localhost:8080` you used in your host operating system will be served by daemon running on port 80 of the guest operating system. If your machine is available as example.net, then everyone can use `http://example.net:8080`. The requests will be forwarded to your guest daemon running port 80. The information about forwarding 8080 on host to 80 on guest is presented during booting in this way:

```
[default] Forwarding ports...
[default] -- 80 => 8080 (adapter 1)
```

By default, Vagrant uses the following rule:

```
config.vm.network :forwarded_port, guest: 22, host: 2222
```

presented as:

```
[default] Forwarding ports...
[default] -- 22 => 2222 (adapter 1)
```

That's why you can connect to the guest operating system with `$ vagrant ssh` or standard ssh clients. When you boot the virtual system, the port 2222 is forwarded to ssh daemon running on the guest operating system on the standard port 22. The connections to port 22 on the guest operating system are by default restricted to the IP address 127.0.0.1. That's why if you want to use ssh to your guest operations system through the network you have to use the following configuration settings:

```
config.vm.network :forwarded_port, guest: 22, host: 22
```

The above rule turns on port forwarding: the connections to port 22 on the host machine will be served by service 22 on the guest machine. The IP addresses are not restricted, thus everyone on the network can use ssh to your virtual machine.

The configuration used in this recipe:

```
config.vm.network :forwarded_port, guest: 9418, host: 9418
```

turns on forwarding for port 9418. This is the standard port used by git daemon. All the requests to your host machine to port 9418 are served by daemon running on the guest operating system on the same port.

■ **Hint**   The documentation for git daemon is available as `$ git daemon --help`

What happens if you boot two virtual machines?

When you boot two virtual machines they both cannot use the same ports. Therefore, the port 2222 can be forwarded to only one of them. The first virtual machine you boot will get the port number 2222 for its ssh daemon:

```
# Booting the first virtual machine
[default] Forwarding ports...
[default] -- 22 => 2222 (adapter 1)
```

The second virtual machine will obtain the 2200 port:

```
# Booting the second virtual machine
[default] Forwarding ports...
[default] -- 22 => 2200 (adapter 1)
```

It is very easy to forget which port is used for which machine. Therefore I advise you to have only one virtual machine running at any given time.

The command:

```
$ vagrant ssh
```

is immune to changed port number. It will always connect you with the machine started from the current server. You can check the ssh settings with:

```
$ vagrant ssh-config
```

But some other commands, such as scp, need to be adjusted.

11-7. Hosting git repositories over http

Problem

You wish to set up hosting with public read-only access to the repository. By public read-only access we mean that everyone can clone and fetch from the repository. You want to use http protocol.

Solution

Initialize a new virtual machine:

```
# Host OS (e.g., Windows, Linux, OS X)
$ cd git-recipes
$ mkdir 11-07
$ cd 11-07
```

Create the Vagrantfile shown in Listing 11-6. The path to git-recipes needs to be adjusted to suit your system.

Listing 11-6. Vagrantfile in Recipe 11-6

```
VAGRANTFILE_API_VERSION = "2"
Vagrant.configure(VAGRANTFILE_API_VERSION) do |config|
  config.vm.box = "precise32"
  config.vm.box_url = "http://files.vagrantup.com/precise32.box"
  config.vm.synced_folder "c:\\some\\where\\git-recipes", "/pub/git"
end
```

Boot the virtual machine and open the ssh session:

```
$ vagrant up
$ vagrant ssh
```

Update the system dependencies and install the git and apache2 packages:

```
# Guest OS (Ubuntu 12.04)
$ sudo apt-get update -y
$ sudo apt-get install -y git apache2
```

Install the repository you want to share.

```
# Guest OS (Ubuntu 12.04)
$ cd /var/www
$ sudo git clone --bare /pub/git/03-01 03-01.git
$ sudo chown -R vagrant:www-data /var/www/03-01.git
```

Create the hook:

```
# Guest OS (Ubuntu 12.04)
$ cd /var/www/03-01.git/hooks
$ mv post-update.sample post-update
```

Run post update for the first time:

```
# Guest OS (Ubuntu 12.04)
$ cd /var/www/03-01.git/
$ git update-server-info
```

The repository is now available to the public with the following URL: `http://localhost/03-01.git`. Clone it with:

```
# Guest OS (Ubuntu 12.04)
$ cd
$ git clone http://localhost/03-01.git
```

Close ssh:

```
# Guest OS (Ubuntu 12.04)
$ exit
```

Stop the virtual machine:

```
# Host OS (e.g., Windows, Linux, OS X)
$ vagrant halt
```

How It Works

The method of hosting described in this recipe provides read-only anonymous access to the repository /var/www/03-01.git. Everyone who can access the host using HTTP protocol can clone this repository. But the clone created with HTTP, as in:

```
$ git clone http://localhost/03-01.git
```

cannot be used to push to the original repository. HTTP allows read-only access.

If you want to host a repository over HTTP protocol in a read-only anonymous mode you have to:

- Make the directory with the repository available through HTTP protocol
- Update the information about branches
- Create the hook that will update the information about branches with every push

The command `$ git update-server-info` creates a text file `.git/info/refs` with all your branches and references. When you use HTTP protocol to access the repository, as in `$ git clone` http://localhost/03-01.git, then git first downloads the `.git/info/refs`. That's how the client knows about the references in the cloned repository.

The file `.git/info/refs` has to be updated after every push. Otherwise the client would get stale references. This is achieved with the hook stored in `.git/hooks/post-update`. This shell script executes a single `$ git update-server-info` command.

■ **Hint** If you want to push to `/var/www/03-01.git` you have to use the SSH protocol described in Recipe 11-4 or the local protocol described in Recipe 10-2.

11-8. Using Gitweb CGI application
Problem

You want to install and run the web application named Gitweb. This is a CGI script written in Perl, which offers an intuitive web interface to git repositories. You want allow browsing all the repositories under the `git-recipes` directory.

Solution

Initialize a new virtual machine:

```
# Host OS (e.g., Windows, Linux, OS X)
$ cd git-recipes
$ mkdir 11-08
$ cd 11-08
```

Create the Vagrantfile presented in Listing 11-7. If you work on the Unix-like system remember to change the path to a `git-recipes` directory.

Listing 11-7. The Vagrantfile from Recipe 11-8 for Windows

```
VAGRANTFILE_API_VERSION = "2"
Vagrant.configure(VAGRANTFILE_API_VERSION) do |config|
  config.vm.box = "precise32"
  config.vm.box_url = "http://files.vagrantup.com/precise32.box"
  config.vm.network :forwarded_port, guest: 80, host: 8080
  config.vm.synced_folder "c:\\some\\where\\git-recipes", "/pub/git"
end
```

Boot the virtual machine and open the ssh session:

```
$ vagrant up
$ vagrant ssh
```

Update the system dependencies and install the git and gitweb packages:

```
# Guest OS (Ubuntu 12.04)
$ sudo apt-get update -y
$ sudo apt-get install -y git gitweb
```

Next modify Gitweb's configuration. Open the /etc/gitweb.conf file with $ sudo vi /etc/gitweb.conf and change the line:

```
$projectroot = "/var/cache/git";
```

to:

```
$projectroot = "/pub/git";
```

Finally, open your web browser (on the host machine) and visit the following address:

```
http://localhost:8080/gitweb
```

You should see the web page presented in Figure 11-2. The name of every repository is the hyperlink. If you follow it you will see the page presenting detailed information about the repository. Figure 11-3 presents the detailed information about repository 03-01. The description:

```
Unnamed repository; edit this file 'description' to name the repository.
```

that is visible on both figures can be changed. It comes from the .git/description file.

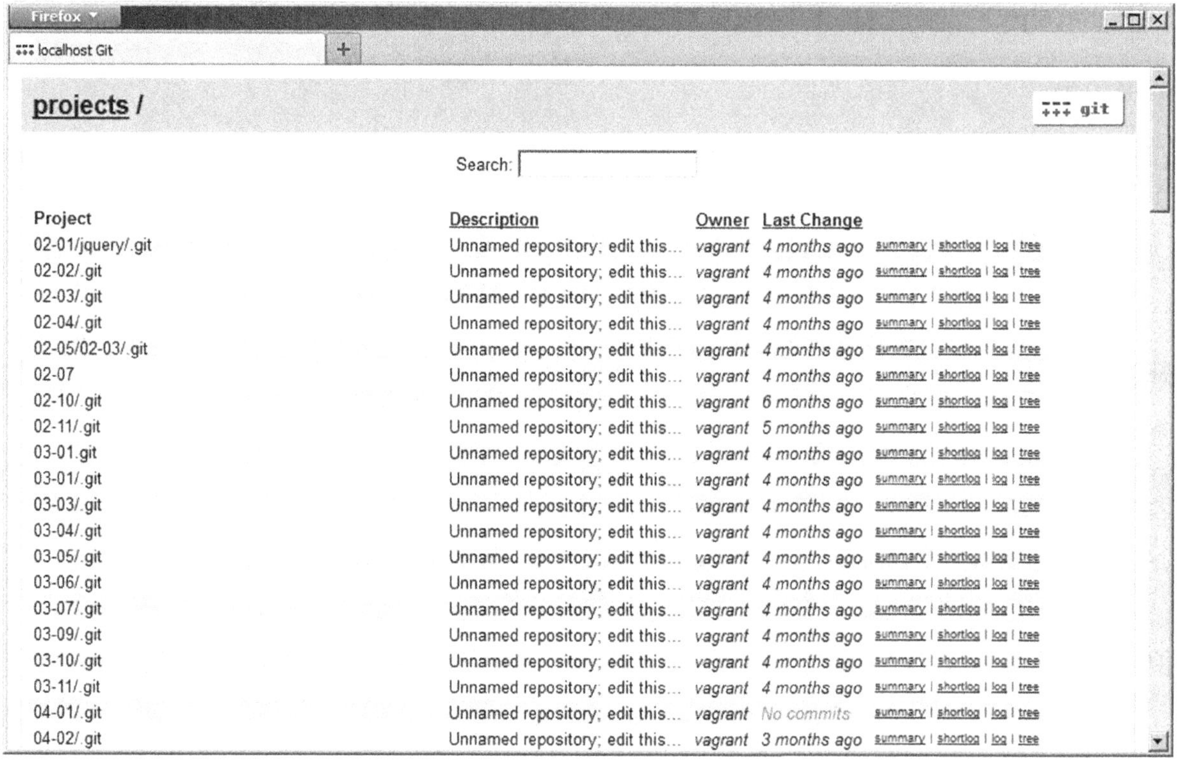

Figure 11-2. *The main page of the Gitweb application lists all available repositories*

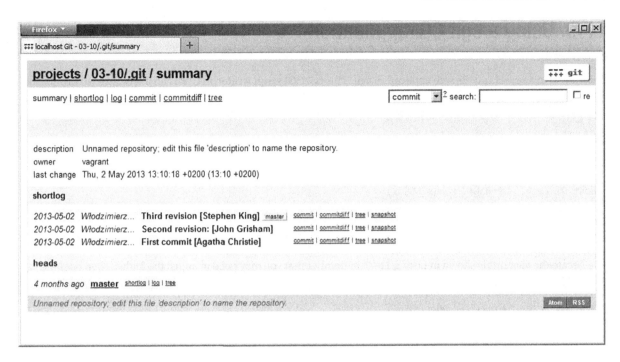

Figure 11-3. *The main page of 03-10 repository presented by Gitweb*

■ **Hint**   Take a good look at Figure 11-3. Gitweb doesn't provide URLs to clone a repository. You can only browse them with a web interface.

How It Works

You want to serve web pages by the apache daemon on the guest machine. To do it configure forwarding for port 8080:

```
config.vm.network :forwarded_port, guest: 80, host: 8080
```

The second option in Vagrantfile, which is:

```
config.vm.synced_folder "c:\\some\\where\\git-recipes", "/pub/git"
```

turns on synchronization of the git-recipes directory on the host machine (i.e., your Windows system) with /pub/git on the guest machine (i.e., virtual Ubuntu system).

By default, Gitweb scans the /var/cache/git directory for repositories. That's why you need to change the project root in the /etc/gitweb.conf file. We set it to the directory git-recipes on the host operating system. This is why we need to synchronize /pub/git on the guest machine with git-recipes on host machine.

Default configuration for apache is stored in /etc/apache2/sites-available/default. That's where you should look to change the configuration of the web server. You may need it to configure url rewriting rules.

11-9. Using a cgit CGI application

Problem

You want to install and run the web application cgit. This is a CGI script written in C. It is an alternative to Gitweb. You want to allow browsing in all the repositories under the `git-recipes` directory.

Solution

Initialize the virtual machine:

```
# Host OS (e.g., Windows, Linux, OS X)
$ cd git-recipes
$ mkdir 11-09
$ cd 11-09
```

Create the Vagrantfile shown in Listing 11-7. Remember that you may need to adjust the folder. Then boot the virtual machine and open the ssh session:

```
# Host OS (e.g., Windows, Linux, OS X)
$ vagrant up
$ vagrant ssh
```

Update the system packages and install git, apache2, and all the tools and libraries necessary to compile cgit:

```
# Guest OS (Ubuntu 12.04)
$ sudo apt-get update -y
$ sudo apt-get install -y git
$ sudo apt-get install -y apache2
$ sudo apt-get install -y make libssl-dev libz-dev gettext libexpat1-dev libcurl4-openssl-dev
```

Download cgit sources:

```
# Guest OS (Ubuntu 12.04)
$ git clone --recurse-submodules --depth 1 git://git.zx2c4.com/cgit
```

Compile and install cgit with the following commands:

```
# Guest OS (Ubuntu 12.04)
$ cd cgit
$ make
$ sudo make install CGIT_SCRIPT_PATH="/var/www"
```

Adjust cgit's configuration to suit your needs:

```
# Guest OS (Ubuntu 12.04)
$ sudo mv /var/www/cgit.cgi /usr/lib/cgi-bin
$ sudo touch /etc/cgirc
$ sudo sh -c "echo scan-path=/pub/git >> /etc/cgitrc"
$ sudo sh -c "echo clone-prefix=ssh://vagrant@localhost:2222/pub/git >> /etc/cgitrc"
```

And finally run your web browser and open the following URL:

```
http://localhost:8080/cgi-bin/cgit.cgi
```

You will see the web page shown in Figure 11-4. Figure 11-5 presents the detailed information about the repository 03-10. As you can see this time the page contains an URL that allows you to clone the repository.

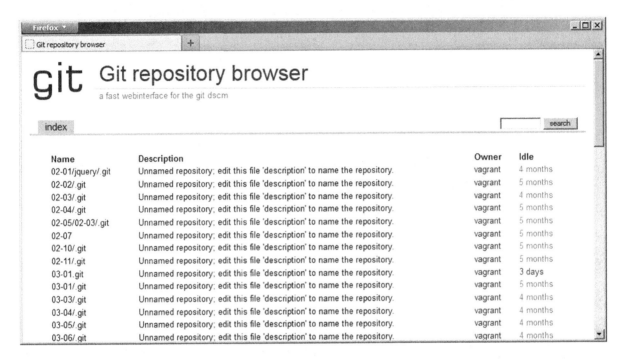

Figure 11-4. *The main page of cgit*

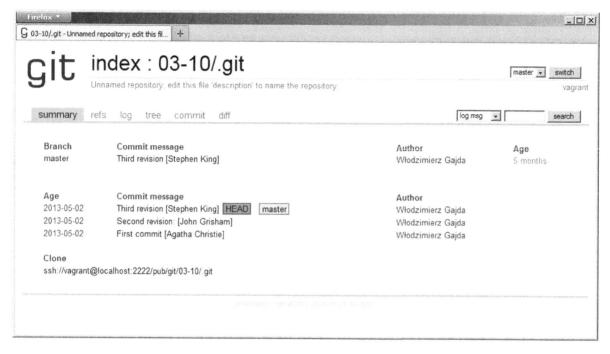

Figure 11-5. *The main page of 03-10 presented by cgit*

How It Works

The latest version of cgit is always available at:

```
http://git.zx2c4.com/cgit/
```

The sources of cgit include a source code of git. This is done with *submodules*. The switch `--recurse-submodules` clones the repository and all submodules. Unfortunately, the `--depth 1` option is not used for submodules. The cloning of git sources in this recipe will last much longer than in Recipe 11-3.

The configuration file `/etc/gitrc` allows easy configuration of URLs for cloning. This type of URL is visible in the lower part of Figure 11-3. If you want to use cgit with ssh and git daemon, try the following configuration:

```
clone-prefix=ssh://vagrant@localhost:2222/pub/git git ://localhost/git
```

11-10. Working with gitolite
Problem

You want to set up git hosting for your organization using ssh and gitolite. This will give you the ability to grant access using three different rights:

- Read
- Write
- Forced write

Each of these rights can be assigned on a per user, per repository, and per branch basis.

Your task in this recipe is to set up a virtual machine for hosting git repositories over ssh with gitolite. You want to create two gitolite accounts: admin and peter and one repository abc. Admin will be the administrator and peter will be ordinary user. Using the administrator's account you will set the following privileges for peter:

- Branch a—read/write access with forced pushes

- Branch b—read/write access without forced pushes

- Branch c—read-only access

The repository abc in this recipe will be a clone of the repository from Recipe 6-7.

Solution

Initialize a new virtual machine with:

```
# Host OS (e.g., Windows, Linux, OS X)
$ cd git-recipes
$ mkdir 11-10
$ cd 11-10
$ vagrant init precise32 http://files.vagrantup.com/precise32.box
```

Add the configuration option responsible for synchronizing the git-recipes directory:

```
config.vm.synced_folder "c:\\some\\where\\git-recipes", "/pub/git"
```

Boot the virtual machine and open the ssh session:

```
# Host OS (e.g., Windows, Linux, OS X)
$ vagrant up
$ vagrant ssh
```

Installation of a gitolite package

Upgrade the dependencies and install gitolite:

```
# Guest OS (Ubuntu 12.04)
# as vagrant user
$ sudo apt-get update -y
$ sudo apt-get install -y gitolite
```

Creating the git and peter accounts

Create a new user with:

```
# Guest OS (Ubuntu 12.04)
# as vagrant user
$ sudo adduser --gecos Git git
$ sudo adduser --gecos Peter peter
```

Configuring a git and RSA key for the vagrant user

Configure the git settings for the vagrant user:

```
# Guest OS (Ubuntu 12.04)
# as vagrant user
$ git config --global user.name vagrant
$ git config --global user.email vagrant@localhost
```

Generate the ssh key for the vagrant user on your guest machine

```
# Guest OS (Ubuntu 12.04)
# as vagrant user
$ ssh-keygen -t rsa -C vagrant@localhost -N "" -f .ssh/id_rsa
```

Copy vagrant's public key to the home directory of the git account:

```
# Guest OS (Ubuntu 12.04)
# as vagrant user
$ scp ~/.ssh/id_rsa.pub git@127.0.0.1:admin.pub
```

Use git account's password to complete the above command.

Configuring a git and RSA key for the peter user

Switch to peter's account:

```
# Guest OS (Ubuntu 12.04)
# as vagrant user
$ sudo su - peter
```

Configure the git settings for the peter user:

```
# Guest OS (Ubuntu 12.04)
# as peter user
$ git config --global user.name peter
$ git config --global user.email peter@localhost
```

Generate the ssh key for the peter user on your guest machine

```
# Guest OS (Ubuntu 12.04)
# as peter user
$ mkdir .ssh
$ ssh-keygen -t rsa -C vagrant@localhost -N "" -f .ssh/id_rsa
```

Copy peter's public key to the home directory of the vagrant account:

```
# Guest OS (Ubuntu 12.04)
# as peter user
$ scp ~/.ssh/id_rsa.pub vagrant@127.0.0.1:peter.pub
```

Use the vagrant account's password to complete the above command.

Close Peter's shell:

```
# Guest OS (Ubuntu 12.04)
# as peter user
$ exit
```

Configuring gitolite for the git account

Log in as a git user with:

```
# Guest OS (Ubuntu 12.04)
# as vagrant user
$ sudo su - git
```

Now, the $ ls command:

```
# Guest OS (Ubuntu 12.04)
# as git user
$ ls
```

should print one file: admin.pub. Set up gitolite for the git account:

```
# Guest OS (Ubuntu 12.04)
# as git user
$ gl-setup admin.pub
```

The above command is executed only once—when you initialize the work with gitolite on the git@localhost account. It opens the vi editor with the gitolite configuration. Save the file and close the ssh session to the git account:

```
# Guest OS (Ubuntu 12.04)
# as git user
$ exit
```

Creating repositories

To create a new repository open the ssh session to the git account:

```
# Guest OS (Ubuntu 12.04)
# as vagrant user
$ sudo su - git
```

Clone the repository from Recipe 6-7:

```
# Guest OS (Ubuntu 12.04)
# as git user
$ git clone --bare file:///pub/git/06-07 /home/git/repositories/abc.git
```

Log out from the git account:

```
# Guest OS (Ubuntu 12.04)
# as git user
$ exit
```

Setting up privileges

As a vagrant user clone the gitolite-admin repository:

```
# Guest OS (Ubuntu 12.04)
# as vagrant user
$ git clone git@localhost:gitolite-admin.git
```

Copy the peter.pub key from the vagrant's home directory to the gitolite-admin/keydir directory:

```
# Guest OS (Ubuntu 12.04)
# as vagrant user
$ mv /home/vagrant/peter.pub /home/vagrant/gitolite-admin/keydir
```

As a vagrant user edit the /home/vagrant/gitolite-admin/conf/gitolite.conf file and insert the contents presented in Listing 11-8.

Listing 11-8. The contents of the /home/vagrant/gitolite-admin/conf/gitolite.conf file

```
repo    gitolite-admin
        RW+     =   admin

repo    testing
        RW+     =   @all

repo    abc
        RW+     a   =   peter
        RW      b   =   peter
        R       c   =   peter
```

Commit the changes in the gitolite-admin repository and push it to the server:

```
# Guest OS (Ubuntu 12.04)
# as vagrant user
$ cd /home/vagrant/gitolite-admin
$ git add -A
$ git commit -m "Peter's priviledges for abc repo"
$ git push origin master
```

Working within the gitolite controlled repository

Now you are faking the work by Peter. Log in to Peter's account:

```
# Guest OS (Ubuntu 12.04)
# as vagrant user
$ sudo su - peter
```

Clone the abc repository:

```
# Guest OS (Ubuntu 12.04)
# as peter user
$ git clone git@localhost:abc
```

The clone will succeed only because peter has R rights for some references. If you try to clone gitolite-admin repository using peter's account:

```
# Guest OS (Ubuntu 12.04)
# as peter user
$ git clone git@localhost:gitolite-admin
```

the operation will be rejected because Peter has no privileges for the gitolite-admin repository.

Now enter the abc repository with the cd command and switch to branch a, remove the last commit, and perform a forced push:

```
# Guest OS (Ubuntu 12.04)
# as peter user
$ cd abc
$ git checkout a
$ git reset --hard HEAD~
$ git push -f origin a
```

The above push will be accepted because Peter has RW+ access to branch a.

Next, switch to branch b and try to remove the last commit and perform the forced push for branch b:

```
# Guest OS (Ubuntu 12.04)
# as peter user
$ git checkout b
$ git reset --hard HEAD~
$ git push -f origin b
```

This time the forced push will be rejected because Peter has only RW privileges to branch b.

Update your local branch b to the state of origin/b, then create a new revision and push it:

```
# Guest OS (Ubuntu 12.04)
# as peter user
$ git rebase origin/b
$ echo x > x.txt
$ git add -A
$ git commit -m x
$ git push origin b
```

The above operation is a fast-forward push. Peter has RW rights, therefore the fast-forward is accepted.

Switch to branch c and try to perform a fast-forward push:

```
# Guest OS (Ubuntu 12.04)
# as peter user
$ git checkout c
$ echo y > y.txt
$ git add -A
$ git commit -m y
$ git push origin c
```

This time the push is rejected even if it is a fast-forward. That is because Peter has only R rights to the branch c.

How It Works

The best solution to host git repositories for the private projects of your team is to use SSH with git account and public keys, as shown in Recipe 11-5. The problem with this approach is that every user whose public key is appended to git user's authorized_keys file has full read/write access with forced pushes for every repository stored in the git user's account. In other words every user who is successfully authenticated by SSH to access that git account, gains full access to every git account. The only restriction that you can enforce using built-in git features is to disable shell access as we did in Recipe 11-5 with changing git user's shell to git-shell.

Gitolite is a tool to circumvent these shortcomings. It is very simple to install and to work with.

▓ **Hint**   The complete gitolite documentation is available at `http://gitolite.com/gitolite/master-toc.html`.

To start using gitolite you need a host serving git repositories over ssh using a git account. The git account cannot be restricted with git-shell. It needs an ordinary ssh shell. The access to the shell of a git account will be restricted by gitolite itself. Thus, the first account we need is git.

The second account we will use is the administrator who sets the privileges. He creates new repositories, removes repositories that are not used anymore, adds new users, removes stale users, and defines appropriate rights for every user to every repository. We will use the vagrant account in this role.

To fake the work by an ordinary user we will need another account. It will be named peter.

Summarizing, in this recipe we work with three accounts:

- git—this is the account used for ssh access

- vagrant—he is the administrator, who assigns access rights

- peter—he is ordinary developer who works in one of the repositories

The gitolite package is installed in the system by the vagrant user with the $ sudo apt-get install command. Once the package is installed we can configure it for any arbitrary account. The command to configure gitolite for an account is $ gl-setup. The only necessary parameter of this command is the filename of the public key for the administrator. We want to use vagrant as the administrator, thus we first have to generate the RSA key for vagrant:

```
# Guest OS (Ubuntu 12.04)
# as vagrant user
$ ssh-keygen -t rsa -C vagrant@localhost -N "" -f .ssh/id_rsa
```

The key has to be copied to git account. We use the scp command for this:

```
# Guest OS (Ubuntu 12.04)
# as vagrant user
$ scp ~/.ssh/id_rsa.pub git@127.0.0.1:admin.pub
```

You should notice that vagrant's public key ~/.ssh/id_rsa.pub will be copied to the git@localhost account and stored in the admin.pub file. The file is renamed from id_rsa.pub to admin.pub. This is very important. Gitolite uses filenames as usernames. If you name the public key file as sarah.pub, then gitolite will treat this key as the user named sarah.

When the file admin.pub is copied to the git@localhost account you can configure gitolite to run at the git@localhost account. Open the shell connection to the git account with:

```
$ sudo su - git
```

and then run the following command:

```
$ gl-setup admin.pub
```

It will configure gitolite for the git@localhost account.

Managing users and privileges

All management tasks concerning users are performed by someone who can be authenticated with the admin.pub key. In this recipe it is vagrant user. The admin.pub key is the parameter passed to the $ gl-setup command.

Gitolite doesn't have a user interface. The management is done through a gitolite-admin repository available under the following URL: git@localhost:gitolite-admin. The first step is to clone this repository:

```
$ git clone git@localhost:gitolite-admin
```

The above command will succeed only if it is issued by the user whose one of the RSA keys is the same as admin.pub. Thus the vagrant user can clone the repository gitolite-admin. When Peter tries to clone it he will only see the message about insufficient rights.

Once the gitolite-admin repository is cloned by vagrant, he can perform the administrative tasks. To add users he copies public keys into gitolite-admin/keydir directory. To assign rights he edits the gitolite-admin/conf/gitolite.conf file. The changes are applied when the administrator pushes them to the server:

```
# the command issued by administrator
# in his or her gitolite-admin repository
# applies the rights
$ git push origin master
```

The simplest syntax to assign privileges in gitolite.config file is the following:

```
repo foo
    RW+         =   sarah
    RW          =   paul
    R           =   ann
```

It assigns RW+ rules to sarah, RW rule to paul, and R rule to ann. All these rules are defined for foo repository. The keys for sarah, paul, and ann should be stored in:

```
gitolite-admin/keys/sarah.pub
gitolite-admin/keys/paul.pub
gitolite-admin/keys/ann.pub
```

Keep in mind that usernames for their accounts are not important. Sarah can use the account rose@some-host as long as her ~/.ssh/id_rsa.pub file contains the same key as in gitolite-admin/keys/sarah.pub.

Managing repositories

The repositories managed by gitolite are stored within the /home/git/repositories directory. The easiest way to manage them is to use the git account. After opening the ssh session go to git@localhost with:

```
$ ssh git@localhost
```

You can enter the directory:

```
$ cd
$ cd repositories
```

And list all available repositories:

```
$ ls -la
```

If you want to initialize a new repository use the following command:

```
$ git init --bare /home/git/repositories/lorem.git
```

To clone an existing project use:

```
$ git clone --bare some-existing-repo /home/git/repositories/ipsum.git
```

You can also remove a repository with:

```
$ rm -rf /home/git/repositories/some-repo.git
```

The command $ ssh git@localhost will succeed only when issued by administrator. If any other user tries to use ssh to git@localhost he or she will only see the information about his or her current privileges:

```
hello peter, this is gitolite 2.2-1 (Debian) running on git 1.7.9.5
the gitolite config gives you the following access:
    R   W     06-07
   @R_ @W_    testing
```

Summary

The recipes in this chapter concern mainly the tasks that are usually performed by someone with root access to your host. To avoid the risk of messing with the host your organization uses for its every day work, I decided to explain administrative tasks using the virtual machine. Working that way you can drill and practice how to install and remove packages in your system without the slightest risk.

I prepared these recipes for beginners without previous experience with vagrant or ssh. The only assumption I made was that you would be familiar with all the recipes from previous chapter. Therefore, I included all the necessary background. Moreover, every recipe is complete. This may make the recipes a little longer to run, but I believe they will be easier to follow.

Depending on your needs, in my opinion, the following are the best choices you can make:

- If you want to host private repositories with the ability to define access rules—follow Recipe 11-10.

- If you want to host private repositories without the ability to define access rules (every user has full access to all repositories)—follow Recipe 11-5.

- If you want to host publicly available repositories—follow Recipe 11-6.

- If you need web interface for your repositories use cgit—follow Recipe 11-9.

The protocols used by git

Along with the four network protocols presented in Table 11-1, git can handle local URLs. You already are quite familiar with commands such as:

```
$ git clone a/local/path/repo.git
```

This command clones a repository available in local directory a/local/path/repo.git. A local clone also can be created with:

```
$ git clone file:///a/local/path/repo.git
```

The difference between the two URLs:

```
a/local/path/repo.git
file:///a/local/path/repo.git
```

is that the first one allows git to use a standard filesystem operations (such as copy) and hard links. The second URL doesn't allow git to create hard links and the data transfer is executed in networked style, not with cp command. This is less efficient, of course, but creates a fresh copy, without any hard links.

When we combine the four networked protocols from Table 11-1 with the two local ones we get the complete list of protocols used by git. The protocol used for a repository is encoded in the URL. Table 11-2 presents an example of URLs for all protocols used by git. If you know the URL of the repository you can easily guess the protocol that git will use.

Table 11-2. *The protocol used by git can be guessed from the repository's URL*

Protocol	URL used for cloning
local	`$ git clone some/local/path/dir/repo.git`
file	`$git clone file:///pub/git/dir/repo.git` `$git clone file:///c/dir/repo.git`

ssh	`$git clone ssh://user@host:dir/repo.git`
	`$git clone user@host:dir/repo.git`
	`$git clone host:/dir/repo.git`

http	`$git clone http://host/dir/repo.git`
https	`$git clone https://host/dir/repo.git`
git	`$git clone git://host/dir/repo.git`

■ ■ ■

## CHAPTER 12

Working with Github.com

In this chapter I discuss using Github to host repositories. Currently this is a popular hosting platform for open-source projects.

We begin by creating a Github account and configuring the SSH keys. When this is done you will learn how to:

- Clone from public Github repositories

- Clone and push to your repositories

Later, I will show you how to start a new Github-hosted project from scratch, and how to import an existing project. Then we will proceed with a pull request. To exercise the work in the role of both contributor and administrator, we will use two Github accounts: your personal account and an organizational account. Working in this way you can fork projects owned by your organization into your personal account.

12-1. Creating a Github account
Problem

You want to use Github.com for one of two reasons:

- To host your own git repositories

- To contribute to some open-source projects

You cannot do this unless you are a registered Github.com user. Therefore your first task is to create a new Github account.

Solution

Start your web browser and visit Github.com. Follow the link "Sign up for GitHub". Fill in the registration form and submit it. When you finish log in using your newly created account.

If you want to use an avatar for your Github account, go to the http://gravatar.com website. Create an account in Gravatar.com, upload your avatar, and associate it with the email you used for your Github account.

When you have finished configuring an avatar on Gravatar.com, go to Github.com, log out, and then log in to your account again. Your account should now use the new avatar.

How It Works

The signing-up procedure is trivial and should be easy to use. The point of this recipe is to emphasize the fact we mentioned in Recipe 2-1: Github doesn't allow the use of SSH protocol until you have configured your own SSH keys. The command:

```
$ git clone git@github.com:jquery/jquery.git
```

fails, producing the following message:

```
Permission denied (publickey).
fatal: Could not read from remote repository.

Please make sure you have the correct access rights
and the repository exists.
```

This error is produced:

- If you don't have Github account.

- If your account is not configured to use SSH keys.

The URL in the above $ git clone command:

```
git@github.com:jquery/jquery.git
```

uses SSH protocol. You will find a complete reference of protocol used by git in Table 11-2.

12-2. Configuring a Github account with SSH keys
Problem

You want to configure your Github account in such a way that git allows you to clone, fetch, and push using SSH URLs.

Solution

To complete this recipe you will need an SSH key pair. Check if your ~/.ssh/ directory contains them. Open a bash window and list the contents of the .ssh directory:

```
$ ls ~/.ssh
```

If this directory doesn't contain the id_rsa and id_rsa.pub files, then you have to generate them. The command you need is:

```
$ ssh-keygen -t rsa -C your.email@example.net
```

This command will ask you two questions that were explained in Recipe 11-5 under the RSA keys section. The first question sets the names for the two files with keys; the second sets the use of a passphrase to protect your keys. If you press *ENTER* the files will be stored in default location and the passphrase will not be used.

When the id_rsa and id_rsa.pub files are ready, start your web browser and visit Github.com. Follow the link titled "Sign up for GitHub;" when you finish, log in using your newly created account.

To use key-based authentication, you have to upload your public key to your account. Copy the contents of your public key stored in ~/.ssh/id_rsa.pub onto the clipboard. If you work on Windows you can use the following command:

```
$ clip < ~/.ssh/id_rsa.pub
```

Readers working on other systems can open the file with their favorite text editor and use the edit/copy commands.

Go to your Github account settings, open the *SSH Keys* menu option, and then press the *Add SSH key* button. When you see a form titled *Add an SSH Key*, paste the contents of your clipboard into the form. Then press the *Add key* button. The process of adding an SSH key is illustrated in Figure 12-1. Follow the arrows labeled A, B, C, D, and E. When you have finished, the uploaded key will be listed under SSH Keys, as shown in Figure 12-2.

Figure 12-1. *Adding a new SSH key on Github account*

Figure 12-2. *Succesfully uploaded keys are listed under SSH Keys*

The configuration is finished. You can verify this by cloning the arbitrary public repository using SSH protocol. If the command:

```
$ git clone git@github.com:jquery/jquery.git
```

succeeds, then your keys are correct. You can use SSH protocol to access repositories hosted on Github.

How It Works

SSH protocol doesn't allow anonymous access. To use it you need an account on the server. Github uses a single account named git for all users. That's why all clone commands include git@github, as in:

```
$ git clone git@github.com:jquery/jquery.git
```

The above command means that you are accessing a git account at the host github.com. SSH daemon working on github.com grants access to a git account only if the key-based authentication succeeds—that happens if your public SSH key was configured for your git@github.com account. If not, you will not be allowed access to any of the resources. This hosting solution was explained in Recipes 11-5 and 11-10. The web interface presented in Figures 12-1 and 12-2 just simplifies the task of managing your public SSH keys.

12-3. Creating a Github-hosted repository for a new project
Problem

You want to start a new project and host it on Github.

Solution

Start your web browser and log in to Github.com. Then click the *Create a new repo* button. The button *Create a new repo* is on the menu displayed in the upper-right corner of the Github webpage (see A in Figure 12-3). You will find the same button in Figures 12-1 and 12-2 as well.

Figure 12-3. *Creating a new repository on* Github.com

When you press the *Create a new repo* button you will see the form presented in Figure 12-3. Enter 12-03 in the *Repository name* edit box and then press the *Create repository* button (see B and C in Figure 12-3).

After this you will see the page shown in Figure 12-4, which displays the URL for this repository and the two procedures you can use to start your work. Assuming that your Github account is named john-doe, the URL for your repository will look like:

```
git@github.com:john-doe/12-03.gi
```

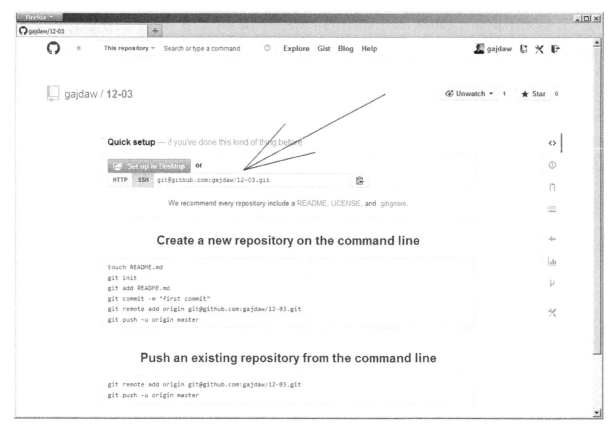

Figure 12-4. *Webpage for the newly created repository*

You will find it in the edit box shown in Figure 12-4.

The work on Github is finished for now. Open your bash command line and execute the following commands:

```
# the commands should be executed in git-recipes directory
$ cd git-recipes
$ git clone git@github.com:john-doe/12-03.git
$ cd 12-03
$ git simple-commit a b c
$ git push -u origin master
```

Now go back to Github.com and follow the link identified in Figure 12-5 with A. You will see the list of files stored in the repository. The list will include three files: a.txt, b.txt, and c.txt, as pointed by the B arrow in Figure 12-5.

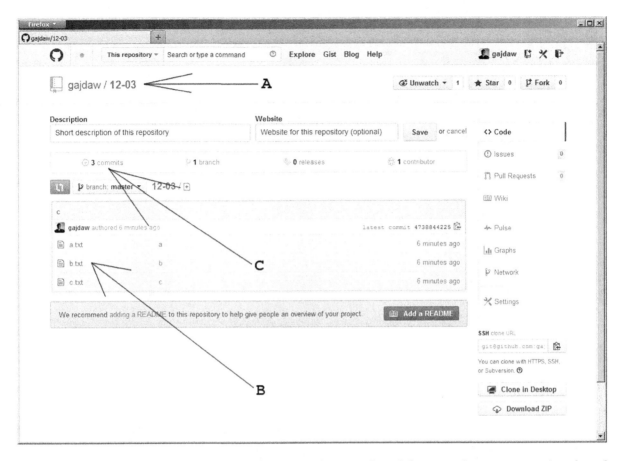

Figure 12-5. *The $ git push -u origin master command sent the master branch from your drive to your repository hosted by Github*

How It Works

To create a new repository hosted on Github you should use web interface. When the new repository is created you can clone it. Use the local clone to create new commits and when you want to send the updated repository on Github use the $ git push command. Using the button pointed by the C arrow in Figure 12-5 you can display the list of revisions stored in repository. The list is shown in Figure 12-6.

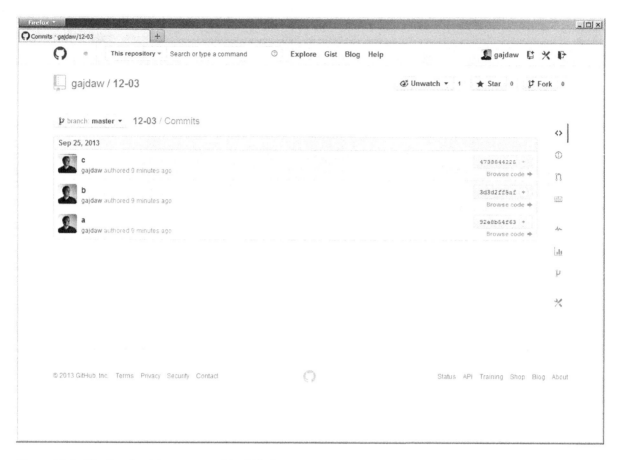

Figure 12-6. *The list of revisions presented by Github*

As you will remember from Recipe 8-1, every revision stores two special attributes to assign authorship. They are `Author` and `Commit`. `Author` is the name of the person who created the code. `Commit` is the name of the person who created the revision. For the revisions presented in Figure 12-6 both `Author` and `Commit` are set to the same person, Włodzimierz Gajda and email gajdaw@gajdaw.pl. Github uses this email to guess the name of the account. Therefore my commits are captioned as authored by `gajdaw`. Because the `Author` and `Commit` data are the same, the authorship is reduced to simple `gajdaw`. This means that `gajdaw` created the code and the commit.

What happens if the commit contains a different name for `Author` and a different name for `Commit`? Github presents this information as shown in Figure 12-7. The revision presented in Figure 12-7 was authored by John Doe and rebased by gajdaw. Github displays these messages:

```
John Doe authored...
Gajdaw committed...
```

foo

John Doe authored a minute ago

➡ gajdaw committed just now

Figure 12-7. For revisions with different Author and Commit data, Github presents both

---

■ **Hint**   How to create revisions such as the one shown in Figure 12-7? You can use $ git commit --amend as described in Recipe 8-1. You can use the $ git cherry-pick, $ git am, and $ git rebase commands in a similar way.

12-4. Creating a Github-hosted repository for an existing project

Problem

You have worked on your project for some time, and now you want to publish it on Github.

Solution

Create a project with the following commands:

```
$ cd git-recipes
$ git init 12-04
$ cd 12-04
$ git simple-commit a b c d
```

Start your web browser, log in to Github.com, and create a new empty repository named 12-04 using the procedure shown in Figure 12-3.

When you get to the page shown in Figure 12-4 you will see instructions for uploading: how to upload an existing project to this newly created repository. Go to the bash command line and execute two commands hinted by Github:

```
# the commands should be executed in git-recipes/12-04 directory
$ git remote add origin git@github.com:your-github-username/12-04.git
$ git push -u origin master
```

When the commands are executed, your Github repository should contain all the revisions from your project: a, b, c, and d.

How It Works

If you want to publish an existing project using Github, you have to create a new empty repository and then execute two commands:

```
$ git remote add origin git@github.com:your-github-username/12-04.git
$ git push -u origin master
```

12-5. Creating an organization account on Github

Problem

Github interface contains a special operation called a pull request. It simplifies the workflow for open-source projects. If you want to exercise how to work with pull requests as:

- A developer who sends his contributions

- A project owner who accepts the contributed code you need two Github personalities.
  In this recipe you want to create your own organization hosted on Github. This will give you the opportunity to work under two different personalities:

    - As an ordinary user

    - As the organization's owner

We will use these two accounts to practice pull requests in the next recipes.

Solution

To create your own organization, visit your Github account and go to the settings of your account, then to *Organizations* and press the *Create new organization* button. Follow the buttons in Figure 12-8.

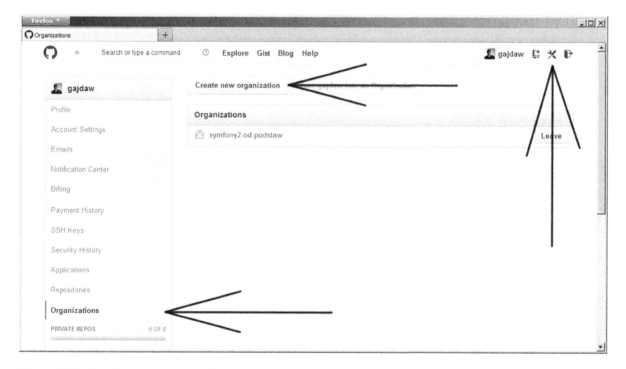

Figure 12-8. *Creating a new organization*

The *Create new organization* button will open the dialog box shown in Figure 12-9. Enter the name of your organization and email address. My username on Github is gajdaw and I used gajdaw-learning-git as the name for my organization, but you can choose any name you like. Then click *Create Organization* at the bottom of the page.

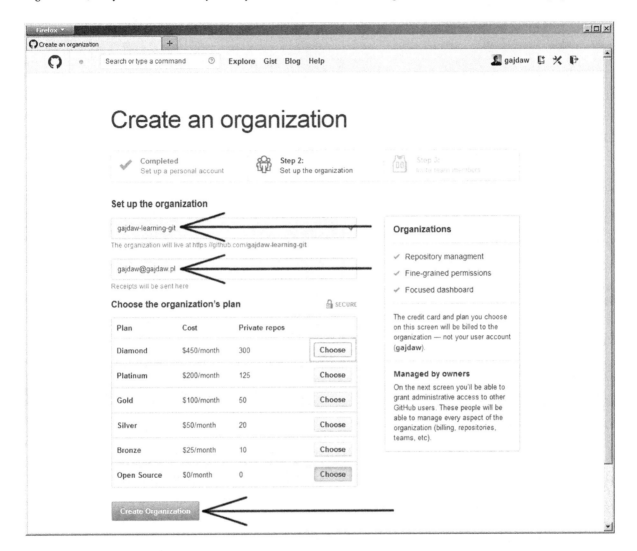

Figure 12-9. *Properties of the new organization*

Once the organization is created you can visit its page using the following URL:

```
https://github.com/gajdaw-learning-git
```

Instead of gajdaw-learning-git use the name you typed in the dialog box shown in Figure 12-9. The main page of my organization gajdaw-learning-git is shown in Figure 12-10.

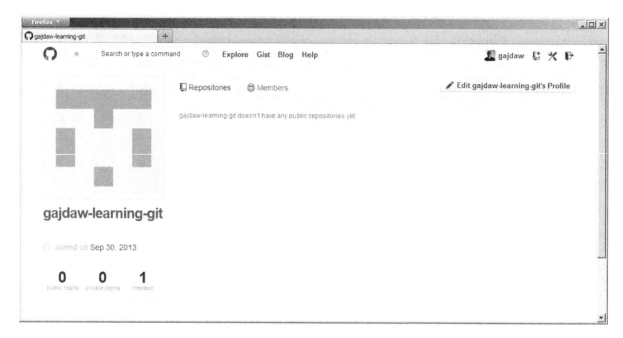

Figure 12-10. The homepage of the gajdaw-learning-git organization is available at https://github.com/gajdaw-learning-git

How It Works

Github interface allows you to create organizations. Because every Github can own repositories you can use your organization to simulate the work with pull requests.

Beware that the Github database license strictly forbids creation of multiple accounts by a single person. Therefore you cannot create two different user accounts to work with pull requests.

12-6. Creating a new project hosted by an organization
Problem

You want to start a new project hosted by your organization.

Solution

Visit your Github account and:

1. Press *Create a new repo* button

2. Choose your organization name from the *Owner drop down* list

3. Fill the name of a new repository as 12-06

4. Press *Create repository* button in the lower part of the page

All the steps are shown in Figure 12-11.

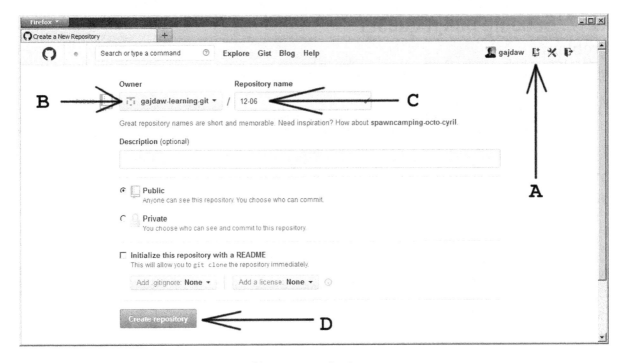

Figure 12-11. *Creating a new repository owned by your organization*

Now open a bash command line and execute the following commands:

```
$ cd git-recipes
$ git clone git@github.com:your-github-organization/12-06.git
$ cd 12-06
$ git config --local user.name admin
$ git config --local user.email admin@example.net
$ git simple-commit a b c
$ git push -u origin master
```

You have to replace the name your-github-organization with the name you used in the form shown in Figure 12-9. When you run the above commands your repository hosted on Github should now contain revisions a, b, c authored by admin.

How It Works

The work with repositories owned by your organization is identical to the work with repositories that you own. The only difference in Recipes 12-3 and 12-6 is that in the latter you changed the owner from your personal account to your organization.

In the repository stored in `git-recipes/12-06` you will work using admin identity.

12-7. Sending pull requests

Problem

Github hosts a project titled 12-06. The project is available at the following URL:

```
https://github.com/your-github-organization/12-06
```

You want to contribute to this project sending a pull request with three commits.

Solution

Start the web browser, log in to your Github account, and go to following URL:

```
https://github.com/your-github-organization/12-06
```

You will see the webpage presented in Figure 12-12. Make sure that you are visiting the project your-github-organization/12-06 identified by A.

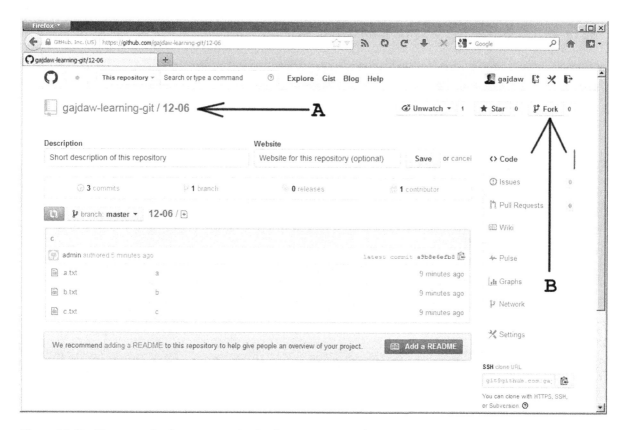

Figure 12-12. *Homepage for the your-organization/12-06 repository that you wish to contribute*

Use the *Fork* button identified as B to create your personal copy of this repository. When you press the button, you will be asked the question "Where should we fork this repository?" Answer the question by choosing your personal account (not your organization). This will redirect you to webpage shown in Figure 12-13. You should notice that this time the repository is available under your username, as in:

```
your-github-username/12-06
```

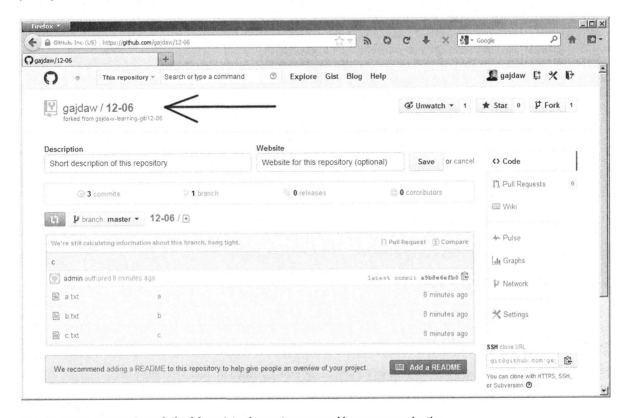

Figure 12-13. *Your private fork of the original repository owned by your organization*

The place where you can verify the name of the repository is shown in Figure 12-13.
There are two repositories that we will use in this recipe. Their URLs are:

- Original repository: git@github.com:your-organization/12-06.git
- Your fork: git@github.com:your-github-username/12-06.git

Now it's time to create a clone stored on your hard drive. Open a bash command line and type the following commands:

```
$ cd git-recipes
$ mkdir 12-07
$ cd 12-07
$ git clone git@github.com:your-organization/12-06.git.
```

Take a good look at the above commands. This should be the URL for the original repository.

Now add the remote URL aliased by me and pointing to your fork:

```
$ git remote add my git@github.com:your-github-username/12-06.git
```

Your local repository saved in git-recipes/12-07 contains two remote aliases. The command $ git remote -v prints the following results:

```
$ git remote -v
my       git@github.com:your-github-account/12-06.git (fetch)
my       git@github.com: your-github-account/12-06.git (push)
origin   git@github.com:your-organization/12-06.git (fetch)
origin   git@github.com: your-organization/12-06.git (push)
```

Check your identity with two following commands:

```
$ git config user.name
$ git config user.email
```

The output of the above commands should include your real name and your real email address. You are ready to contribute to the original repository. To do this, create a new branch:

```
$ git checkout -b numbers
```

Create three revisions one, two, three with:

```
$ git simple-commit one two three
```

Push your branch named numbers to your fork on Github with:

```
$ git push -u my HEAD
```

Go to the web browser and check if your fork contains the newly pushed branch. Use the buttons shown in Figure 12-14.

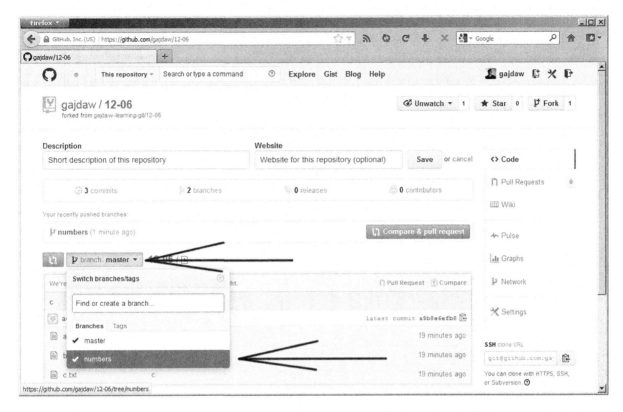

Figure 12-14. *The branch you pushed is available in your fork. You can check it out using the buttons pointed to by the arrows*

Now you are ready to send your commit to the original repository. Press *Compare & pull request* as shown in Figure 12-15.

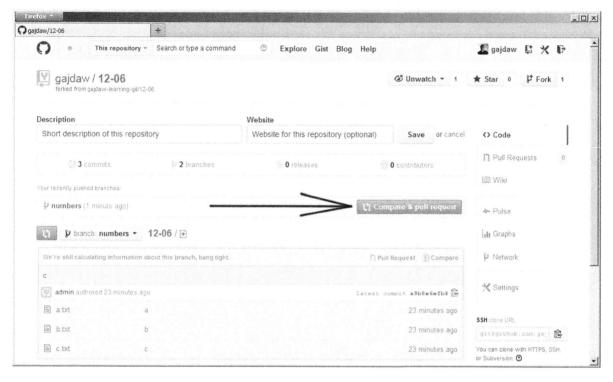

Figure 12-15. *The button Compare & pull request*

The button in Figure 12-15 will open the dialog box shown in Figure 12-16. The letter A shows the accurate information about:

- The branch that will receive the pull request

  your-organization:master

- The branch that will be pushed

  your-github-username:numbers

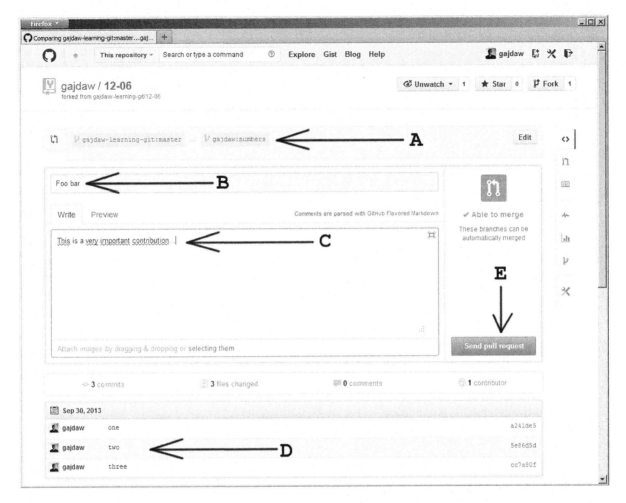

Figure 12-16. *The dialog box to send a pull request*

The letter B in Figure 12–16 contains the title you need to type. I used foo bar as a title. The C points to the full description of the purpose behind your pull request. D lists the commits that will be pushed. To proceed with the pull request, click *Send pull request.*

After clicking *Send pull request* you will be redirected to the webpage shown in Figure 12-17. This is the original repository that you forked.

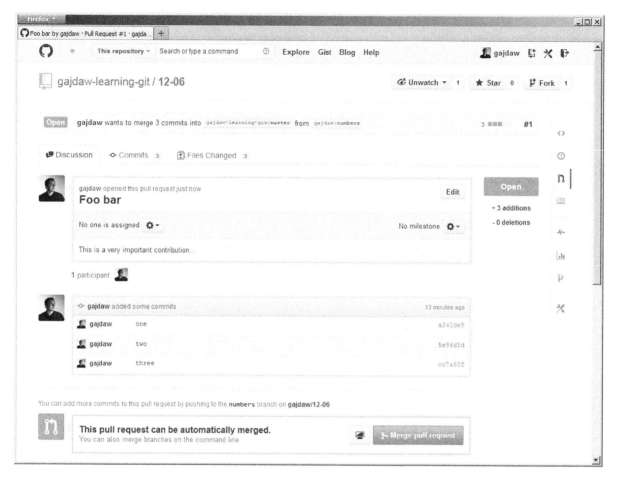

Figure 12-17. *The pull request was succesfully sent and is available in the original repository owned by your organization*

Your work is finished. The pull request was sent to the original repository. It is up to the owner of this repository to accept your pull request.

How It Works

The work with pull requests includes three repositories and looks like this:

- Original repository hosted on Github
- Your fork hosted on Githhub
- Your local repository stored on your machine

You are responsible for two of them: your fork and your local repository. The first is created by clicking *Fork* in the Githhub interface shown in Figure 12-8. The local repository is created as a clone of the original repository. The relationship between the three repositories is depicted in Figure 12-18.

Figure 12-18. *The relationship between the three repositories needed for work with pull requests*

When using pull requests, the workflow is organized as follows:

- You commit, merge, and rebase in your local repository only.
- You push the changes from your local repository to your fork.
- You send pull requests from your fork to the original repository.
- You fetch the latest updates from the original repository to your local repository.

The flow of commands is presented in Figure 12-19.

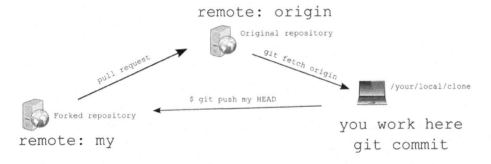

Figure 12-19. *The flow of commands when working with pull requests*

Because your local repository is a cloned original repository, the origin alias points to the repository owned by the organization. You can fetch the latest updates made by other developers with:

```
$ git fetch origin
```

As you know fetch doesn't move your local tracking branches. To merge the latest revisions in your local master branch you would have to execute merge or rebase, for example:

```
$ git rebase origin/master master
```

To make pushing to your fork easier you need to set an alias for this repository. The command:

```
$ git remote add my git@github.com:your-github-username/writers.git
```

defines an alias named my. Therefore, if you want to push to your fork you can use commands such as:

```
$ git push my branch-name
$ git push my HEAD
```

The first command pushes the branch with the given name and the second pushes your current branch. When your branch with your contributions is available in your forked repository, you can send a pull request.

I prefer to create a local repository stored on my machine by cloning an original hosted by organization. Then the alias original is used to fetch the most recent contributions made by others and my alias is used to push my new contributions to the forked repository. But you can use the other setting as well. You can clone your fork and define a new remote named upstream for an original repository hosted by organization. Then you will use origin alias to push your contributions to your fork and the upstream alias to download the latest contributions. There is really no difference in these two solutions other then renamed remotes.

12-8. Reworking your pull requests
Problem

You contributed to an open-source project sending a pull request. But your contribution was not accepted. You were asked to make some improvements. You want to add two new commits to your pull request.

Solution

Go to your local repository in which you created the revisions that were sent as the pull request. It is in the git-recipes/12-07 directory:

```
$ cd git-recipes/12-07
```

I assume that you sent a pull request to merge the revisions from your local numbers branch into the master branch in original repository. To get a clear linear history you should update your local branch with the latest revisions in remote master branch. Execute the following commands:

```
$ git fetch origin
$ git rebase origin/master numbers
```

These commands will move your revisions on top of the origin/master branch. Now you can add some commits to your pull request. Your current branch after rebasing is numbers. Create two new revisions in it:

```
$ git simple-commit red green
```

Push it to your fork with:

```
$ git push -f my HEAD
```

Your pull request should now contain two new revisions red and green. You can check it in the following way. Go to the original repository and follow *Pull Requests* button shown in Figure 12-20.

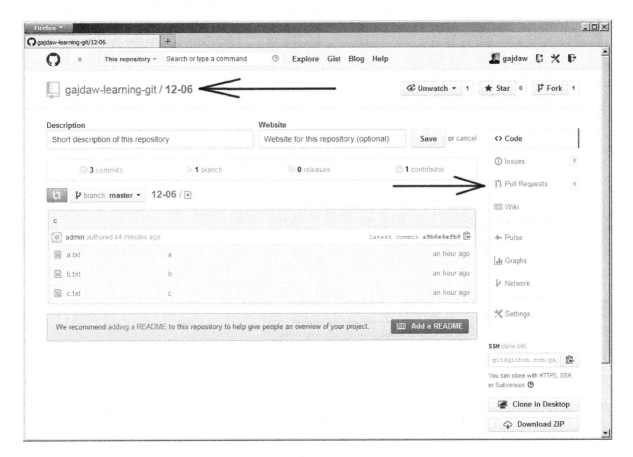

Figure 12-20. *The list of all pull requests is available with the Pull Requests button*

Now check your pull requests from the list. You will see your two revisions in the lower part of the window as shown in Figure 12-21.

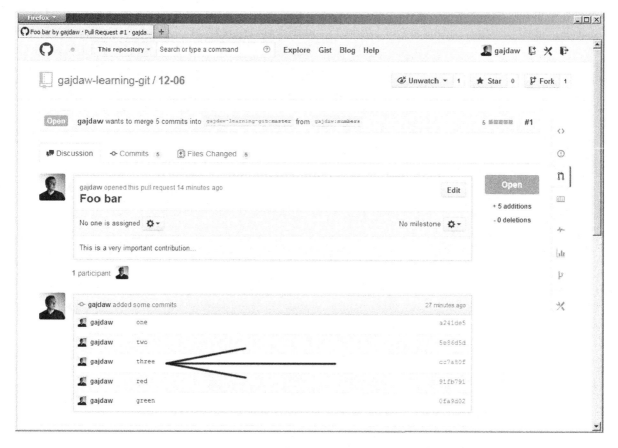

Figure 12-21. *New revisions pushed to the appropriate branch in the forked repository are automatically added to the pull requests*

How It Works

Your branch in the forked repository can be used to add more commits to the pull requests. As long as the pull request was not accepted you can push to this branch.

It can happen that the master branch in the original repository moved forward. If that is the case, you should update your local repository with:

```
$ git fetch origin
$ git rebase origin/master numbers
```

When new commits are ready you can append them to the existing pull request with single command:

```
$ git push -f my numbers
```

The flag -f is necessary if during the update phase your revisions were rebased. If there were no new revisions in the original master branch than you can use the command without -f flag:

```
$ git push my numbers
```

Keep in mind that your local branch, as well as the branch in your fork, is considered your private work until they are accepted. This means that you can use the arbitrary methods described in chapter 8 to adjust the history. You add new commits, you can reorder commits, you can delete commits, and finally, you can squash all commits into a single commit.

And remember, whenever you want to contribute to a project hosted on Github use branches. Do not work in your master branch for this purpose. If you prepare your pull request in a separate branch it will not complicate your work. When a pull request is rejected you will simply delete the branch. Otherwise you would need to adjust the master branch using $ `git reset --hard HEAD~n` to remove rejected revisions.

12-9. Accepting a pull request

Problem

You own a popular repository. Developers often contribute to your project. You want to accept a pull request that you just received.

Solution

In this recipe you will work only in the web interface provided by Github. Go to your organization, then select the repository 12-06 and open the list of available pull requests. Next open the page with the detailed information about the pull request. You can do this following the links shown in Figure 12-22.

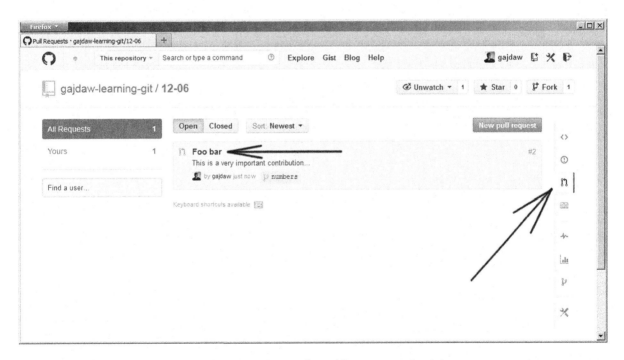

Figure 12-22. *The list of all pull requests in the repository hosted by your organization*

The details of pull requests are shown in Figure 12-23. You can analyze all contributed codes. When you are sure that the code is correct you can merge it by clicking the button shown in Figure 12-23.

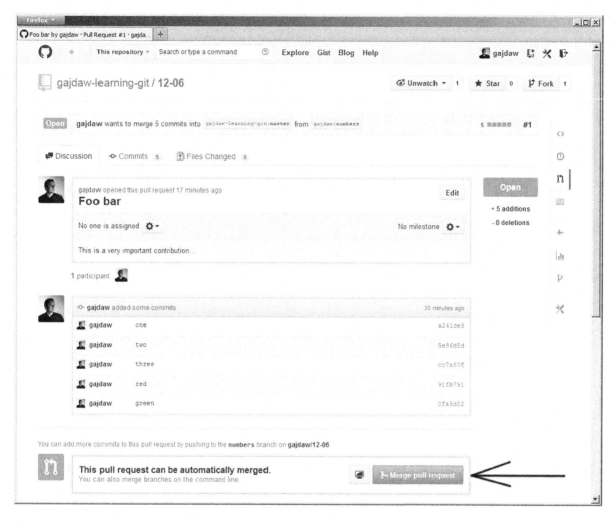

Figure 12-23. *The button for merging pull requests*

When the pull request is merged it will be included in the projects history as shown in Figure 12-24.

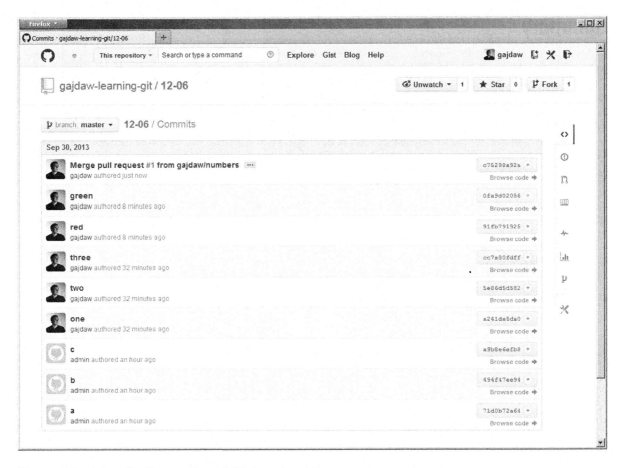

Figure 12-24. *Merged pull request is available in projects history*

How It Works

All pull requests that were sent to the repository are listed on the page shown in Figure 12-22. You can thoroughly inspect every one of them. In particular, Github allows you:

- To list the commits contained in the pull request

- To list the files modified by pull request

- To list modified lines

- To discuss the pull requests with other developers

When you decide that the pull request is correct you can accept it using the *Merge pull request* button shown in Figure 12-23.

Summary

In this chapter I have provided you with basic information for using Github as a hosting platform for your projects as well as the procedures for contributing to projects owned by others.

If you want to host an open-source project using Github, follow Recipes 12-3, 12-4, and 12-6. Whenever you receive a pull request you can accept it by following Recipe 12-9.

Maybe you want to contribute to an open-source project? You can do this by using the method explained in Recipes 12-7 and 12-8.

If you host a project that is developed by a team of developers that you trust, you can avoid using pull request by you and your friends. Setting appropriate rights you can allow other Github users to push directly to the original repository. The dialog box to do this is available under the team management link shown in Figure 12-25.

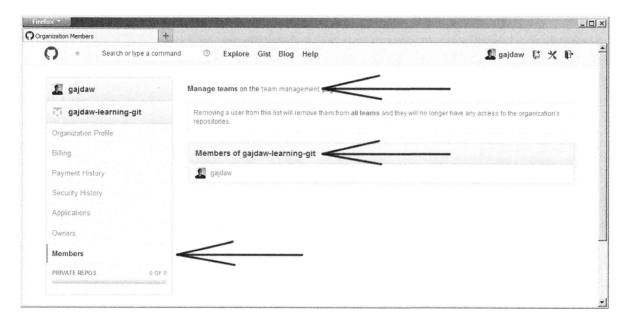

Figure 12-25. *The team management link leads you to the page where you can assign rights for other developers*

If you need some more arguments to give Github a try, take into account that it contains an embedded issue tracker. All contributors participating in the project can use it to discus submitted code. All these features make Github a really great platform for sharing your code.

CHAPTER 13

More Recipes

In this closing chapter, I discuss some details that have not been covered and sooner or later can become indispensable to you. You will learn:

- How to use the command $ git diff to compare different versions of files.
- How to overcome the problems concerning line endings.
- Three different methods to configure ignored files
- Using tags
- The command $ git archive to generate zipped package containing your project

13-1. Working with the $ git diff command
Problem

You want to learn how to use the $ git diff command to analyze the difference between two versions of the same file.

Solution

Create a new repository:

```
$ cd git-recipes
$ mkdir 13-01
$ cd 13-01
$ git init
```

Then create the file named numbers.txt with the contents shown in Listing 13-1.

Listing 13-1. The first version of the file numbers.txt

```
one
two
three
four
five
six
```

```
seven
eight
nine
ten
```

Commit the file using the following commands:

```
$ git add -A
$ git commit -m "Numbers: en"
```

Right now, the repository is clean and the three snapshots—the first stored in HEAD, the second stored in the staging area, and the third in the working directory—all contain the same version of numbers.txt file.

Next, change the contents of the file. Replace the four words four, five, six, and seven with two lines containing the words foo and bar. The file you should obtain is shown in listing 13-2.

Listing 13-2. The second version of the file numbers.txt

```
one
two
three
foo
bar
eight
nine
ten
```

The command $ git status -sb now prints the file as:

```
_M numbers.txt
```

The file was modified but not yet staged.

The command $ git diff will now produce the output shown in Listing 13-3. When executed without any parameters, the command $ git diff compares the working directory and the staging area.

Listing 13-3. The output of the $ git diff command

```
index f5ef170..a769e64 100644
--- a/numbers.txt
+++ b/numbers.txt
@@ -1,10 +1,8 @@
 one
 two
 three
-four
-five
-six
-seven
+foo
+bar
 eight
 nine
 ten
```

Stage the file numbers.txt with:

```
$ git add -A
```

After this command the file is in the M_ state. The command $ git status -sb would print:

```
M_ number.txt
```

Now, the command $ git diff prints empty results. This means that the file in the staging area is identical to the file in the working directory. If you want to compare the file in the staging area to the file stored in HEAD, you can use the additional parameter --staged:

```
$ git diff --staged
```

The above command compares the file stored in HEAD and the file in the staging area. The result will be exactly the same as in Listing 13-3.

■ **Hint** The command $ git diff compares the working directory to the staging area. The command $ git diff --staged compares the staging area to the version stored in the revision pointed by HEAD.

Now commit the staged changes with:

```
$ git commit -m "Numbers: foo bar"
```

The command $ git status -sb proves that your repository is clean. All three snapshots, HEAD, the staging area, and the working directory, contain exactly the same version of file numbers.txt. Thus both commands:

```
$ git diff
$ git diff --staged
```

print empty results.

Finish the recipe by comparing the next to the last revision, HEAD~, and the last revision, HEAD, with the following command:

```
$ git diff --unified=1 HEAD~ HEAD
```

The output of the above command is shown in Listing 13-4.

Listing 13-4. The output of the $ git diff --unified=1 HEAD~ HEAD command

```
diff --git a/numbers.txt b/numbers.txt
index f5ef170..a769e64 100644
--- a/numbers.txt
+++ b/numbers.txt
@@ -3,6 +3,4 @@ two
 three
-four
-five
-six
```

```
-seven
+foo
+bar
 Eight
```

The additional parameter `--unified=1` changed the number of lines preceding and following the changed content.

How It Works

The command `$ git diff` uses the format defined by GNU diffutils tools available at:

`http://www.gnu.org/software/diffutils/`

The `$ git diff` command produces the output conforming to the following format:

```
--- a/some-file-name
+++ b/some-file-name
@@ -a,b +c,d @@
xxx
+yyy
-zzz
qqq
```

The above description unambiguously defines two versions of the file: the version before we apply the changes and the version after we apply the changes. Using the above output we can construct the file in two states: before and after the change.

The first two lines inform you that the output describes the changes of the file named `some-file-name`. The version before the change can be retrieved by removing the lines that begin with + and writing the lines that begin with - without the leading dash. The above output describes the file before the change contained:

```
xxx
zzz
qqq
```

The version after the change can be retrieved by removing the lines that begin with a dash and writing the lines that begin with + without the leading plus. The file after the change looks like:

```
xxx
yyy
qqq
```

The special line:

`@@ -a,b +c,d @@`

defines two ranges of lines: `a,b` and `c,d`. The first range `a,b` describes the first version of file. The second range, `c,d` describes the second version of file.

The range a,b indicates that this version before the change:

```
xxx
zzz
qqq
```

starts at line a and contains b lines.

The second range c,d indicates that this version after the change:

```
xxx
yyy
qqq
```

starts at line c and continues for d lines.

The $ git diff command allows you to change the number of lines used in the output. The command:

```
$ git diff --unified=4
```

changes the behavior of $ git diff in such a way that every change will be surrounded by four unmodified lines, as in:

```
--- a/some-file-name
+++ b/some-file-name
@@ -a,b +c,d @@
xxx
xxx
xxx
xxx
+yyy
-zzz
qqq
qqq
qqq
qqq
```

The output shown in Listing 13-4 was produced with --unified=1, therefore the description is surrounded by single lines (they contain the words three and eight):

```
@@ -3,6 +3,4 @@ two
  three         <- the first surrounding line
-four
-five
-six
-seven
+foo
+bar
  eight         <- the last surrounding line
```

Thanks to 3,6 we know that the first version of the file starts at line 3 and consists of 6 lines:

```
three
four
five
six
seven
eight
```

The 3,4 tells us that the second version of the file starts at line 3 and consists of 4 lines:

```
three
foo
bar
eight
```

To produce the output shown in Listing 13-4, we passed the two identifiers HEAD~ and HEAD to compare different revisions. In similar way you can compare different branches:

```
$ git diff master dev
```

and the files stored in different branches:

```
$ git diff master dev -- some-file
```

By default, $ git diff compares lines. You also can change its behavior to search for changed words. This can be done with:

```
$ git diff --word-diff
```

And if you want to find the revisions in which a given file some-file was modified you can use both:

```
$ git diff --name-only master dev -- some-file
```

and

```
$ git log --name-only master dev -- some-file
```

■ **Hint** The command $ git diff has a very useful parameter --check that can be used to verify that the commit does not introduce changes that affect only white characters. The command $ git diff --check reports problems with the handling of white characters.

13-2. Committing files without line-ending conversion
Problem

You want to start a new repository that contains text files with different types of line endings. Some of them use Linux-like line endings that consist of a single LF character, some of them use Windows-like line endings consisting of two characters CRLF. Your repository even contains files using both types: LF and CRLF that are mixed in a single file. You want to commit all the files without any conversion of line-ending characters.

■ **Hint**   At first, you may consider the files using both LF and CRLF to be corrupted. But you may need them anyway. I found them very useful as the static fixtures to tests when I was working on a library to process text files produced by external tools. It turned out that the applications I used generated corrupted files containing not only LF and CRLF but also CR as line endings. All three were mixed in a single file!

Solution

Initialize a new repository:

```
$ cd git-recipes
$ mkdir 13-02
$ cd 13-02
$ git init
```

Create three files stored in separate directories:

```
$ mkdir linux
$ mkdir mixed
$ mkdir windows

$ printf "linux \n a \n b \n c \n d" > linux/abcd.txt
$ printf "mixed \n a \r\n b \n c \r\n d" > mixed/abcd.txt
$ printf "windows \r\n a \r\n b \r\n c \r\n d" > windows/abcd.txt
```

The first named linux/abcd.txt uses LF line endings (they are usually encoded as \n in strings). The second file named mixed/abcd.txt contains both LF and CRLF line endings. The last file named windows/abcd.txt uses CRLF line endings. These, when embedded in strings, are written as \r\n. You can verify line endings using the following commands:

```
$ hexdump -c linux/abcd.txt
$ hexdump -c mixed/abcd.txt
$ hexdump -c windows/abcd.txt
```

To commit files without any conversion of new lines turn off the core.autocrlf setting:

```
$ git config --local core.autocrlf false
```

Commit the files:

```
$ git add -A
$ git commit -m "Three files: linux, windows and mixed line endings"
```

Now the most recent commit stored in the database .git/objects contains the following line endings:

- linux/abcd.txt uses LF

- mixed/abcd.txt uses both LF and CRLF

- windows/abcd.txt uses CRLF

The files in the working directory and in the staging area are exactly the same.

How It Works

Git configuration contains an option `core.autocrlf`. This option governs the way git handles line-ending conversion. It can take three different values: `true`, `input`, and `false`. Because conversion of line endings can be performed during checkout or when you commit your files, we have to analyze the meaning of every value in both situations.

The first value, `true`, affects both checkout and check-in. During checkout git converts LF characters to CRLF. When you commit, reversed conversion is performed: CRLF line endings are converted to LF.

The second value, `input`, turns on conversion from CRLF to LF during check-in operation. There is no conversion when you perform checkout with this setting.

The last value, `false`, turns off all conversions. The files stored in the object database have the same line endings as the files in your working directory.

The meaning of three values of `core.autocrlf` is summarized in Table 13-1.

Table 13-1. *All values of the core.autocrlf option and their influence on checkout and commit*

Value	Checkout	Commit
true	LF => CRLF	CRLF => LF
input	None	CRLF => LF
false	None	None

As you remember from Recipe 8-4 and from Table 8-1, your repository consists of three snapshots. We can denote them as HEAD, the staging area, and the working directory. In the repository 13-02 these three areas contain the line endings shown in Table 13-2.

Table 13-2. *The line endings in the three snapshots in the repository 13-02*

	linux/abcd.txt	mixed/abcd.txt	windows/abcd.txt
HEAD	LF	LF/CRLF	CRLF
The staging area	LF	LF/CRLF	CRLF
The working directory	LF	LF/CRLF	CRLF

All three snapshots use exactly the same line endings.

13-3. Checking out files without line-ending conversion
Problem

Your git configuration contains the `core.autocrlf` option set to `true`. Therefore when you clone a repository the line endings in the working directory are converted to CRLF.

You have just cloned the repository with `core.autocrlf` set to `true`. Your intention was to make the files in the working directory exactly the same as in the database. Because `core.autocrlf` was set to `true` you have created a clone that you consider corrupted. You want to correct your mistake.

Your task is to checkout all the files once again. This time you want to avoid any conversion of line endings. You want the line endings in your working directory to match the line endings stored in HEAD revision in the database.

Solution

To understand the solution, you first need to create a repository containing corrupted files.

Set the core.autocrlf to true with:

```
$ git config --global core.autocrlf true
```

and then clone the repository from previous recipe:

```
$ cd git-recipes
$ git clone 13-02 13-03
```

Setting core.autocrlf to true caused the conversion of the linux/abcd.txt file. It now contains the CRLF line endings. The file with the mixed line endings, that is, mixed/abcd.txt, was not converted. The line endings you get after the clone with core.autocrlf set to true are summarized in Table 13-3.

Table 13-3. *Line endings in three snapshots in the repository 13-03 right after the $ git clone command with core.autocrlf set to true*

	linux/abcd.txt	mixed/abcd.txt	windows/abcd.txt
HEAD	LF	LF/CRLF	CRLF
The staging area	CRLF	LF/CRLF	CRLF
The working directory	CRLF	LF/CRLF	CRLF

Right now, the working directory contains different line endings that are stored in the HEAD revision. Therefore you may think that your repository is dirty; however, that is not the case. If you use the $ git status command you will see that the repository is clean. This is because git handles the conversion of line endings for you. This can cause another problem: how to commit the files exactly as they are with CRLF line endings? We will come to this problem in Recipe 13-4.

Right now, you consider your working directory to be corrupted. Your intention was to get the files in the working directory with the same line endings as in HEAD. To perform the checkout operation once again, this time without any conversion of line endings, follow this procedure:

1. Remove all tracked files: $ git ls-files | xargs rm

2. Remove the staging area: $ rm .git/index

3. Turn off conversion of new lines: $ git config --local core.autocrlf false

4. Recreate the working directory and the staging area: $ git reset --hard

Now the staging area and the working directory contain the files exactly as they were stored in the HEAD revision. The line endings used in your repository are the same as in Table 13-2.

How It Works

If you set the option core.autocrlf to true and then clone the repository, the files using LF line endings will be converted to use CRLF line endings. Thus right after:

```
$ git clone 13-02 13-03
```

the file linux/abcd.txt now contains CRLF line endings. The files that contain both LF and CRLF, such as mixed/abcd.txt, are not converted.

To perform a checkout that recreates all the files in the working directory and in the staging area you have to:

- Remove all tracked files

- Remove the staging area

- Use the $ git reset command with the --hard option

The list of all tracked files is returned by the $ git ls-files command. If you pass the resulting list to the $ rm command with xargs:

```
$ git ls-files | xargs rm
```

all tracked files will be removed from your working directory.

The staging area is stored in the .git/index file. You can remove this file with the $ rm .git/index command.

After the above commands the staging area and the working directory do not contain the files stored in HEAD anymore. As you already know you can recreate the working directory and the staging area with the $ git reset --hard command. This command recreates the working directory and the staging area using the snapshot stored in HEAD. If the operation is executed with core.autocrlf set to false both the staging area and the working directory will be populated with files using the original line endings (the ones stored in HEAD snapshot).

When you finish Recipe 13-3 the repository would contain the line endings presented in Table 13-2.

13-4. Converting line endings to CRLF in the working directory during checkout and committing the change

Problem

You work in a repository that contains text files using different line endings. You want to:

- Convert all the files in the working directory to use CRLF line endings

- Commit the files with CRLF line endings into the repository

This revision should internally (i.e., in the git database) use CRLF encodings. If someone clones this repository without any conversion of new lines (i.e., with autocrlf set to false), they should get the working directory with all text files using CRLF.

Solution

Clone the repository from Recipe 13-1:

```
$ cd git-recipes
$ git clone 13-02 13-04
$ cd 13-04
```

Now convert the line endings in the working directory to CRLF:

1. Set the core.autocrlf option to true with $ git config --local core.autocrlf true

2. Remove all tracked files with $ git ls-files | xargs rm

3. Restore all tracked files with $ git reset --hard

The file `linux/abcd.txt` stored in the working directory now uses CRLF line endings. You want to commit this file into the repository in such a way that the object stored in the database uses CRLF line endings. But the command `$ git status -sb` prints the information that the working directory is clean. Therefore you cannot commit this file with the simple `$ git add` and `$ git commit` commands.

To commit the `linux/abcd.txt` file with a CRLF line ending you have to update the staging area. Follow this procedure:

4. Set the `core.autocrlf` option to `false` with `$ git config --local core.autocrlf false`

5. Remove the staging area with `$ rm .git/index`

6. Recreate the `.git/index` file with `$ git reset`

Check the status of all files with `$ git status -sb`. As you can see the file `linux/abcd.txt` is listed as modified. The command:

```
$ git diff
```

outputs:

```
-linux
- a
- b
- c
+linux ^M
+ a ^M
+ b ^M
+ c ^M
```

In the above output the characters ^M represent CR. We can say that the file `linux/abcd.txt` was changed in such a way that every line contains a new CR character.

Because `$ git status -sb` prints the information that the repository is dirty, you can create a new commit. Finish the recipe committing all changed files with

```
$ git add -A
$ git commit -m " Standardization: committing line endings changed to CRLF"
```

Now the most recent revision stored in the database in the repository 13-04 contains the line endings presented in Table 13-4.

Table 13-4. *The line endings in the three snapshots in the final state of the repository 13-04*

	linux/abcd.txt	mixed/abcd.txt	windows/abcd.txt
HEAD	CRLF	LF/CRLF	CRLF
The staging area	CRLF	LF/CRLF	CRLF
The working directory	CRLF	LF/CRLF	CRLF

How It Works

If you:

- Turn on the conversion of line endings with `$ git config --local core.autocrlf true`

- Remove the tracked files

- Check the tracked files out

the files that previously used LF, such as `linux/abcd.txt`, will use CRLF. The content of the file is changed—it was LF and now it is CRLF, but `$ git status` reports that the working directory is clean. This causes the following problem: how to commit a file with changed line endings?

To do this you have to recreate the staging area with the line endings used in the working directory:

- Turn off the conversion of line endings `$ git config --local core.autocrlf false`

- Remove the staging area with `$ rm .git/index`

- Recreate `.git/index` file with `$ git reset`

Now `$ git status` prints the information that the working directory is dirty. You can commit the `linux/abcd.txt` file with CRLF line endings into the database.

13-5. Converting line endings to LF and committing the change

Problem

You work in a repository that contains different encodings of new lines. You want to:

- Convert the files in the working directory in such a way that they use LF line endings

- Commit the files with line endings converted to LF as a new revision.

The objects stored in the git database should contain LF line endings.

Solution

Clone the repository from Recipe 13-1:

```
$ cd git-recipes
$ git clone 13-02 13-05
$ cd 13-05
```

and follow this procedure:

1. Create the file `.gitattributes` files with one rule `* text=auto`. You can do it with `$ echo "* text=auto" >>.gitattributes`

2. Remove the staging area with `$ rm .git/index`

3. Recreate the `.git/index` file with `$ git reset`

Check the status of all files with `$ git status -sb`. As you can see this time both `mixed/abcd.txt` and `windows/abcd.txt` are listed as modified. Finish the recipe committing all changed files with:

```
$ git snapshot Standardization: line endings changed to LF.
```

All three snapshots HEAD, the working directory, and the staging area now contain LF line endings. The result of Recipe 13-5 is summarized in Table 13-5.

Table 13-5. *The line endings in the three snapshots in the final state of the repository 13-05*

	linux/abcd.txt	mixed/abcd.txt	windows/abcd.txt
HEAD	LF	LF	LF
The staging area	LF	LF	LF
The working directory	LF	LF/CRLF	CRLF

Notice that this recipe converted the file mixed/abcd.txt.

How It Works

The procedure described in this recipe uses the following .gitattributes entry:

```
* text=auto
```

Thanks to the above rule, when checked-in, all text files will be converted to use LF.

If you recreate the staging area with the two commands $ rm .git/index and $ git reset then $ git status will inform you that the files are changed. The next commit operation will save in the database, files with LF line endings.

13-6. Unintended conversion of all line endings
Problem

You want to learn how to avoid unintentional conversion of all line endings in an open-source project. To gain a deeper understanding of this problem you want to reproduce this failure. Your task is to clone a reveal.js project hosted on github at https://github.com/hakimel/reveal.js and then to change the repository configuration in such a way that git will consider all the files changed.

Solution

Set the global git configuration to perform LF=>CRLF conversion during checkout and CRLF=>LF conversion during check-in:

```
$ git config --global core.autocrlf true
```

Then clone the reveal.js repository:

```
$ cd git-recipes
$ git clone https://github.com/hakimel/reveal.js.git 13-06
$ cd 13-06
```

Right after the clone command, all the text files in 13-06 directory will use CRLF line endings. This encoding will be used regardless of your operating system. CRLF will be used in Windows, Linux, and MacOS. The repository is in clean state—you can verify it with $ git status -sb.

Now, turn off all conversions of line endings with:

```
$ git config --global core.autocrlf false
```

and recreate the staging area with:

```
$ rm .git/index
$ git reset
```

Even though the files in your working directory were not touched the above change will confuse git. The command $ `git status -sb` will inform you that git considers all the text files changed.

You can verify the changes in the working directory using the following command:

```
$ git diff --check
```

It will print the warnings about the changed line endings.

■ **Hint** If you are using Linux, you can skip the two commands: $ `rm .git/index` and $ `git reset` in this recipe; you will get the same results.

How It Works

The project `reveal.js` uses LF line endings. All text files stored in object database use the line ending LF. When you perform a clone with `autocrlf` set to `true`, git will—during a checkout—perform LF=>CRLF conversion; your working directory will contain files with CRLF. The staging area, however, will use the original line endings, that is, LF.

As long as you have `autocrlf` turned on, git will use the CRLF=>LF conversion when comparing the working directory to the staging area. Therefore the repository remains clean.

If you use $ `git config --global core.autocrlf false` to turn off the conversion performed during check-in, git compares the working directory to the staging area without any conversions. Because the files stored in these two locations use different line endings, the $ `git status` command reports that there are unstaged changes in your working directory.

This is a situation you should always avoid.

Imagine that right now in this state you want to contribute to `reveal.js`. You change a single line in one of the files and then commit the change with the $ `git add -A` and $ `git commit` commands. This revision, when accepted, would cause a headache for the project leader and other developers as it introduces hundreds of changes. All but one are not only unnecessary but would be probably reverted by the next contributor who uses different line endings.

This recipe presents a pattern that you should always avoid.

13-7. Defining line endings for individual files and directories
Problem

You start a new project. You want to configure it in such a way that:

- Text files stored under the `linux/` directory always use LF line endings.

- Text files stored under the `windows/` directory always use CRLF line endings.

- Text files stored under the `mixed/` directory are never converted—they always preserve the original line endings.

Solution

Initialize a new repository:

```
$ cd git-recipes
$ git init 13-07
$ cd 13-07
```

Create the directories and files:

```
$ mkdir linux
$ mkdir mixed
$ mkdir windows

$ printf "linux \n a \n b \n c \n d" > linux/abcd.txt
$ printf "mixed \n a \r\n b \n c \r\n d" > mixed/abcd.txt
$ printf "windows \r\n a \r\n b \r\n c \r\n d" > windows/abcd.txt
```

Next create the .gitattributes file with the following contents:

```
*          eol=lf
windows/*   eol=crlf
mixed/*     -text
```

Finally commit all files using the $ git snapshot Initial commit command.

The repository now contains the very accurate rules that define the line endings conversion. Now, if anyone clones the repository, then, no matter what his or her settings are, the cloned repository will contain exactly the same line endings that we used within $ print commands. To verify this set the core.autocrlf to true with:

```
$ git config --global core.autocrlf true
```

And then clone the repository:

```
$ cd ..
$ git clone 13-07 13-07-verification
$ cd 13-07-verification
```

The command:

```
$ hexdump -c linux/abcd.txt
```

prints the contents of the file with LF line endings. This proves that even though core.autocrlf was set to true no conversion was performed.

How It Works

The rule * eol=lf forces git to always checkout all files using LF line endings. Thus, by default, all the files will use LF encoding. Files stored under the linux/ directory in particular. The second rule, which is windows/* eol=crlf, defines an exception to the first rule. When checking out files stored under the windows/ directory, CRLF will be used. The last rule, mixed/* -text, turns off all the conversions of line endings for all files stored under the mixed/ directory.

The configuration written in the .gitattributes file overrides settings defined with the $ git config command. Therefore, no matter what your settings are, the working directory of the project will always stick to the predefined assumptions:

- All text files stored under windows/ will use CRLF
- All text files stored under mixed/ will always preserve original line endings
- All other text files will use LF

■ **Hint** This solution is used within a jQuery project. Thanks to the * eol=lf rule stored in the .gitattributes file, all text files are always encoded using LF as an end-of-line character; no matter what your platform and configuration.

13-8. Ignoring automatically generated files
Problem

You start a new project in which some tools generate temporary files. You do not want to commit them into the repository. The temporary files in your project conform to the following rules:

- They are stored within the /tmp/ directory.
- Their name ends with the .abc extension.

Therefore, you want to ignore the files that match the two following patterns:

```
/tmp/
*.abc
```

You want to share the rules for ignoring files with all the developers who work on this project.

Solution

Initialize a new repository:

```
$ cd git-recipes
$ mkdir 13-08
$ cd 13-08
$ git init
```

Create an empty initial revision with:

```
$ git commit --allow-empty -m "Initial commit"
```

Create the file named .gitignore with the following contents:

```
/tmp/
*.abc
```

You can do this with the following two commands:

```
echo /tmp/ > .gitignore
echo "*.abc" >> .gitignore
```

Commit the file `.gitignore` into the repository with:

```
$ git add -A
$ git commit -m "Gitignore: new rules to ignore files"
```

The repository is ready; you can share it with other developers.

To test whether the files stored within the `/tmp/` directory and the files with the `.abc` extension are really ignored create two files:

```
$ echo abc > some-file.abc
$ mkdir tmp
$ echo def > tmp/some-file.txt
```

and check the status of the repository with the `$ git status` command. The files that match the patterns defined in `.gitignore` file are not reported by `$ git status`.

How It Works

If your project contains some files that are automatically generated, you should probably ignore them. The best way to do this is to create a special file named `.gitignore`. The file should contain the patterns to be ignored by git. As a result, if you commit the file into your repository, all your colleagues working on the same project will share the rules.

The rules stored in `.gitignore` are the following.

- If the rule starts with a slash / it will match only the entries that are stored in the root directory of your project. The rule `/foo` will only match the file `/foo` it will not match the file `some/dir/foo`.

- If the rule ends with a slash / it will match only the directories. Thus the rule `bar/` will match the directories `bar/` and `some/other/dir/bar/` but it will not match the file `some/special/bar`.

You can use `.gitignore` files on a per directory basis. The `.gitignore` file stored within a directory will affect this directory and its subdirectories.

Three types of settings

The patterns for files that should be ignored can be defined on three different levels:

- `.gitignore`—this file is committed into the directory; it affects only the repository in which it is committed.

- Global `.gitignore`—this file resides in your home directory. It affects all of your repositories. This is your private file: you do not commit this file into the repository.

- `.git/info/exclude`—this file is stored in .git directory; it is your private file—you do not share it with others. The `exclude` file affects only one repository: the one that contains the file.

How to clean a project that contains ignored files?

If the repository contains ignored files you can remove all the tracked files with:

```
$ git ls-files | xargs rm
```

If you want to remove all of the untracked files use:

```
$ git clean -f
```

13-9. Customizing a project with .dist files
Problem

You want to start a new Internet application for publishing blogs. You plan to publish the application as an open source. Blog entries will be stored in the database and the credentials to access the database server will be stored in a file.

To make life easier for those who plan to use your application you need to:

- Define the rules to ignore configuration files
- Create the general structure of the configuration file

Both the .gitignore file and the generic configuration file should be committed with the code for your application.

Solution

Initialize a new repository:

```
$ cd git-recipes
$ mkdir 13-09
$ cd 13-09
$ git init
```

Create an empty initial revision with:

```
$ git commit --allow-empty -m "Initial commit"
```

Create the configuration file named database.ini-dist. The contents of the file are shown in Listing 13-5.

Listing 13-5. The configuration file database.ini-dist

```
[parameters]
    database_host     = your.host.example.net
    database_name     = dbname
    database_user     = admin
    database_password = sEcrEtPaSSword
```

Create the .gitignore file containing a single rule:

```
/database.ini
```

You can produce the file with the following command:

```
$ echo /database.ini > .gitignore
```

Commit both files with:

```
$ git add -A
$ git commit -m "Generic database configuration"
```

How It Works

If someone wants to use your application he has to clone it and customize the configuration. The user has to rename the file database.ini-dist to database.ini and change its contents with his settings. Thanks to the .gitignore file his personal settings will never be committed into the repository.

13-10. Using the .git/info/exclude file

Problem

You want to contribute to the open-source project http://github.com/symfony/symfony.git using NetBeans IDE.

Solution

Clone the repository you want to contribute to:

```
$ cd git-recipes
$ mkdir 13-10
$ cd 13-10
$ git clone http://github.com/symfony/symfony.git.
```

When you open a new project with NetBeans the IDE creates the nbproject/ directory in the root directory of the project. To avoid committing the directory nbproject/ create the following entry in .git/info/exclude file:

```
/nbproject/
```

You can do this with the following command:

```
$ echo /nbproject/ > .git/info/exclude
```

Now start NetBeans and open the project you just cloned. IDE will create its /nbproject/ directory, but thanks to the pattern /nbproject/ stored in the .git/info/exclude file, the repository remains clean. The command:

```
$ git status -sb
```

doesn't report changes within the /nbproject/ directory.

How It Works

Many contemporary IDEs store their configuration on a per project basis using special directories. NetBeans stores its configuration in the /nbproject/ directory, PhpStorm and other tools produced by JetBrains store the configuration within the /.idea/ directory. Because every developer can use different tools and editors these files and directories are not usually committed with the project.

Because the configuration is stored within the working directory of your repository by default, git will report these files with the $ git status command. To avoid this you can ignore the configuration files using either .git/info/exclude or your personal .gitignore file.

If you choose to ignore the configuration with the .git/info/exclude file you will have to define the pattern /nbproject/ in every new project.

If you choose to use your personal .gitignore file you can define the patterns that will be used in all your projects.

13-11. Using tags
Problem

You want to use tags to label releases of your project.

Solution

Initialize a new repository:

```
$ cd git-recipes
$ mkdir 13-11
$ cd 13-11
$ git init
```

Create the history of your project with:

```
$ git simple-commit a b c d
```

Now you want to tag the current state of your project with v1.2.3. You can do this with the following command:

```
$ git tag -a v1.2.3 -m "Release 1.2.3"
```

Create some more commits with:

```
$ git simple-commit e f g
```

The state is not yet ready for the next release. Yet for some reason, you want to keep the reference to the most recent commit using a lightweight tag. To create this, execute the following command:

```
$ git tag temp-version
```

Your repository now contains seven commits a, b, c, d, e, f, g and two tags v1.2.3 and temp-version.

How It Works

Git allows you to label arbitrary revisions with tags. There are two types of tags:

- Annotated
- Lightweight

Annotated tags are stored in your repository as objects. They contain the information about:

- Author
- The date when the tag was created
- The comment
- The SHA-1 of the revision that is tagged

Lightweight tags contain just the SHA-1 of the revision they point to.
You can list all the tags, both annotated and lightweight, with this command:

```
$ git tag
```

Both types of tags are stored in the `.git/refs/tags` directory. Your `.git/refs/tags` repository now contains two files. You can check this with:

```
$ ls .git/refs/tags
```

The files stored in `.git/refs/tags` contain the SHA-1 hashes. In the case of a lightweight tag this hash points to the revision. For annotated tags, the hash points to the tag object stored in the database.
The command:

```
$ git show -s tagname
```

prints the detailed information about the tag. When executed for an annotated tag:

```
$ git show -s v1.2.3
```

prints the detailed information about the tag object:

- Tag name (the SHA-1 hash of the tag)
- Tagger (the person who created the tag)
- Date
- Comment
- Revision

Here is the example output:

```
tag v1.2.3
Tagger: Włodzimierz Gajda <gajdaw@gajdaw.pl>
Date:   Sun Nov 3 10:32:10 2013 +0100

Release 1.2.3

commit b2e1f624d8c7ce5e6a0917ed55d3bfc69bbefd9e
```

When used for a lightweight tag the command produces only the commit's data:

```
commit e2833c1517a3873661a35f808349b473f56aff7c
Author: Włodzimierz Gajda <gajdaw@gajdaw.pl>
Date:   Sun Nov 3 10:33:32 2013 +0100
```

Creating, deleting, and listing tags

To create an annotated tag use:

```
$ git tag -a tag-name -m "tag comment" [REVISION]
```

Lightweight tags are created with:

```
$ git tag tag-name [REVISION]
```

To remove both annotated and lightweight tags use:

```
$ git tag -d tag-name
```

You can list tags with:

```
$ git tag
```

If you want to list all the tags sorted by date use the following command:

```
$ git log --tags --simplify-by-decoration --pretty="%ai %d"
```

And here is the command to check the most recent annotated tag:

```
$ git describe
```

Publishing tags

You can publish your tags with:

```
$ git push --tags
```

Whenever you execute the command:

```
$ git fetch
```

it will fetch all the tags from the server.

If for any reason you want to delete a remote tag, you should use:

```
$ git push origin :refs/tags/tag-name
```

Similar to branches, when tags in a remote repository are deleted, your local repository is not affected. The command $ git fetch will fetch any new tags but will not remove any tags that were removed in the remote repository. To synchronize your tags with remote tags use:

```
$ git fetch --tags
```

Using tags

Tags can be used just as any other identifiers of revisions. You can pass them to $ git branch, $ git checkout, and $ git reset commands, such as:

```
$ git reset --hard v1.2.3
$ git checkout -b my-new-branch v1.2.3
```

■ **Hint** You can treat tags as branches that cannot move.

13-12. Exporting repositories to zipped archives
Problem

You have worked on a project that has just reached a stable release. You want to generate a zipped archive containing all the files that are important to anyone who would wish to use your project. You don't want to include the files that are important only to the developers who worked on this project in the zipped archive.

Solution

Initialize a new repository:

```
$ cd git-recipes
$ mkdir 13-12
$ cd 13-12
$ git init
```

Create an empty initial revision with:

```
$ git commit --allow-empty -m "Initial commit"
```

Now create the directories src/ and doc/ and commit some files in them:

```
$ mkdir src
$ echo "/* code */" > src/main.c
$ mkdir doc
$ echo "<DOCTYPE html>" > doc/index.html
$ git add -A
$ git commit -m "Source code and documentation"
```

Finally create some tests in the Test/ directory:

```
$ mkdir Tests
$ echo "/* tests */" > Tests/TestMain.c
$ git add -A
$ git commit -m "Tests"
```

Now your project contains three directories: src/, doc/, and Tests/. The files stored in src/ and doc/ are important to the users of your project. The files stored in the Tests/ directory are only important to the developers who contributed to your project. They are not important to anyone who would want to use your project.

Create the file named .gitattributes with the following contents:

```
/Tests/ export-ignore
/.gitattributes export-ignore
```

You can do this with the following commands:

```
$ echo "/Tests/ export-ignore" > .gitattributes
$ echo "/.gitattributes export-ignore" >> .gitattributes
```

Commit this file with:

```
$ git add .gitattributes
$ git commit -m "Gitattributes to exclude /Tests/ and /.gitattributes from ZIP"
```

The project has reached a stable point in its history. Tag it as v2.3.4 with the following command:

```
$ git tag -a v2.3.4 -m "Release 2.3.4"
```

Finally, produce the zipped archive containing the version v2.3.4 of your project:

```
$ git archive --format=zip --output=../project-v2.3.4.zip v2.3.4
```

This command will create the file git-recipes/project-v2.3.4.zip. The file will contain your project without the Tests/ directory and without the .gitattributes file. To list the contents of a zipped file, you can use the following command:

```
$ unzip -l ../project-v2.3.4.zip
```

How It Works

The command:

```
$ git archive --format=zip --output=filename.zip [REVISION]
```

exports the project in the version stored in [REVISION] to the file named filename.zip. The file is stored in a ZIP format. Thanks to this command you don't have to create zipped versions of your project, such as:

```
project-v0.1.2.zip
project-v2.8.4.zip
project-v5.15.89.zip
```

to preserve your project in a specific version. All you have to do is to create tags, such as:

```
$ git tag -a v0.1.2 -m "Release 0.1.2"
$ git tag -a v2.8.4 -m "Release 2.8.4"
$ git tag -a v5.15.89 -m "Release 5.15.89"
```

If you want to get a zipped file with a specific version all you have to do is to execute a command, such as:

```
$ git archive --format=zip --output=project-v0.1.2.zip v0.1.2
$ git archive --format=zip --output=project-v2.8.4.zip v2.8.4
$ git archive --format=zip --output=project-v5.15.89.zip v5.15.89
```

All the versions are stored in the same repository and can be produced on demand with the $ git archive command. There is no need to back up files such as project-v2.8.4.zip. If you back up your repository you will always be able to generate all of the specific versions that were tagged.

Gitattribute file allows you to exclude some files from the automatically generated archive. When the .gitattributes file contains the following rule:

```
/Tests/ export-ignore
```

then the generated archive will contain all the files except those stored within /Tests/ directory.

Summary

The first command introduced in this chapter, $ git diff, will help you check the state of your project. It reports the changes using the format defined by GNU diffutils tools. By default, when called without parameters:

```
$ git diff
```

compares the working directory to the staging area. Using the --staged parameter you can compare the staging area to HEAD:

```
$ git diff --staged
```

Called with two revisions, git diff compares the files in these revisions:

```
$ git diff master beta
```

The additional parameter --unified can be used to specify the number of unchanged lines that will be printed.

Recipes 13-2 to 13-7 presented various problems concerning line endings. Because git is a tool that synchronizes the work of a group of developers and because every developer can use a different platform, you have to be aware of possible issues that may complicate the work of your team.

The first item discussed was how to commit and how to checkout the files exactly as they are, without any conversions performed by git. These matters, covered in Recipes 13-2 and 13-3, are essential in cases when you have problems with your line endings and you want to get rid of them. Remember, that to get a clean checkout, you can remove the tracked files:

```
$ git ls-files | xargs rm
```

and the staging area:

```
$ rm .git/index
```

The command $ git reset --hard recreates the working directory and the staging area using the snapshot stored in HEAD.

Recipes 13-4 and 13-5 explain in greater detail the procedures you should follow if you want to commit the files with the line endings converted to CRLF and LF, respectively.

Recipe 13-6 presents an anti-pattern that should convince you how important line endings are. When followed, it will produce the following error: even though no files were edited, git reports them as all changed. If any developer commits and submits this type of change it will confuse other developers. And, by the way, the `$ git diff` command also can be helpful when dealing with problems concerning white characters, line endings in particular. When called with `--check` parameter:

```
$ git diff --check
```

outputs the changes that can be regarded as problems with white characters. And remember that one of the best and easiest solutions to prevent all problems with line endings is to use the `.gitattributes` file—defining line endings on a per pattern basis. Using the simple rule `* eol=lf`, you can avoid all problems concerning line endings. This solution was presented in Recipe 13-7.

Recipes 13-8, 13-9, and 13-10 present the three most typical problems that you can solve by defining appropriate rules to ignore files. The first problem concerns the binary files that are automatically generated by various tools. Here are the examples:

- The files generated during compilation: `*.o`, `a.out`, `*.exe`, `*.lib`

- Cached configuration generated when the application is executed; it can be stored in some special directory, such as `cache/`

- Dependencies—the external libraries embedded in the project; they can be stored in some specific directory, such as `vendor/`

Because all developers will from time to time generate all of the above files, the best solution for these files is to ignore them using the `.gitignore` file that is committed with the project.

The second case concerns the files that contain some private information. It can be the configuration with credentials to access external resource, such as database. Here again all the developers and users will struggle with the same problem: how to avoid inadvertent publication of these sensitive data. Thus, the rules to exclude these types of files should be also stored in the `.gitignore` file that is committed in the repository.

The third case concerns the private settings of every developer. I use specific tools that create specific files inside the project. In this case it makes no sense to commit the rules into the repository. Thus, to ignore the files and directories generated by the tools that I use, I can either use the `.git/info/exclude` file stored within the specific repository or the user's global `.gitignore` file stored in his or her home directory.

Two final recipes showed how to work with tags and with the `$ git archive` command. Remember that git offers two different types of tags: annotated tags and lightweight tags. Annotated tags are stored in the `.git/objects` database. They contain detailed information about who, when, and why created the tag. Lightweight tags are just aliases for referencing commits. As in the case of branches: there is no information who, when, or why created a lightweight tag or a branch. Some projects, such as jQuery, use lightweight tags. Others, such as Symfony, use annotated tags. The choice is up to you, although because annotated tags contain author, date, and comment, they are generally considered a better choice. Both types of tags are published with:

```
$ git push --tags
```

To synchronize your tags with the remote repository use:

```
$ git fetch --tags
```

To delete a remote tag, you should use the same command as to delete a remote branch:

```
$ git push origin :remote-branch-to-delete
$ git push origin :refs/tags/remote-tag-to-delete
```

Index

H

■ I, J, K

■ L

■ M

Get the eBook for only $10!

Now you can take the weightless companion with you anywhere, anytime. Your purchase of this book entitles you to 3 electronic versions for only $10.

This Apress title will prove so indispensible that you'll want to carry it with you everywhere, which is why we are offering the eBook in 3 formats for only $10 if you have already purchased the print book.

Convenient and fully searchable, the PDF version enables you to easily find and copy code—or perform examples by quickly toggling between instructions and applications. The MOBI format is ideal for your Kindle, while the ePUB can be utilized on a variety of mobile devices.

Go to www.apress.com/promo/tendollars to purchase your companion eBook.

THE EXPERT'S VOICE™